Bitcoin and Beyond

Since the launch of Bitcoin in 2009, several hundred different 'cryptocurrencies' have been developed and become accepted for a wide variety of transactions in leading online commercial marketplaces and the 'sharing economy', as well as by more traditional retailers, manufacturers, and even by charities and political parties.

Bitcoin and its competitors have also garnered attention for their wildly fluctuating values as well as implication in international money laundering, Ponzi schemes and online trade in illicit goods and services across borders. These and other controversies surrounding cryptocurrencies have induced varying governance responses by central banks, government ministries, international organizations, and industry regulators worldwide. Besides formal attempts to ban Bitcoin, there have been multifaceted efforts to incorporate elements of blockchains, the peer-to-peer technology underlying cryptocurrencies, in the wider exchange, recording, and broadcasting of digital transactions. Blockchains are being mobilized to support and extend an array of governance activities. The novelty and breadth of growing blockchain-based activities have fuelled both utopian promises and dystopian fears regarding applications of the emergent technology to Bitcoin and beyond.

This volume brings scholars of anthropology, economics, science and technology studies, and sociology together with global political economy (GPE) scholars in assessing the actual implications posed by Bitcoin and blockchains for contemporary global governance. Its interdisciplinary contributions provide academics, policymakers, industry practitioners, and the general public with more nuanced understandings of technological change in the changing character of governance within and across the borders of nation-states.

Malcolm Campbell-Verduyn is an SSHRC Postdoctoral Fellow at the Balsillie School of International Affairs, Canada.

RIPE Series in Global Political Economy

Series Editors:
James Brassett (*University of Warwick, UK*),
Eleni Tsingou (*Copenhagen Business School, Denmark*)
and
Susanne Soederberg (*Queen's University, Canada*)

The RIPE Series published by Routledge is an essential forum for cutting-edge scholarship in international political economy. The series brings together new and established scholars working in critical, cultural, and constructivist political economy. Books in the RIPE Series typically combine an innovative contribution to theoretical debates with rigorous empirical analysis.

The RIPE Series seeks to cultivate:
- field-defining theoretical advances in international political economy
- novel treatments of key issue areas, both historical and contemporary, such as global finance, trade, and production
- analyses that explore the political economic dimensions of relatively neglected topics, such as the environment, gender relations, and migration
- accessible work that will inspire advanced undergraduates and graduate students in international political economy.

The *RIPE Series in Global Political Economy* aims to address the needs of students and teachers.

For a full list of titles in this series, please visit www.routledge.com/RIPE-Series-in-Global-Political-Economy/book-series/RIPE

Beyond Defeat and Austerity
Disrupting (the Critical Political Economy of) Neoliberal Europe
David Bailey, Monica Clua-Losada, Nikolai Huke and Olatz Ribera-Almandoz

Civil Society and Financial Regulation
Consumer Finance Protection and Taxation after the Financial Crisis
Lisa Kastner

Bitcoin and Beyond
Cryptocurrencies, Blockchains, and Global Governance
Edited by Malcolm Campbell-Verduyn

Bitcoin and Beyond

Cryptocurrencies, Blockchains, and Global Governance

Edited by Malcolm Campbell-Verduyn

Routledge
Taylor & Francis Group

LONDON AND NEW YORK

First published 2018 by Routledge

2 Park Square, Milton Park, Abingdon, Oxfordshire OX14 4RN
52 Vanderbilt Avenue, New York, NY 10017

Routledge is an imprint of the Taylor & Francis Group, an informa business

First issued in paperback 2019

British Library Cataloguing in Publication Data
A catalogue record for this book is available from the British Library

Library of Congress Cataloging in Publication Data
A catalog record for this book has been requested

ISBN: 978-0-415-79214-1 (hbk)
ISBN: 978-0-367-26492-5 (pbk)

Typeset in Times New Roman
by Wearset Ltd, Boldon, Tyne and Wear

Contents

Figures

Tables

Contributors

Malcolm Campbell-Verduyn is an SSHRC postdoctoral fellow at the Balsillie School of International Affairs. His research combines a general focus on language and ideas in the global political economy, with a specific interest in the roles of private actors, technologies, and technical artefacts in contemporary global governance. His research has appeared in the journals *Business and Politics, Competition and Change, Global Society, Journal of European Public Policy, New Political Economy*, and *New Political Science*. He is the author of *Professional Authority after the Global Financial Crisis*, published in 2017 by Palgrave Macmillan.

Quinn DuPont is a postdoctoral researcher at the University of Washington. He studies human and social dimensions of cybersecurity, cryptography, and code. He has a PhD in information science (Toronto), and is an ALA-accredited librarian (Western), with a decade of industry experience as a senior information specialist at IBM, an IT consultant, and a usability and experience designer. He is currently writing a book on cryptocurrencies and blockchains (Polity).

Marcel Goguen is a PhD candidate in political science at McMaster University, Hamilton, Canada. He studied political science at l'Université de Moncton and the University of Ottawa. His research focuses on the interstice between international relations theory, political theory, and global finance. Under the supervision of Tony Porter, he is participating in research funded by the Social Sciences and Humanities Research Council of Canada (SSHRC) on 'Numbers in the changing fabric of global governance'.

William W. Grimes is Associate Dean for Academic Affairs and Professor of International Relations and Political Science at the Frederick S. Pardee School of Global Studies at Boston University. He is the author of *Unmaking the Japanese Miracle: Macroeconomic Politics, 1985–2000* (Cornell University Press, 2001) and *Currency and Contest in East Asia: The Great Power Politics of Financial Regionalism* (Cornell University Press, 2009). He has published extensively on financial policy and the political economy of East Asia.

Ying-Ying Hsieh is a PhD candidate at Ivey Business School (Canada). Having received her education and worked in the technology sector, Ying-Ying is deeply interested in the overarching theme of innovation. Her research sets out to explore how technologies enable novel organizational design, which in turn enables new forms of organizing. Specifically, she focuses on coordination and governance in the cryptocurrency and fintech industries. Ultimately, she aspires to theory-building for mechanisms by which organizations in these sectors create and capture value to achieve superior performance.

Moritz Hütten is a graduate student of financial and economic sociology at Goethe University Frankfurt. His research interests include cryptocurrencies, banking regulation in Europe, and financial literacy. He has been involved in several research projects at Goethe University Frankfurt and Darmstadt Business School, as well as the research centre Sustainable Architecture for Finance in Europe (SAFE).

Kai Jia is an assistant professor in the School of Political Science and Public Administration, University of Electronic Science and Technology of China, Chengdu, China. Kai Jia completed his doctorate at the School of Public Policy and Management in Tsinghua University, Beijing. He has been a Fulbright Scholar, a visiting scholar at the University of California at Davis. He has extensive research experience in internet and data governance. His research topics include the internet platform economy and its regulations, individual production models and value distribution studies, the Bitcoin open resource community and its governance, sovereign data and privacy. He has several publications in the *FTChinese* and *21st Century Business Herald.*

Alexandre Mallard is Director of the Centre de Sociologie de l'Innovation at MINES ParisTech, PSL Research University. Originally trained as a sociologist of science and technology, he now works in the field of economic sociology. He has conducted research on sales activity, on very small businesses, and on the rise of network interactions in the corporate environment. His current research projects investigate the social inscription of innovation, at the crossroads between economic sociology and political science.

Cécile Méadel is a sociologist, professor at the Department of Communication (*Institut français de Presse*-IFP) of Pantheon Assas University in Paris, and associate researcher at the Center for the Sociology of Innovation. Her work focuses on the uses and users of communication technologies, investigating the mutual adjustment between a means of communication, the professionals specialized in it, its resources, and its users. Her most recent work is on internet regulation of e-communities and on industrial making of audiences (through audience measurement tools or devices for internet users' contributions).

Francesca Musiani (PhD, MINES ParisTech, 2012) is an associate research professor (*chargée de recherche*), French National Centre for Scientific

Research (CNRS), Institute for Communication Sciences (ISCC-CNRS/Paris-Sorbonne/UPMC), associate researcher at the Centre for the Sociology of Innovation of MINES ParisTech-PSL, and academic editor for the *Internet Policy Review*. Her research explores internet governance 'by infrastructure', and draws upon an interdisciplinary training in information and communication sciences, science and technology studies, and international law. Francesca is the author of *Internet et vie privée [Internet and Privacy]* (Uppr Editions, 2016) and *Nains sans géants. Architecture décentralisée et services Internet [Dwarfs Without Giants. Decentralized Architecture and Internet Services]* (Presses des Mines, 2013 [2015], *Prix Informatique et Libertés* 2013 of the French Privacy and Data Protection Commission, CNIL).

Daivi Rodima-Taylor is a lecturer and research associate at the Frederick S. Pardee School of Global Studies of Boston University. She is a social anthropologist and Africanist, with a doctorate from Brandeis University. Her research focuses on fiduciary culture and financial inclusion, diaspora and migration, informal economies, land and natural resource tenure, and innovation and entrepreneurship. Dr Rodima-Taylor has taught sustainable development and anthropology, and contributed to international development work in financial inclusion, participatory planning, and community governance. She has conducted longitudinal ethnographic research in Africa and published in academic and policy-oriented journals.

Matthias Thiemann is an assistant professor of European public policy at Sciences Po, Paris. His research investigates the patterns of interaction of public and private actors in the financial system post-crisis in terms of the development as well as the enforcement of regulation or the intervention of state actors directly in financial markets. His work has appeared in the journals *American Journal of Sociology, Review of International Political Economy, Business and Politics*, and *Competition and Change*, among others.

Jean-Philippe (JP) Vergne is an associate professor at Ivey Business School (Canada) who examines how socially contested and/or illegal organizations affect the birth, death, and renewal of industries operating at the vanguard of capitalism. JP is the founding coordinator of the Crypto Capitalism Center and co-director of the Scotiabank Digital Banking Lab, where he coordinates a research programme on fintech. In 2013, JP co-authored the book *The Pirate Organization: Lessons from the Fringes of Capitalism* (Harvard Publishing), and in 2017 the graphic novel *Déjà Vu*, whose chapters can be found recorded in the bitcoin blockchain.

Sha Wang is a PhD candidate in economics at Western University (Canada). Her research area focuses on the new trends in financial markets and their impact on asset returns. She has co-authored with Professor JP Vergne on drivers of cryptocurrency returns. Her PhD thesis studies the impact of speculative activities on major currencies' exchange rate fluctuations. She has benefited from her industry experience in the currency hedging arm of an investment institution to incorporate additional insight into her theoretical framework on currency values.

Falin Zhang earned his PhD in International Relations from McMaster University (Hamilton, Canada) in 2015 and is now a postdoctoral research fellow at the School of International Studies, Peking University (Beijing, China). His principal research interests lie in international relations, international political economy, global financial governance, foreign policy analysis, and Chinese politics. His recent research focuses on China's foreign policy in global financial governance and recent works include journal articles published, respectively, in the *Journal of Contemporary China* ('Holism Failure: China's Inconsistent Stances and Consistent Interests in Global Financial Governance', 2016) and the *Journal of International Relations and Development* ('The Chinese Developmental State: Standard Accounts and New Characteristics', 2017), a book chapter, 'Determinants and Fluctuations of China's Exchange Rate Policy', in *The Political Economy of Chinese Finance* (edited by J. Jay Choi *et al.*, Emerald, 2016), and a translated Chinese textbook, *Global Political Economy* (Robert O'Brien and Marc Williams, 2016).

Acknowledgements

The support of John Ravenhill and the Balsillie School of International Affairs as well as the Social Sciences and Humanities Research Council of Canada (grant no. 611-2016-0318) is gratefully acknowledged for having enabled fruitful discussions of this research in Waterloo, Canada at the end of February 2017. Sincere thanks are also due to Eleni Tsingou and Eric Helleiner for providing continuous support from the inception to the final production of this volume.

1 Introduction

What are blockchains and how are they relevant to governance in the global political economy?

Malcolm Campbell-Verduyn

Imagine having almost instantaneous access to a permanent record of all digital transactions undertaken across the world. Without revealing precisely who and what is involved in these transactions, this digital database grants you nearly real-time overviews of peer-to-peer exchange within and across national borders. Such unprecedented capacity to monitor direct Internet-based interaction between quasi-anonymous individuals who undertake, verify, and publish records of their digital transactions is at the core of promises and fears surrounding blockchains. This volume explores governance implications for the actors and processes involved in ordering, managing, and organising an increasingly digital global political economy arising from growing applications of this set of emergent technologies to Bitcoin and beyond.

At their essence, blockchains are digital sequences of numbers coded into computer software that permit the secure exchange, recording, and broadcasting of transactions between individual users operating anywhere in the world with Internet access. Like most technological changes, the development of blockchains drew on and combined several existing technologies. Blockchains incorporate digital encryption technologies that mask, to varying degrees, the specific content exchanged as well as the identities of individual users. Algorithms, pre-coded series of step-by-step instructions, are also mobilised in solving complex mathematical equations and arriving at a consensus on the validity of transactions within networks of users. Time-stamping technologies then periodically bundle verified transactions into datasets, or 'blocks'. Linked together sequentially, these 'blocks' form 'chains' that make up larger 'blockchain' databases of transactions that broadcast a permanent record of transactions whilst maintaining the anonymity of users and specific content exchanged. Blockchains are intended to be maintained by all users in manners meant to be immutable, unless users arrive at a clear consensus to undertake changes.

Ledgers of user-verified transactions were envisioned by the science fiction writer H.G. Wells (2005) in the 1930s and advocated by 'cypherpunk' computer hackers seeking to ensure digital privacy as the Internet began evolving later in the twentieth century (Jeong, 2013). The technical blueprint for developing blockchain technology was originally proposed in a white paper published by one Satoshi Nakamoto in 2008. Efforts to identify this individual or group of individuals have remained unsuccessful, adding a substantial aura of mystery to this information communication technology (ICT).[1] The technical design for blockchains initially circulated on the cryptography mailing list was quickly taken up by an online community of technology enthusiasts, who developed Bitcoin as the first time-stamped ledger of user-verified transactions in 2009. Initially intended to enable the transactions of monetary-like 'coins' between users, the Bitcoin blockchain was later adapted for the digital exchange, verification, and broadcasting of a range of other information. As non-proprietary and open-source software, the original Bitcoin 'protocol' was replicated in developing other blockchains that exchange not only 'cryptocurrencies' (CCs), but also a much wider range of information on everything from ownership rights and contractual obligations to votes and citizenship.

Applications of blockchain technologies began being noticed beyond technologists and technology enthusiasts a half-decade following the publication of the 2008 white paper. Attention to Bitcoin in particular exploded in 2013 because of a confluence of events internal and external to esoteric online 'crypto-communities'. Internally, the rise and fall of both the leading 'exchange' converting CCs to and from state-backed currencies, Tokyo-based Mt. Gox, as well as the infamous online marketplace for illicit goods and services, the Silk Road, received widespread media coverage. Primarily negative and sensationalistic, this attention alerted citizens, firms, and governments to what appeared as the 'new wild west' surrounding Bitcoin (Singh, 2015). At the same time, a host of external events focused more positive attention to the potential benefits of the original application of blockchain technologies as alternatives to the widespread government and corporate surveillance revealed in the Edward Snowden leaks; financial instabilities in the eurozone that included the confiscation of deposits in the 'bailout' of Cypriot banks; technical glitches at major banks that left customers unable to access their savings; and confirmation that controversial central bank quantitative easing programmes would be extended well beyond their original intention as emergency responses to the 2007–08 global financial crisis. Whether for philosophical, speculative, or security reasons, wider public interest in the promises and perils of Bitcoin occurred in a period of unprecedented volatility in the exchange values of the original CC, which rose nearly tenfold from just over US$10, only to fall by nearly half and eventually end 2013 at around US$750.

In the wake of this pivotal year, Bitcoin and blockchain technologies became increasingly integrated into the very global economic system that their earliest developers had explicitly sought to provide alternatives to. Bitcoin became progressively accepted for a wide variety of transactions in leading online commercial marketplaces, such as eBay, in the 'sharing economy' of AirBnB and Uber, as well as by more traditional retailers, manufacturers, and even by some political parties. Beyond merely accepting Bitcoin for transactions, some multinational firms began developing their own CCs and integrating blockchains into their operations. The world's largest retailer, Wal-Mart, trialled the technology for enhancing quality control over its global food supply chain. Several investment banks and stock market operators also began integrating blockchains in efforts to streamline their back-office operations. Even some governments began developing blockchain-based land and health registries as well as benefits payments systems. A wider variety of applications[2] beyond the esoteric online communities and illicit market-places in which the technology had originally been applied heralded the growing integration of blockchains into key segments of the global political economy.

While surveys nearly continually hint at ever-greater roles and applications of blockchains (e.g. World Economic Forum, 2015: 24), even traditionally enthusiastic consultants have begun to consider whether 'peak hype' has been reached in the excitement this technology has generated (Gartner, 2016). Leading media, such as *The Economist* (2015), stress the 'extraordinary potential' of the block-chain 'as a piece of innovation on a par with the introduction of limited liability for corporations, or private property rights, or the internet itself'. Scholars have characterised blockchains as 'the most important innovation in fundamental architecture since the tubes of the internet were first developed' (Lawrence Lessig, cited in Eyers, 2015). The first book dedicated to blockchains compares the technology to the Magna Carta and the Rosetta Stone, providing 'the potential for reconfiguring all human activity' (Swan, 2015: viii).

Further context and nuance is clearly necessary for evaluating the wider socio-economic implications of blockchains in a global political economy that is more interconnected than ever before as a result of the increasing spread and application of these and other Internet-based technologies. In specifically addressing the implications posed by blockchains for *governance* in the contemporary global political economy, this book provides wider insights into the changing character and role of emergent technologies in organising, ordering, and managing the increasingly instantaneous and multifaceted relationships between actors and processes within and beyond the borders of nation-states.

Implications for, and insights into, contemporary global governance

How does examining a relatively esoteric set of emergent technologies yield useful insights into the character of contemporary global governance? Journalists and technology enthusiasts regularly hint at how applications of blockchains have been transforming key facets of twenty-first-century global governance. Gillian Tett (2014) at the *Financial Times*, for instance, has emphasised how blockchains shift trust from traditional centralised institutions towards decentralised users interacting directly through digital cryptography and computer code. Technologists, meanwhile, celebrate how blockchains foster nearly instantaneous exchange to occur amongst individuals that bypasses a range of intermediaries and centralised 'trust actors', governments in particular (e.g. Cox, 2013; Brito *et al.*, 2015; Koenig, 2015). Rather one-sided praise of such curtailment of centralised authority, along with journalistic assessments hampered by formats more conducive to sensationalistic claims than nuanced analysis, provide some, albeit limited, insight into the changing character of twenty-first-century global governance (e.g. Kaminska, 2015; Soltas, 2013; Rifkind, 2013; Vigna and Casey, 2015; for an exception see Popper, 2015).

Scholarly treatments of Bitcoin, CCs, and blockchains began to emerge in 2011. With some exceptions, early studies have remained technical and narrowly focused, largely avoiding consideration of the wider implications that blockchain applications pose for contemporary global governance.[3] Legal scholarship detailing the varied manners in which Bitcoin, CCs and blockchains fit within existing formal laws and regulations often loses sight of the wider governance implications presented (Bollen, 2013; Farmer, 2014; Hughes and Middlebrook, 2014; Penrose, 2013; Kiviat, 2015; Pflaum and Hateley, 2013; Ponsford, 2015). Studies by computer scientists focused on the technical properties of blockchains are largely concerned with testing the immutability and pseudo-anonymity of blockchain applications (Arvind *et al.*, 2016; Böhme *et al.*, 2014; Yli-Huumo *et al.*, 2016). Economists, the most prominent public commentators on CCs and blockchain technologies (Foley, 2015), largely contemplate whether or not CCs can be considered as currencies or central elements of the so-called 'Internet of Money' (Wladawsky-Berger, 2014; e.g. Dwyer, 2015; Lo and Wang, 2014; Selgin, 2015; Weber, 2016).[4]

While pioneering in their analysis of complex technological developments, initial scholarly studies tend to be economistic, legalistic, and technical in manners that overlook, or merely hint at, wider considerations for global governance in the 'digital age' (Der Derian, 2003). Key questions of governance often remain unaddressed in this literature, such as how and where exactly are decisions made and discontent voiced in blockchain-based activities? Do blockchains overcome the flaws of existing decision-making processes? Do blockchains give rise to *new* governance problems and pathologies? Is 'blockchain-based governance' desirable for *all* actors in the global political economy?

Social scientists, and scholars of global political economy (GPE) in particular, have long addressed questions more generally pertaining to the nexus of technology and global governance, and in regards to ICTs in particular (Singh and Rosenau, 2002; see also Ruggie, 1975; Talalay and Farrands, 1997; Porter, 2002). The turn of the millennium technology stock bubble and rise of Internet technologies were analysed in nuanced debates, such as over the opportunities and threats presented for traditional forms of monetary governance posed by electronic moneys (Cohen, 2001; Helleiner, 1998; Kobrin, 1997). More widely, GPE studies provide a range of insights on key questions of agency, ethics, legitimacy, and power arising from applications of novel technologies. For example, scholarship on 'digital gaps' draws attention to how technology-enabled decision-making can become dominated by specialists and exclude those less familiar or less able to remain appraised with intricate sets of technologies (Wade, 2002; Youngs, 2007). New and emergent technologies are regarded not only as fostering the cooperation and progress stressed in liberal and more techno-uptopian accounts, but also as giving rise to technocratic forms of governance characterised by the inequalities and power asymmetries emphasised in critical and more techno-dystopian perspectives.

However, GPE scholars have yet to extend such insights to the governance implications raised by applications of blockchains. Detailed GPE analysis of technological changes in the aftermath of the 2007–08 global financial crisis (e.g. Gabor and Brooks, 2016; Hansen and Porter, 2017; Langley and Leyshon, 2016; Nesvetailova, 2014; Rogers and Clarke, 2016) considers neither the advent of blockchain technologies nor their primary application with CCs. Analysis in the related interdiscipline of International Relations (IR) similarly overlooks blockchains despite a growing focus on interlinkages between governance and technologies (Mayer *et al.*, 2014a, 2014b) and 'large technical systems' more generally (Mayer and Acuto, 2015), as well as the Internet specifically (Carr, 2016; Choucri, 2012; Mueller, 2010).

This book provides an initial of many sets of bridges across the gap between wider and longstanding GPE consideration of the governance implications presented by technologies and the more specific analysis of blockchains emerging in related academic disciplines. To understand the wider socio-economic implications of blockchains and the changing nature of global governance, key issues at the heart of GPE, including the agency, legitimacy, and power of specific actors and processes underpinning global governance, need to be integrated into technical, legal, and economic scholarship on Bitcoin and blockchain technologies that is beginning to consider such issues (e.g. Bjerg, 2016; Böhme *et al.*, 2015; De Filippi and Loveluck, 2016). This volume brings together scholars of anthropology, economics, and sociology as well as science and technology studies (STS) in conversation with GPE scholars. To ensure overall degree of coherence across chapters by interdisciplinary groups of scholars, all contributors were asked to contemplate three core questions:

1   What opportunities and challenges do blockchain applications provide for global governance?
2   Who specifically is (dis)empowered by applications of blockchain technologies?
3   How are certain actors and processes (dis)empowered by applications of blockchain technologies?

Unlike the technical consensus required to process blockchain transactions, no artificial agreement on a single set of answers to these questions was imposed in generating this volume. Rather, varying and at times divergent insights into how a rapidly evolving set of emergent technologies are impacting key facets of contemporary global governance were promoted in the recognition that a diversity of analyses is necessary for understanding their nuanced implications. The central findings of this volume previewed in the final section of this chapter are therefore necessarily provisional. The following sections more widely situate the analysis of contributors within existing GPE and social scientific debates on emerging technologies and global governance.

Technologies and global governance

A conceptual starting point of debate shared amongst contributions to this volume relates to the nature and evolution of technological change. In their specific assessments of applications of blockchains to Bitcoin and beyond, contributors assess whether this set of technologies can be considered as 'emergent'. Emergence here refers to how practical applications of novel types of knowledge in the global political economy remain largely, if not wholly, unsettled. Science and technology policy scholars identify emergent technologies, first, by the new dimensions of knowledge or principles they apply in novel manners; second, by rapid growth in funding and research their attempted applications receive; third, by their core community of supporting actors; and fourth, by uncertain yet ambitious projections of the significance that their applications will have on existing socio-economic systems (Rotolo *et al.*, 2015). Many applications of emergent technologies remain theoretical in nature, at 'proof of concept' stages rather than underlying existing practices in the global political economy. Despite what are often highly publicized allusions to their 'revolutionary' nature, the actual potential of the novel set of knowledge remains indeterminate. In other words, widespread 'projections of potential applications remain just that – projected aspirations and hopes' (Einsiedel, 2009: 3).

How and when do emergent technologies become 'established' in the relationships between actors and processes that underpin global governance? This question can productively be explored by examining blockchain applications that, as noted above, have grown exponentially CCs in the second half-decade since the advent of Bitcoin. Rotolo *et al.* (2015) consider that technologies cease to be characterised as emergent once either their practical applications become *less* ambiguous and *more* widespread in activities beyond their initial niche, or once their rapid growth in funding and potential applications declines and they become abandoned by their supportive community. In neither scenario, however, are transitions from emerging to established technologies entirely clear-cut. To take perhaps the most well-known contemporary example, the Internet spread from initial development and application in security and academic communities to underpin vast tracks of activity across the global political economy. Novel applications of this technology continue expanding relentlessly, however, with the 'Internet of things', for instance, slated to contribute to a 'fourth industrial revolution' (Schwab, 2016). The evolution of the Internet thus illustrates the unclear boundary between established and emergent technologies.

In enhancing clarity of what emergent technologies *are* and *how* they evolve, this volume draws on earlier insights from IR and GPE studies of technology. A shared starting point is the 'Skolnikoff principle'. In *The Elusive Transformation*, the scholar of technology and international affairs, Eugene Skolnikoff (1993: 35), stressed how 'new technologies, whatever their source, often will have applications far from the original purposes for which they were developed'. The still unknown designer(s) of blockchain technologies likely never contemplated nor foresaw the diverse range of applications with this technology as their 'shared *genus*' (Russell, 1997: 55). So-called wider 'blockchain 2.0' applications building on and going beyond CCs have challenged seemingly established notions of what this emergent technology fundamentally consists of. Consistent efforts have been made to substitute the term blockchains with 'distributed ledger technologies' (DLTs). However, DLTs subtly yet importantly change the original decentralised and 'permissionless' character of blockchains by developing *closed* ledgers that require specified actors to serve as formal gatekeepers in granting permission to select users. These experiments and the different governance implications they prompt are characterised by much of the ambiguous, experimental, and provisional character that GPE and legal scholars have identified as increasingly prevalent in contemporary global governance (e.g. Best, 2008; Brassett *et al.*, 2012; Broome and Seabrooke, 2008; De Búrca *et al.*, 2014).

Wider blockchain '2.0' applications are also indicative of the uncertain and difficult to predict paths the evolution of emergent technologies take in becoming increasingly established within the activities of existing actors and existing processes in the global political economy. As the Skolnikoff principle suggests, each process of development occurs in unique ways that are often lacking in precise historical parallel. Though frequently compared with the Internet, blockchain applications more precisely build *on top of* existing Internet infrastructures. Consequently, blockchain applications might be more appropriately compared with specific Internet-based technologies such as Voice over Internet Protocols (VoIPs), like Skype. In turn, DLTs can be understood as the reverse of ongoing efforts to develop 'open source' operating systems (OS) such as Linux from original 'closed-source' Windows and Mac OS. Yet even such specific comparisons may be thrown into doubt, for instance by ongoing efforts to apply blockchain technologies to newer, more decentralised versions of the Internet itself (Kastelein, 2016).[5]

Beyond considering *what* emergent technologies *are* and *how* their evolution can be conceived, this volume engages wider debates on the implications of what practical applications of novel types of knowledge actually *do*. Technologists, consultants, and other market actors tend to stress the 'disruption' that the enhanced competition applications of emergent technologies *may* provide. This competition is often implicitly understood in liberal framings as normatively desirable for all socio-economic actors and processes in capitalist political economies (e.g. Schwab, 2016). Yet, as critical GPE studies have explicitly countered, competition inevitably produces both winners and losers, may not *always* be desirable in *all* areas of social activity, and may actually reinforce longstanding processes and actors (e.g. Clarke, 2017; Wigger and Buch-Hansen, 2013).

This volume therefore shifts beyond the widespread tendency to merely implicitly invoke the *potential* benefits of 'disruption' by more explicitly considering the *actual* implications arising from technological change. Contributors detail both normatively positive as well as negative consequences posed for both the actors and process underpinning contemporary global governance. These implications are more widely linked to the interrelated forms of governance *by* emergent technologies, *through* emergent technologies, and *with* emergent technologies that scholars of science and technology policy and of GPE are beginning to identify (Campbell-Verduyn *et al.*, 2016; Pelizza and Kuhlmann, forthcoming; see more widely Chwierut, 2016). The following sub-sections illustrate examples of the insights that interdisciplinary studies of blockchains are beginning to yield into broader GPE debates on the consequences of technological change for global governance, and which contributors to this volume build upon.[6]

The normative implications of governance by emergent technologies

In an initial instance, analysing blockchains and their various applications provides insight into how the specific characteristics of technologies *themselves* have profound implications for contemporary global governance. Constructivist scholars in GPE and other disciplines consider technologies as deeply social phenomena that are underpinned by specific ideologies and ideas with the power to constitute the interests and incentives of their users. These processes can broadly be conceived as forms of governance *by* technologies. Technologies here are understood as 'powerful forces acting to reshape that activity and its meaning' (Winner, 1986: 6; see e.g. Barbrook and Cameron, 1996). The implicit and often backgrounded ideas and norms underpinning computer code, for example, give rise to regularised patterns of behaviour (Berry, 2012). Understanding computer code as a form of law (Lessig, 2006) stresses the manners in which specific features of technologies themselves can reframe, redefine, and reconstitute the mundane activities of the social actors and social process underpinning global governance. The specific arrangements and architectures of technologies, such as the Internet, are regarded as crucial 'arrangements of power' (DeNardis, 2014: 7), with key implications for 'what is possible' (Auld *et al.*, 2010: 21).

Governance *by* emergent technologies is revealed in several existing interdisciplinary studies that have examined blockchain applications. The incentives for actors to hoard Bitcoins imposed by technical limits on the creation of a maximum 21 million monetary tokens in the original blockchain have been linked to a particular monetary philosophy alternatively identified as 'digital metallism' (Maurer *et al.*, 2013) and 'neo-metalism' (Jeong, 2013). Rather than assuming blockchains to be overly complex and incomprehensible 'black boxes' (Rosenberg, 1982: vii), the specific properties of these technologies are increasingly being drawn out and linked to forms of governance *by* emergent technologies. One example is how the 'permissionless' character of blockchains has positioned their users as 'dispersed, atomized, self-interested individuals' operating in what has been compared with Hobbesian states of nature (Atzori, 2017). Lacking recourse to higher authority, the computer code underlying blockchains has been regarded as forming a type of 'techno-Leviathan' that structures the activities and incentives of its users in important yet often implicit manners (Scott, 2015). The monetary-like coins or tokens granted as rewards for verifying blockchain transactions have further been considered as forms of 'gamification' (DuPont and Maurer, 2015) that extend the principles of Milton Friedman (1970) in incentivising users to maximise self-interest in order to contribute to the wider benefit of the communities they operate within. That the original Bitcoin blockchain is explicitly underpinned by liberal and libertarian ideologies has been increasingly recognised by critics and promoters alike as constituting users as particular types of 'consumer-citizens' (Swan, 2015; for a critique see Karlstrøm, 2014).

Yet what exactly do the principles underlying blockchains entail for specific actors and processes in contemporary global governance? Contributors to this volume extend the findings of existing interdisciplinary blockchain studies by not only drawing out further instances of governance *by* emergent technologies but also by assessing the governance implications posed. In doing so, they navigate between the claims of liberal commentators that implicitly consider governance *by* emergent technology to be normatively positive and those of critical scholars who more explicitly lament the negative consequences stemming from how blockchain applications enable individualistic and capitalist relations to be extended into further spheres of social activity (e.g. Golumbia, 2015).

(Dis)empowerment in governance with emerging technologies

In a second instance, this volume builds on blockchain studies yielding insights into longstanding GPE debates on the specific actors and processes that are (dis)empowered through forms of governance *with* technologies. In contrast to constructivist understanding of technology as fundamentally shaping its users, these approaches assume rationalist conceptions of technologies as *tools* for advancing predetermined and unchanging actor self-interests. Emergent technologies here enable some actors to exercise power *over* others in zero-sum games that inevitably yield winners and losers. These debates engage traditional GPE concerns with how a specific technology 'is (or is not) adopted when it is, and for whom' (Underhill, 1997: 141; e.g. Huo, 2015). In other words, emergent technologies are considered to *enhance* global governance capacities by helping 'a wide range of state and non-state actors to acquire new interaction capacities thereby becoming more effective and influential players on the global stage' (Fritsch, 2014: 120).

Who precisely is empowered in governance *with* emergent technologies such as blockchains? Existing studies by scholars and formal governance actors suggest that instrumental uses of blockchains may empower several sets of historically underprivileged actors. Blockchain applications for remittances have been widely praised for enhancing the 'inclusion' of migrants, temporary 'guest workers', and the 'unbanked' into key processes of market-based governance (Ammous, 2015; Athey, 2015; European Banking Authority, 2014; Her Majesty's Treasury, 2015). CCs such as Ripple[7] are specifically designed to facilitate cross-border money flows in manners that reduce the fees and pathologies involved with longstanding global remittance processes (Kunz, 2011). Along with competing CCs such as Stellar,[8] these applications of blockchains have been less enthusiastically recognised as helping other individuals, such as whistleblowers, and organisations such as Wikileaks to gain further prominence in global governance by holding powerful actors accountable (Banque de France, 2013; Simser, 2015; see more generally Pieterse, 2012).

At the same time, existing studies of blockchains also suggest that applications of these technologies may disempower established non-state actors at the heart of global governance. The roles of financial intermediaries in the credit card and money transfer industries, for instance, are bypassed in peer-to-peer CC transactions. Blockchains also threaten the longstanding governance roles of insurers and accountants in interpreting insurance claims and auditing transactions, respectively (von Gunten and Mainelli, 2014; Spoke and Steel, 2015). By automatically verifying and triggering pre-encoded contractual terms, blockchain-based 'smart contracts' challenge the interpretations of ambiguous contractual language by lawyers (DuPont and Maurer, 2015; Swanson, 2014; Campbell, 2016). Blockchains may thereby contribute to the wider technological challenges faced by traditional professionals whose expert knowledge has long underpinned global governance whilst empowering new sets of professionals such as computer coders and ICT developers (Susskind and Susskind, 2015; Campbell-Verduyn, 2017). At the organisational level, layered sets of smart contracts may further displace established processes of corporate governance. The crowdfunding campaign for the first decentralised autonomous organisation (DAO), a venture capital fund that was to be managed by layered sets of smart contracts rather than human executives and board members, raised a sum of CCs equivalent to a record $170 million in 2016.

Applications of blockchain technologies thereby appear to be disintermediating the roles of key centralised actors and processes traditionally underpinning global governance in manners that may not always be normatively desireable. Enabling transactions that circumvent the banks and other financial institutions charged with monitoring and supplying states with income information, whilst generally being beyond the reach of traditional global tax governance processes, has led one legal scholar to characterise CCs as 'super tax havens' (Marian, 2013). Blockchain applications may be indicative of shifting governance authority enabled by emergent technologies in an age in which, as the Internet governance scholar Laura DeNardis (2014: 9–10) puts it, '[t]raditionally dominant institutions of power – whether nation states, religious institutions, or multinational corporations – have lost some of their historic control'. In principle, applications of blockchain technologies appear to contribute to the 'decentralization of political power within societies' (Skolnikoff, 1993: 240) that GPE scholars have recognised as shifting 'power and the locus of authority away from the state' (Singh and Rosenau, 2002: 2; see more widely Junne, 1997; Cerny, 1994; Auld *et al.*, 2010; Youngs, 2007: 10). Such loss of centralised governance capacity may be celebrated in enhancing the competition, for instance, to state monopolies over national currencies, as CC supporters tend to stress in invoking the liberatarian arguments of deceased Austrian economist Friedrich Hayek in

The Denationalisation of Money (Hayek, 1976; Paul, 2016). Yet, whilst praising the limits imposed on overtly political forms of state-driven governance, CC supporters tend to overlook both the normative and practical problems that have remained unresolved in such applications of blockchain technologies. For instance, the lack of recourse to a centralised entity to rectify a loss or theft of CCs leaves 'altcoin' users without remedy, which business ethicists have recognised as unfair (Dierksmeier and Steele, 2016).

Yet instrumental uses of blockchain technologies may actually empower the centralised actors and processes that have long underpinned global governance. States are not solely at the whims of technological change but, as GPE and other scholars have long recognised, still the predominant actors in global governance are often active in developing and applying emergent technologies (Datz, 2008; Mazzucato, 2015; Strange, 1998). Even small states have 'partnered' with blockchain firms, for instance, to provide 'e-residency' identity documents for foreign investors (Sullivan and Burger, 2017).[9] Blockchain-based registries of government data and blockchain-based issuance of public social welfare benefits have been trialled by governments in both large and small jurisdictions who have worked in partnership with blockchain firms to fight corruption and abuse (Aitken, 2016; Chavez-Dreyfuss, 2016, 2017; Plimmer, 2016; Shin, 2016). State actors are furthermore employing this set of emergent technologies as tools for tracking and tracing digital transactions in prosecuting crime (Bohannon, 2016: 1145). The Netherlands, for example, has drawn on blockchains in prosecuting individuals alleged to have undertaken and facilitated money laundering through Bitcoin and other applications of the emergent technology (Eikelenboom and Dobber, 2017). Rather than necessarily undermining state capacities, therefore, governance *with* blockchains may be empowering established centralised actors and processes.

In addition to states, centralised multinational firms and quasi-state institutions may also be further empowered by blockchain applications. The Big Four accounting firms, for instance, have repositioned themselves as 'conduits' to help clients implement blockchain technologies (Allison, 2015).[10] Large global banks have not disappeared but are rather strengthening the back-office operations of longstanding financial processes in working together to develop common standards for uses of blockchain technology in global finance (e.g. R3, n.d.; Society for Worldwide Interbank Financial Telecommunication, 2017). Central bankers, moreover, have contemplated the uses of blockchain-backed digital currencies for eliminating paper money (Haldane, 2015; Spence, 2015). So-called 'state-sponsored' CCs (Deloitte, 2015) are being explored by central banks to provide these historically powerful actors with enhanced 'real-time' capacities to monitor aggregate transactions and extend control over interest rates (Eyers, 2016; Shubber, 2016; e.g. Stafford, 2016). These trends are indicative of how emergent technologies can both 'induce firms to cooperate' (Cutler *et al.*, 1999: 8) as well as empower the already powerful by reinforcing status quo power relations in global governance. In examining how the *actual* uses of blockchains as tools provide actors with relative power *over* one another, contributors to this volume draw out specific implications of governance *with* technology for organising, ordering, and managing a global political economy in which increasingly rapid and complex interrelationships are occurring between actors beyond and within nation-states.

Coercion and flexibility in the governance of emerging technologies

In a third instance, contributors to this volume provide insights into contemporary forms of governance *of* technologies in building on and extending recent analysis of whether and how applications of blockchains should be formally governed at various levels of authority. At the national level, countries including Bangladesh, Bolivia, and Ecuador have pursued a centralised approach banning the most prominent application of blockchain technology. Similarly, the People's Bank of China and State Bank of Vietnam have issued formal laws prohibiting financial services firms and their employees from handling and conducting any transactions in CCs. Studies by computer scientists, legal scholars, and economists (e.g. Böhme *et al.*, 2015) have all warned that such 'heavy-handed' (Singh, 2015) approaches fail to prevent the illegitimate uses of blockchain activities. Centralised forms of coercion are regarded in existing interdisciplinary scholarship as merely pushing blockchain-based activities towards less stringent jurisdictions and murkier corners of the Internet whilst also harming their more legitimate and beneficial applications, such as facilitating migrant remittances (Scott, 2016; see also Commonwealth Working Group, 2015: 15–18).

Recognising the digital and globe-spanning nature of blockchain activities, governments and formal regulators in other countries and regions have adopted less restrictive and decentralised approaches to the governance *of* this emerging technology. On the one hand, supranational agencies in the European Union have issued stern yet rather general warnings concerning the risks involved with blockchain experiments in order to informally discourage financial institutions from dealing in CCs (European Banking Authority, 2014; European Central Bank, 2016: 2). Similarly, in the United States, a commissioner of the Commodity Futures Trading Commission has publicly advocated for federal regulators to 'avoid undue restrictions' and 'do no harm' by relying on the 'nature of the technology' and the 'bottom–up' decentralised forms of governance (Giancarlo, 2016). On the other hand, formal regulatory agencies in Australia, Singapore, the United Kingdom, and elsewhere have developed so-called 'regulatory sandboxes' in which existing laws are temporarily relaxed to permit controlled and monitored blockchain experiments within their jurisdictions. Agreements are also being concluded between countries to permit experimentation in blockchain transactions across jursidctions. In contrast to the centralised and more coercive governance *of* blockchains in some nations, these more flexible approaches allow for multiple types of decentralised rule-making characteristics of the 'provisional' and 'experimentalist' forms of governance that, as noted above, have been identified in several areas of contemporary global governance (Best, 2014; Campbell-Verduyn and Porter, 2014; Nance and Cottrell, 2014; Overdevest and Zeitlin, 2014).

In analysing the formal governance of applications of blockchain technologies, this volume contributes practical lessons and insights into wider debates on the promises and perils of centralised or decentralised approaches to global governance. The latter have become critically important for policy-makers in a period in which even states and regions that have long advocated more flexible, decentralised governance approaches are beginning to consider shifting towards more centralised, formal governance strategies as applications of blockchains have grown in size, scope, and prominence. According to the World Economic Forum head of financial services industries, blockchains are slated to become 'the beating heart' (Giancarlo Bruno, cited in Vanham, 2016) of what the Institute of International Finance (2015) characterises as an emerging 'internet of finance'. Key regulators in the US and elsewhere have begun warning that applications of blockchain technologies, and CCs in particular, may threaten global financial stability (Jopson, 2016). These warnings are instigating shifting perspectives on more active and 'hands-on', formal approaches that are becoming increasingly attractive to regulators pressed to act or at least be seen 'to be doing something' (MacKnight, 2016). Insights into how formal regulatory efforts have and can address problems and governance 'gaps' in blockchain-based activities are provided in several chapters of this volume, whose main arguments are summarised in the following section.

Summary of chapters

The structure of this volume takes inspiration from its title and, more generally, from the growing international recognition that applications and implications of blockchain technologies have shifted beyond crypto-communities and 'beyond Bitcoin' (e.g. Extance, 2015; Kostakis and Giotitsas, 2014; Hutt, 2016; Rosov, 2015; Schatsky and Muraskin, 2015). The initial chapters of this volume focus primarily on Bitcoin and its competitors. The volume progressively moves towards chapters that analyse further blockchain applications whose experimental character is indicative of the continually emergent nature of this set of technologies. There is, however, no clear-cut division between initial chapters focusing *solely* on Bitcoin and latter chapters ignoring the leading CC. While all chapters consider both the initial and more recent applications of the emergent technology, the initial prominence of Bitcoin steadily gives way to other blockchain applications as the volume progresses.

The justification for this chapter structure is that, as the previous section of this chapter indicated, emergent technologies are often framed by their initial or their most prominent applications. Yet, what exactly Bitcoin *is* and what initial applications of blockchain *are* both remain fundamentally contested. Contributors to this volume, while all employing the term 'cryptocurrencies', stress that CCs are radically different from traditional state-backed currencies. Chapter 2 tackles debates over the specific *monetary* nature of Bitcoin and its digital competitors head on. From an innovative combination of heterodox perspectives, sociologists Moritz Hütten and Matthias Thiemann stress the politically charged nature of all attempts to develop money, whether or not these are in digital formats. Their analysis reveals surprising governance activities undertaken by combinations of activists, market actors, and states in 'money games' that include both longstanding national currencies and recent applications of blockchain technology. Examining the frequent formal and informal actions undertaken by state and non-state governance actors alike, Hütten and Thiemann stress the paradoxical nature of attempts to develop 'apolitical' forms of money. Through a detailed periodisation of the politics underpinning the evolution of Bitcoin, their chapter contributes to wider interdisciplinary understanding of the politically charged nature of emergent technologies and their evolving forms of governance.

Chapter 3 identifies a further plethora of actors involved in blockchain-based governance. Analysing the specific factors driving the values of leading CCs, management researchers Ying-Ying Hsieh, Jean-Philippe Vergne and economist Sha Wang distinguish varied yet interconnected roles of several underacknowledged non-state actors in what they refer to as the 'internal' and 'external' governance of CCs. From software coders to traditional and social media, multiple sets of actors are shown to exercise agency in forms of community governance in CCs, which are understood to be 'global organisations'. The quantitative analysis of this chapter yields a surprising conclusion: that the more centralised CCs are, with clearer decision-making structures, the higher their value in global markets. Despite the attention they receive, decentralised CCs with non-hierarchical governance structures are often valued less and their unclear governance structures tend to be regarded with more suspicion. The counterintuitive findings of this chapter point to the persistent importance of specific organisational forms of self-governance.

Chapter 4 then connects considerations of money and media in the previous chapters by analysing the implications of blockchains for global anti-money-laundering (AML) governance. Political economists Malcolm Campbell-Verduyn and Marcel Goguen assess alarmist claims by media and regulatory actors that CCs and other applications of blockchain technologies are implicated in money laundering and undermine AML efforts. The perception of this emergent technology as a challenge rather than an opportunity for combating international money laundering is linked in this chapter to the particular distributed and quasi-anonymous features of blockchains. Campbell-Verduyn and Goguen detail how the specific nature of formal governance responses by actors such as the Financial Action Task Force have in turn influenced a bifurcation of blockchain applications into activities complying and those not complying with AML efforts. In illustrating the mutually constitutive and continuously evolving relationship between blockchains and the international AML regime, this chapter highlights the often surprising and indeterminate trajectories of technology and its formal global governance.

Chapter 5 then compares the responses of governments to blockchains in yielding insights into the benefits and drawbacks of formal governance *of* emergent technologies more generally. Political economists Kai Jia and Falin Zhang distinguish prohibitive from laissez-faire approaches in the respective Russian and the American approaches to the governance *of* blockchain technologies. Jia and Zhang then illustrate the more nuanced 'middle ground' approach pursued in China, the country that has become the centre of CC production (Popper, 2016). This model of 'prudent enthusiasm' is shown to provide useful regulatory opportunities whilst effectively confronting the risks presented by technological change. Jia and Zhang argue that such governance approaches can be usefully adopted by all countries, and particularly those in the Global South, where 'blockchain evangelists' (Scott, 2016) are becoming increasingly active.

In Chapter 6, anthropologist Daivi Rodima-Taylor and political economist William Grimes combine the discussions of previous chapters on development and money laundering into an original analysis comparing the potential and actual promises of blockchain technologies for overcoming the longstanding inefficiencies associated with global remittances. This chapter stresses the persistent importance of local cultures and governance practices in facilitating the adoption of previous digital payment transactions, such as M-Pesa in East Africa, as well as in preventing more recent efforts to integrate blockchain-based remittance applications. Through an assemblage approach, Rodima-Taylor and Grimes emphasise both the challenges and opportunities faced by formal and informal actors involved in organising and maintaining cross-border financial transactions. Their analysis yields valuable insights into how forms of governance can integrate emergent technologies in processes of 'financial inclusion' and development more generally.

Chapter 7 underlines the need to view the governance of Bitcoin and other applications of blockchain technologies with scepticism. Through a science and technology studies-inspired approach, sociologists Francesca Musiani, Alexandre Mallard, and Cécile Méadel foreground how the discreet and backgrounded governance features of blockchain applications influenced several key moments of tension and crisis since the emergence of Bitcoin in 2009. Dissecting three well-publicised instances of disorder and disorganisation enabled and, to lesser extents, resolved through complex interactions between technical infrastructures and a variety of actors, Musiani, Mallard, and Méadel stress the grounding of digital activities in specific socio-material processes. Their chapter exposes both formal and informal governance mechanisms underlying applications of emergent technologies that are often assumed to be devoid of governance.

In Chapter 8, information scientist Quinn DuPont echoes the stress of Chapter 7 on periods of crisis, yet shifts the empirical focus to consider more recent attempts to apply blockchain technology beyond Bitcoin. The case of the failed decentralised autonomous organisation (DAO) highlights the growing governance roles of so-called 'smart contracts', and the main blockchain-based platform for building them – Ethereum – in experimentation at the fringes of this niche sector of the global political economy. Through an ethnographic approach, DuPont navigates the considerable utopian hype surrounding The DAO's contribution – what is more widely linked to ill-fated attempts to reduce the role of humans in automated forms of governance *by* technology. This chapter stresses the persistence of active, human roles and social relationships, both in the development and programming of smart contracts, and controversially in responses to crises arising from their technical flaws.

In Chapter 9, the contributions of the volume are brought together and positioned within wider debates on emergent technologies and the insights their varying forms of governance provide into the ordering, organising, and managing of an increasingly digital global political economy. Common threads are drawn amongst the empirical and conceptual insights of each chapter. Connections are specifically made between the actors, processes, and outcomes characterising forms of governance *by*, *with*, and *of* blockchain applications. As even a volume dedicated to analysing these governance implications and insights is constrained by limits, an agenda for ongoing research is set out specifying several avenues for continually interrogating Bitcoin, CCs and wider applications of blockchain technologies. In summarising the findings of this volume and proposing further paths forward, this concluding chapter makes the case for persistent interdisciplinary research on the implications and insights that analysis of blockchains and emergent technologies more widely provide for governance in an increasingly digital global political economy.

Acknowledgements

The support of the Social Sciences and Humanities Research Council of Canada (fellowship no. 756-2015-0474) as well as the editors at Routledge and the RIPE Global Political Economy Series, especially Eleni Tsingou, is gratefully acknowledged.

Notes

1 See De Filippi and Loveluck (2016: 26, ft 11) for a coincise overview of efforts to identify the real Satoshi Nakamoto. Most prominently, both a 2014 *Newsweek* investigation and a 2016 announcement by Australian security expert Craig Steven Wright that he was Satoshi Nakomoto were discredited as publicity stunts.
2 For a wider sampling, see for instance Kharif (2014); Carney (2013); Shin (2015); Metz (2015); Office of the Inspectorate General (2016).
3 For an overview of literature on Bitcoin and blockchains, see http://bit.ly/BitcoinResearch
4 Some excellent exceptions do exist, such as Ammous (2015) and Böhme *et al.* (2015).
5 An example of which is the Golem Project at https://golem.network/
6 More than three-quarters of which is focused on Bitcoin, as a recent review found (Yli-Huumo *et al.*, 2016).
7 See https://ripple.com/trade/ripple-for-market-makers/; a similar project is http://saldo.mx/
8 See www.stellar.org/how-it-works/use-cases/
9 See https://e-estonia.com/e-residents/about/
10 See for instance http://rubixbydeloitte.com/

Bibliography

Aitken, R. (2016, 5 April). Bitland's African blockchain initiative putting land on the ledger. *Forbes*.

Allison, I. (2015, 18 August). Deloitte, Libra, Accenture: The work of auditors in the age of Bitcoin 2.0 technology. *International Business Times*.

Ammous, S. (2015). Economics beyond financial intermediation: Digital currencies' possibilities for growth, poverty alleviation, and international development. *Journal of Private Enterprise, 30*(3), 19–50.

Arvind, N., Bonneau, J., Felten, E., Miller, A., and Goldfeder, S. (2016). *Bitcoin and cryptocurrency technologies*. Princeton: Princeton University Press.

Athey, S. (2015, January). 5 ways digital currency will change the world. *World Economic Forum*.

Atzori, M. (2017). Blockchain technology and decentralized governance: Is the state still necessary? *Journal of Governance and Regulation, 6*(1), 45–62.

Auld, G., Cashore, B., Balboa, C., Bozzi, L., and Renckens, S. (2010). Can technological innovations improve private regulation in the global economy? *Business and Politics, 12*(3), 1–39.

Banque de France. (2013). The dangers linked to the emergence of virtual currencies: The example of bitcoins. *Focus*, No. 10–5, December.

Barbrook, R., and Cameron, A. (1996). The Californian ideology. *Science as Culture, 6*(1), 44–72.

Berry, D.M. (2012). The relevance of understanding code to international political economy. *International Politics, 49*(2), 277–96.

Best, J. (2014). *Governing failure: Provisional expertise and the transformation of global development finance*. Cambridge: Cambridge University Press.

Best, J. (2008). Ambiguity, uncertainty, and risk: Rethinking indeterminacy. *International Political Sociology, 2*(4), 355–74.

Bjerg, O. (2016). How is Bitcoin money? *Theory, Culture and Society, 33*(1), 53–72.

Bohannon, J. (2016). The bitcoin busts. *Science, 351*(6278), 1144–6.

Böhme, R., Christin, N., Edelman, B., and Moore, T. (2015). Bitcoin: Economics, technology, and governance. *Journal of Economic Perspectives, 29*(2), 213–38.

Böhme, R., Brenner, M., Moore, T., and Smith, M. (eds) (2014). *Financial cryptography and data security*. Berlin: Springer.

Bollen, R. (2013). The legal status of online currencies: Are bitcoins the future? *Journal of Banking and Finance Law and Practice, 24*(3), 272–93.

Brassett, J., Richardson, B., and Smith, W. (2012). Private experiments in global governance: Primary commodity roundtables and the politics of deliberation. *International Theory, 4*(3), 367–99.

Brito, J., Hoegner, S., Friedman, J., Rae, N., and Osborne, P. (2015). *The law of bitcoin*. Bloomington, IN: iUniverse.

Broome, A., and Seabrooke, L. (2008). The IMF and experimentalist governance in small Western states. *Round Table, 97*(395), 205–26.

Campbell, R. (2016). The digital future of the oldest information profession. In F. Xavier Olleros and M. Zhegu (eds) *Research Handbook on Digital Transformations*. Cheltenham: Edward Elgar.

Campbell-Verduyn, M. (2017). *Professional authority after the global financial crisis*. London: Palgrave Macmillan.

Campbell-Verduyn, M., Goguen, M., and Porter, T. (2016). Big data and algorithmic governance: The case of financial practices. *New Political Economy, 22*(2), 219–36.

Campbell-Verduyn, M., and Porter, T. (2014). Experimentalism in European Union and global financial governance: Interactions, contrasts, and implications. *Journal of European Public Policy, 21*(3), 408–29.

Carney, J. (2015, 27 February). J.P. Morgan goes hunting for disruptors and bitcoin experts. *Wall Street Journal.*

Carney, M. (2013, 16 December). Bitcoin has a dark side: Its carbon footprint. *Pando.*

Carr, M. (2016). *US Power and the internet in international relations: The irony of the information age.* London: Palgrave Macmillan.

Cerny, P. (1994). The dynamics of financial globalization: Technology, market structure, and policy response. *Policy Sciences, 27,* 319–42.

Chavez-Dreyfuss, G. (2017, 19 April). Ukraine launches big blockchain deal with tech firm Bitfury. *Reuters.*

Chavez-Dreyfuss, G. (2016, 16 July). Sweden tests blockchain technology for land registry. *Reuters.*

Choucri, N. (2012). *Cyberpolitics in international relations.* Boston: MIT Press.

Chwierut, M. (2016, 24 March). Intro: Cryptocurrency governance (of, by, for the users?). *Smith + Crown.*

Clarke, C. (2017, 24 February). *The digital disruption of finance: Monopoly, power and data in marketplace lending.* Paper presented to the annual convention of the International Studies Association, Baltimore, MD.

Cohen, B. (2001). Electronic money: New day or false dawn? *Review of International Political Economy, 8*(2), 197–225.

Commonwealth Working Group. (2015). *Commonwealth Working Group on virtual currencies.*

Cox, J. (2013). *Bitcoin and digital currencies: The new world of money and freedom.* Baltimore, MD: Laissez Faire Books.

Cutler, C., Haufler, V., and Porter, T. (1999). Private authority and international affairs. In C. Cutler, V. Haufler, and T. Porter (eds) *Private Authority in International Affairs.* Albany, NY: SUNY Press.

Datz, G. (2008). Governments as market players: State innovation in the global economy. *Journal of International Affairs, 62*(1), 35–49.

De Búrca, G., Keohane, R.O., and Sabel, C. (2014). Global experimentalist governance. *British Journal of Political Science, 44*(3), 477–86.

De Filippi, P., and Loveluck, B. (2016). The invisible politics of Bitcoin: Governance crisis of a decentralised infrastructure. *Internet Policy Review, 5*(3).

del Castillo, M. (2015, August 12). The 'Great Bitcoin Exodus' has totally changed New York's Bitcoin ecosystem. *New York Business Journal.*

Deloitte. (2015). *State-sponsored cryptocurrency: Adapting the best of Bitcoin's innovation to the payments ecosystem.* New York: Author.

DeNardis, L. (2014). *The global war for internet governance.* New Haven, CT: Yale University Press.

Der Derian, J. (2003). The question of information technology in international relations. *Millennium-Journal of International Studies, 32*(3), 441–56.

Dierksmeier, C., and Steele, P. (2016). Cryptocurrencies and business ethics. *Journal of Business Ethics,* pp. 1–14. DOI: 10.1007/s10551-016-3298-0.

DuPont, Q., and Maurer, B. (2015, 23 June). Ledgers and law in the blockchain. *King's Review.*

Dwyer, G. (2015). The economics of Bitcoin and similar private digital currencies. *Journal of Financial Stability, 17,* 81–91.

Eikelenboom, S., and Dobber, J. (2017, 3 January). OM voert strijd op tegen witwassen via bitcoin. *Financieele Dagblad.*

Einsiedel, E. (2009). Making sense of emerging technologies. In E. Einsiedel (ed.) *Emerging technologies: From hindsight to foresight.* Vancouver: UBC Press.

European Banking Authority. (2014). Opinion on 'virtual currencies'. Op/2014/08, pp. 18–19.

European Central Bank. (2016). Opinion of the European Central Bank. Retrieved 23 November 2016 from www.ecb.europa.eu/ecb/legal/pdf/en_con_2016_49_f_sign.pdf.

Extance, A. (2015, 30 September). The future of cryptocurrencies: Bitcoin and beyond. *Nature.*

Eyers, J. (2016, 21 November). Central banks look to the future of money with blockchain technology trial. *Australian Financial Review.*

Eyers, J. (2015, 14 December). Why the blockchain will propel a services revolution. *Australian Financial Review.*

Farmer, P. (2014). Speculative tech: The bitcoin legal quagmire and the need for legal innovation. *Journal of Business and Technology Law, 9.*

Foley, S. (2015, 15 February). Professors stake out territory for bitcoin. *Financial Times.*

Friedman, M. (1970, 13 September). The social responsibility of business is to increase its profits. *New York Times Magazine.*

Fritsch, S. (2014). Conceptualizing the ambivalent role of technology in international relations: Between systemic change and continuity. In M. Mayer, M. Carpes, and R. Knoblich (eds) *The global politics of science and technology, Vol. 1* (pp. 115–39). Berlin: Springer Berlin Heidelberg.

Gabor, D., and Brooks, S. (2016). The digital revolution in financial inclusion: International development in the fintech era. *New Political Economy, 22*(4), 423–36.

Gartner. (2016, 16 August). Gartner's 2016 hype cycle for emerging technologies identifies three key trends that organizations must track to gain competitive advantage. Retrieved from www.gartner.com/newsroom/id/3412017

Giancarlo, C. (2016, 12 April). With blockchain, regulators should first do no harm. *Financial Times.*

Gimein, M. (2013, 12 April). Virtual bitcoin mining is a real-world environmental disaster. *Bloomberg.*

Golumbia, D. (2015). Bitcoin as politics: Distributed right-wing extremism. In G. Lovink, N. Tkacz, and P. de Vries (eds) *MoneyLab reader: An intervention in digital economy* (pp. 118–31). Amsterdam: Institute of Network Cultures.

Haldane, A. (2015, 18 September). *How low can you go?* Speech given at the Portadown Chamber of Commerce, Northern Ireland.

Hansen, H.K., and Porter, T. (2017). What do big data do in global governance? *Global Governance: A Review of Multilateralism and International Organizations, 23*(1), 31–42.

Hayek, F. (1976). *Denationalisation of money: The argument refined.* Auburn, AL: Ludwig von Mises Institute.

Helleiner, E. (1998). Electronic money: A challenge to the sovereign state? *International Affairs, 51,* 387–410.

Her Majesty's Treasury. (2015, March). *Digital currencies: Response to the call for information.* London: Author.

Hesse-Biber, S. (ed.) (2011). *The handbook of emergent technologies in social research.* Oxford: Oxford University Press.

Holley, E. (2015, 28 October). Linq launches blockchain platform Linq at Money 2020 in Las Vegas. *Banking Technology.*

Hughes, S., and Middlebrook, S. (2014). Regulating cryptocurrencies in the United States: Current issues and future directions. *William Mitchell Law Review, 40,* 813–44.

Huo, J. (2015). *How nations innovate: The political economy of technological innovation in affluent capitalist economies.* Oxford: Oxford University Press.

Hutt, R. (2016, 13 December). Beyond bitcoin: 4 surprising uses for blockchain. *World Economic Forum.*

Institute of International Finance. (2015, 16 November). *Banking on the blockchain: Reengineering the financial architecture.* Washington, DC: Author.

Jasanoff, S. (2004). The idiom of co-production. In S. Jasanoff (ed) *States of knowledge: The co-production of science and the social order.* London: Routledge.

Jeong, S. (2013). *The bitcoin protocol as law, and the politics of a stateless currency.* pp. 9–14. Available at SSRN: http://papers.ssrn.com/sol3/papers.cfm?abstract_id=2294124

Jopson, B. (2016, 21 June). Regulators say bitcoin poses 'financial stability risks'. *Financial Times.*

Junne, G. (1997). The end of the dinosaurs? In C. Farrands, M. Talalay, and R. Tooze (eds) *Technology, culture and competitiveness: Change and the world political economy* (pp. 57–71). London: Routledge.

Kaminska, I. (2015, 4 September). Disrupting the nation state. *Financial Times.*

Karlstrøm, H. (2014). Do libertarians dream of electric coins? The material embeddedness of Bitcoin. *Distinktion: Scandinavian Journal of Social Theory, 15*(1), 23–36.

Kastelein, R. (2016, 12 June). World Wide Web creator Tim Berners-Lee wants to decentralise the Internet with P2P and blockchain technologies. *BlockchainsNews.*

Kharif, O. (2014, 28 March). Bitcoin 2.0 shows technology evolving beyond use as money. *Bloomberg.*

Kiviat, T. (2015). Beyond Bitcoin: Issues in regulating blockchain transactions. *Duke Law Journal, 65,* 569–608.

Kobrin, S. (1997). Electronic cash and the end of national markets. *Foreign Policy,* 65–77.

Koenig, A. (2015). *A beginner's guide to bitcoin and Austrian economics.* Munich: FinanzBuch Verlag.

Kostakis, V., and Giotitsas, C. (2014). The (A)Political economy of bitcoin. *tripleC: Communication, Capitalism and Critique, 12*(2), 431–40.

Kunz, R. (2011). *The political economy of global remittances: Gender, governmentality and neoliberalism.* New York: Routledge.

Langley, P., and Leyshon, A. (2016). Platform capitalism: The intermediation and capitalisation of digital economic circulation. *Finance and Society.*

Lessig, L. (2006). *Code: Version 2.0.* New York: Basic.

Lo, S., and Wang, J.C. (2014). Bitcoin as money? *Boston Federal Reserve Current Policy Perspectives,* No. 14–4.

Lucas, L. (2016, 5 December). Supermarkets, pig farmers and cotton traders turn to blockchain. *Financial Times.*

MacKnight, J. (2016, 1 April). Blockchain: Less talk, more action. *The Banker.*

Marian, O. (2013). Are cryptocurrencies super tax havens? *Michigan Law Review, 112*(1), 42–3.

Maurer, B., Nelms, T.C., and Swartz, L. (2013) 'When perhaps the real problem is money itself!': The practical materiality of Bitcoin. *Social Semiotics, 23*(2), 261–77.

Mayer, M., and Acuto, M. (2015). The global governance of large technical systems. *Millennium, 43*(2), 660–83.

Mayer, M., Carpes, M., and Knoblich, R. (eds) (2014a). *The global politics of science and technology, Vol. 1: Concepts from international relations and other disciplines.* Berlin Heidelberg: Springer.

Mayer, M., Carpes, M., and Knoblich, R. (eds) (2014b). *The global politics of science and technology, Vol. 2: Perspectives, cases and methods.* Berlin Heidelberg: Springer.

Mazzucato, M. (2015). *The entrepreneurial state: Debunking public vs. private sector myths.* New York: PublicAffairs.

McCook, H. (2014). *An order-of-magnitude estimate of the relative sustainability of the bitcoin network.* Retrieved from www.scribd.com/doc/228253109/The-Relative-Sustainability-of-the-Bitcoin-Network-by-Hass-McCook

Metz, C. (2015, December 17). Tech and banking giants ditch bitcoin for their own blockchains. *Wired.*

Mueller, M. (2010). *Networks and states: The global politics of Internet governance.* Boston: MIT Press.

Nakamoto, S. (2008). *Bitcoin: A peer-to-peer electronic cash system.* Retrieved 21 August 2017 from https://bitcoin.org/bitcoin.pdf

Nance, M.T., and Cottrell, M.P. (2014). A turn toward experimentalism? Rethinking security and governance in the twenty-first century. *Review of International Studies, 40*(2), 277–301.

Nesvetailova, A. (2014). Innovations, fragility and complexity: Understanding the power of finance. *Government and Opposition, 49*(3), 542–68.

Office of the Inspectorate General. (2016). *Blockchain technology: Possibilities for the U.S. Postal Service.* Retrieved from www.uspsoig.gov/sites/default/files/document-library-files/2016/RARC-WP-16-001.pdf

Overdevest, C., and Zeitlin, J. (2014). Assembling an experimentalist regime: Transnational governance interactions in the forest sector. *Regulation and Governance, 8*(1), 22–48.

Paul, A. (2016). Bitcoin vs. sovereign money: On the lure and limits of monetary reforms. *Behemoth: Journal on Civilisation, 9*(2), 8–21.

Pelizza, A., and Kuhlmann, S. (forthcoming, 2018). Mining governance mechanisms: Innovation policy, practice and theory facing algorithmic decision-making. In E.G. Carayannis, D.F. Campbell, and M.P. Efthymiopoulos (eds) *Handbook of cyber-development, cyber-democracy, and cyber-defense.* Berlin: Springer.

Penrose, K. (2013). Banking on Bitcoin: Applying anti-money laundering and money transmitter laws. *North Carolina Banking Institute, 18*, 529–51.

Pflaum, I., and Hateley, E. (2013). Bit of a problem: National and extraterritorial regulation of virtual currency in the age of financial disintermediation. *Georgetown Journal of International Law, 45*, 1169–215.

Pieterse, J. (2012). Leaking superpower: WikiLeaks and the contradictions of democracy. *Third World Quarterly, 33*(1), 1909–24.

Plimmer, G. (2016, 12 July). Use of bitcoin tech to pay UK benefits sparks privacy concerns. *Financial Times.*

Ponsford, M. (2015). A comparative analysis of Bitcoin and other decentralised virtual currencies: Legal regulation in the People's Republic of China, Canada, and the United States. *Hong Kong Journal of Legal Studies, 9*, 29–50.

Popper, N. (2016, 29 June). How China took center stage in Bitcoin's civil war. *New York Times.*

Popper, N. (2015). *Digital gold: The untold story of Bitcoin*. London: Penguin.

Porter, T. (2002). *Technology, governance and political conflict in international industries*. New York: Routledge

R3. (2017). *About R3*. Retrieved from www.r3cev.com/about/

Rifkind, H. (2013, 30 March). How Bitcoin could destroy the state (and perhaps make me a bit of money). *Spectator.*

Rogers, C., and Clarke, C. (2016). Mainstreaming social finance: The regulation of the peer-to-peer lending marketplace in the United Kingdom. *British Journal of Politics and International Relations, 18*(4), 930–45.

Rosenberg, N. (1982). *Inside the black box: Technology and economics*. Cambridge: Cambridge University Press.

Rosov, S. (2015). Beyond bitcoin. *CFA Institute Magazine, 26*(1).

Rotolo, D., Hicks, D., and Martin, B. (2015). What is an emerging technology? *Research Policy, 44*(10), 1827–43.

Ruggie, J. (1975). International responses to technology: Concepts and trends. *International Organization, 29*(3), 557–83.

Russell, A. (1997). Technology as knowledge: Generic technology and change in the global political economy. In M. Talalay, C. Farrands, and R. Tooze (eds) *Technology, culture and competitiveness: Change and the world political economy*. London: Routledge.

Schatsky, D., and Muraskin, C. (2015). *Beyond bitcoin: Blockchain is coming to disrupt your industry*. Westlake, TX: Deloitte University Press.

Schwab, K. (2016). *The fourth industrial revolution*. Geneva: World Economic Forum.

Scott, B. (2016). Blockchain technology for reputation scoring of financial actors. *Ethics in Finance, Robin Cosgrove Prize Global Edition 2014–2015*, pp. 128–39.

Scott, B. (2015, 1 June). Visions of a techno-Leviathan: The politics of the Bitcoin blockchain. *E-International Relations.*

Selgin, G. (2015). Synthetic commodity money. *Journal of Financial Stability, 17*, 92–9.

Shabab, H. (2014, 9 October). *Regulating Bitcoin and block chain derivatives*. Written statement to the Commodity Futures Trading Commission. SSRN: http://ssrn.com/abstract=2508707

Shin, L. (2016, 21 April). Republic of Georgia to pilot land titling on blockchain with economist Hernando De Soto, BitFury. *Forbes.*

Shin, L. (2015, 28 October). MasterCard, Bain Capital Ventures, New York Life invest in Bitcoin company digital currency group. *Forbes.*

Shubber, K. (2016, 20 January). Blockchain raises fundamental questions. *Financial Times.*

Simser, J. (2015). Bitcoin and modern alchemy: In code we trust. *Journal of Financial Crime, 22*(2), 156–69.

Singh, K. (2015). New Wild West: Preventing money laundering in the Bitcoin network. *Northwestern Journal of Technology and Intellectual Property, 13*(1), 38–64.

Singh, J.P., and Rosenau, J. (eds) (2002) *Information technologies and global politics: The changing scope of power and governance*. New York: SUNY Press.

Skolnikoff, E. (1993). *The elusive transformation: Science, technology, and the evolution of international politics*. Princeton, NJ: Princeton University Press.

Skolnikoff, E. (1967). *Science, technology, and American foreign policy*. Cambridge, MA: MIT Press.

Society for Worldwide Interbank Financial Telecommunication. (2017, 25 April). Leading global transaction banks kick off blockchain proof of concept with SWIFT

GPI. Retrieved from www.swift.com/news-events/press-releases/leading-global-transaction-banks-kick-off-blockchain-proof-of-concept-with-swift-gpi

Soltas, E. (2013, 5 April). Bitcoin really is an existential threat to the modern liberal state. *Bloomberg.*

Spence, P. (2015, 25 Feburary). Bitcoin revolution could be the next internet, says Bank of England. *Telegraph.*

Spoke, M., and Steele, S. (2015, 11 July). How blockchain tech will change auditing for good. *CoinDesk.*

Stafford, P. (2016, 16 June). Canada experiments with digital dollar on blockchain. *Financial Times.*

Strange, S. (1998). *Mad money: When markets outgrow governments.* Manchester: Manchester University Press.

Sullivan, C., and Burger, E. (2017). E-residency and blockchain. *Computer Law and Security Review.* https://doi.org/10.1016/j.clsr.2017.03.016

Susskind, R., and Susskind, D. (2015). *The future of the professions: How technology will transform the work of human experts.* Oxford: Oxford University Press.

Swan, M. (2015). *Blockchain: Blueprint for a new economy.* Farnham: O'Reilly Media.

Swanson, T. (2014). *Great chain of numbers: A guide to smart contracts, smart property and trustless asset management.* Mountain View, CA: Creative Commons.

Talalay, M., and Farrands, C. (1997). *Technology, culture, and competitiveness: Change and the world political economy.* London: Routledge.

Tett, G. (2014, 19 December). Breathe deep and pay in Bitcoin. *Financial Times.*

The Economist. (2015, 9 May). Blockchain: The next big thing.

Underhill, G. (1997). When technology doesn't mean change: Industrial adjustment and textile production in France. In M. Talalay, C. Farrands, and R. Tooze (eds) *Technology, culture and competitiveness change and the world political economy.* New York: Routledge.

Vanham, P. (2016, 12 August). Blockchain will become 'beating heart' of the global financial system. *World Economic Forum.*

Vigna, P., and Casey, M.J. (2015). *The age of cryptocurrency: How bitcoin and digital money are challenging the global economic order.* New York: St. Martin's Press.

von Gunten, C., and Mainelli, M. (2014). Chain of a lifetime: How blockchain technology might transform personal insurance. *Long Finance.* www.cryptolibrary.org:8080/handle/21/495

Wade, R. (2002). Bridging the digital divide: New route to development or new form of dependency? *Global Governance,* 443–66.

Weber, B. (2016). Bitcoin and the legitimacy crisis of money. *Cambridge Journal of Economics, 40*(1), 17–41.

Wells, H.G. (2005 [1933]). *The shape of things to come.* London: Penguin.

Wigger, A., and Buch-Hansen, H. (2013). Competition, the global crisis, and alternatives to neoliberal capitalism: A critical engagement with anarchism. *New Political Science, 35*(4), 604–26.

Wigglesworth, R. (2015, 22 November). Hedge funds poach computer scientists from Silicon Valley. *Financial Times.*

Winner, L. (1986). *The whale and the reactor: A search for limits in an age of high technology.* Chicago: University of Chicago Press.

Wladawsky-Berger, I. (2014, 12 February). Bitcoin and the Internet of money. *Wall Street Journal.*

World Economic Forum. (2015). *Deep shift technology tipping points and societal impact.* Geneva: Author.

Wright, A., and De Filippi, P. (2015). *Decentralized blockchain technology and the rise of lex cryptographia.* SSRN: http://papers.ssrn.com/sol3/papers.cfm?abstract_id=2580664

Yermacka, D. (2015). Is Bitcoin a real currency? An economic appraisal. In D.L. Kuo Chuen (ed.) *Handbook of digital currency: Bitcoin, innovation, financial instruments, and big data* (pp. 31–43). London: Academic Press.

Yli-Huumo, J., Ko, D., Choi, S., Park, S., and Smolander, K. (2016). Where is current research on blockchain technology? A systematic review. *PLOS ONE, 11*(10), e0163477. doi:10.1371/journal.pone.0163477

Youngs, G. (2007). *Global political economy in the information age: Power and inequality.* New York and London: Routledge.

2 Moneys at the margins

From political experiment to cashless societies

Moritz Hütten and Matthias Thiemann

Introduction

At the time of writing, the death of Bitcoin has been announced for a total of 121 times.[1] At the same time, Bitcoin trades at over \$1,000/BTC,[2] with an estimated market cap of over \$16 billion,[3] and Bitcoin increasingly is being integrated into the governance of mainstream monetary systems. How can we square this circle? How can a seemingly illegitimate cryptocurrency (CC) such as Bitcoin prevent its death and become woven into the global fabric of the monetary systems most citizens usually encounter? This chapter examines how Bitcoin came to secure a place as money at the margins of the global monetary system by focusing on the possibly most controversial question surrounding Bitcoin: what makes Bitcoin money? We draw on scholars from heterodox economics and other social sciences to answer this question. We contrast the orthodox functionalist understanding of money as a medium of exchange, measure of value, and unit of account with an alternative approach that views money as a form of game played within a society. When the dominant money game with its two-tiered banking system at the center went into crisis in 2008, activists seized that opportunity to position Bitcoin as an alternative money game. Despite being neither widely accepted by merchants nor backed by any nation-state, Bitcoin was able to not only survive but prevail and flourish, slowly weaving itself into the dominant money games. We track the evolution of the money game of Bitcoin and its leading supporters, tracing the cognitive split between its positive and its more illicit aspects that allowed it to flourish and to maintain itself. From this processual intertemporal perspective, we trace the cooptation and normalization of a project that was initially strongly anti-statist and anti-establishment, and now is becoming integrated within the dominant money game. The rest of the chapter proceeds as follows: *first*, we examine the topic of theorizing money; *second*, we discuss the initial positioning of Bitcoin against the dominant money game; *third*, we develop the original three phases that defined the evolution of Bitcoin as a money game based on our evaluation of recent journalist, academic, and governmental publications; and *fourth*, we summarize our findings, concluding how the Bitcoin money game changed and shifted since its inception, and how this might affect other existing money games.

How can money be?

Since its inception, Bitcoin has been the source of scandal and controversy. However, nothing divided minds as much as the claim of whether Bitcoin can or cannot be money. What may appear as a straightforward question turns out to be anything but clear. If we want to know how Bitcoin can be money, we must first gain clarity on what we mean by money. Just about anywhere in the world today, money is one of the most central institutions organizing society, positing a fundamental puzzle: why would anyone accept inherently useless money for inherently useful goods and services (see Shackle, 1974, in Ganssmann, 2002; Menger, 1892)? Why do people all around the world partake in such an odd endeavor? When one poses the question like this, the answer seems inherent: each individual participates because he or she knows that everyone else does, too. But if the use of money is inherently circular, how can we think about the origin of money without already presuming what we seek to explain? How do we ever get started with money?

One of the most prominent answers to these questions was that money has value because coins are made from valuable materials. The idea of grounding the value of money in a *truly* valuable commodity has re-emerged countless times throughout history, such as the bullionist movements (Carruthers and Babb, 1996), or the gold standard of the post-war Bretton Woods system. This approach, however, is difficult to reconcile with the spread and rise of paper money. The problem paper money posed to this theoretical approach could be postponed for some time with reference to the convertibility of paper money into the *truly* valuable commodity, but with the end of Bretton Woods in 1971 even this tie was cut. How can paper money be valued without a *truly* valuable good backing it? Paper money can work perfectly fine as long as the people using it trust in it. This is what the term "fiat money" (from *fide*, to trust) suggests. However, when the real issue of money is trust, and not what commodity backs it, we quickly run into tautologies. If everybody trusts because everybody else trusts, who started trusting first? Where do we get started with trust?

Heterodox economists and sociologists have offered nuanced answers to this question, providing helpful alternatives to the widespread but limited orthodox positions on trust and money. The economist John Maynard Keynes was convinced that the primary concept of money is the unit of account in which debts are expressed. Keynes went on to describe debts as contracts of deferred payments (Keynes, 1971: 3). Money in this view is closely tied to the concept that debts will be discharged in the future. This understanding is echoed by the sociologist Geoffrey Ingham, who states that the specific feature of money is not so much facilitating "spot" exchanges, but the "projection of *abstract* value through *time*" (Ingham, 2002: 128). In this view, money always bridges from a given present into an uncertain future. Insofar all money is *fiduciary* at heart and society depends on creating stable arrangements that allow for the development of *trust* that money will still be valued when that future arrives. In this sense, the history of money is a history of trust, not between two individuals, but instead between an individual and a community as a whole (Aglietta, 2002: 32ff.).

Michel Aglietta further differentiates between two types of trust that money requires. On the one hand, he describes methodical trust as a form of trust that comes with routines and traditions as well as past experience of successful inter-action, founding a "framework of references and roles within which private agents mould themselves" (Aglietta, 2002: 34). On the other hand, he describes hierarchical trust as trust that originates from political authority that imparts it on money. Both forms of trust correspond to a particular institutional underpinning of money. Methodical trust corresponds to horizontal integration with businesses and individuals trusting that a form of money will be accepted in ongoing exchange. Vertical trust corresponds to vertical integration with a political struc-ture able to enforce or change the conditions under which a form of money is accepted. Most importantly, both forms of trust are not equals: "Hierarchical trust is superior to methodical trust because the political entity with authority over money has the power to change the rules" (Aglietta, 2002: 35). The import-ance of hierarchical trust is a notion that other scholars capture when they speak about the hierarchy of money (Bell, 2001; Mehrling, 2013). However, sovereign authority over money has also been a lasting source of discontent, fueling fears that the state can use political authority to bend the rules when it wants to cover its own financial needs, thus devaluing everyone's money in the process (Keynes, 1971).

Within such tensions, we must find stable institutional arrangements that allow us to believe that money will have value in the future. Yet, finding such an arrangement is not a one-time achievement, but rather a continuous process that allows us to effectively treat value as invariant even when we know it is not (Mirowski, 1991: 579). Money must be produced and reproduced in social set-tings, meaning that we are *doing money* more than anything else (Ganssmann, 2012a: 1). Consequently, we must not ask what money is, but *how* we are *doing* it under different conditions and in different social settings, and most of all *over time*. In his earlier writing, Nigel Dodd (1994) argued that each function of money depends on extended social relations that relate to a geographical or geo-political area and eventually culminates in what he called a *monetary network (p. XII), that is, the governance arrangement that provides institutional stability to a form of money.* In Dodd's analysis, monetary forms are different from each other because monetary networks differ. Such differences include the political means of validation of forms of money and the institutional mechanisms that hold social relations steady. Echoing Aglietta's argument that money requires *systemic* or *impersonal trust*, Dodd described what information participants require to foster the emergence of trust in the monetary network, including a standardized accounting system, information that justifies expectations that money can be reused in the future, information about the spatial and legal proliferation of the network, and information on the behavior and expectations of others. Money is thereby a social fact, or rather a social convention based on an articulate governance network where its social and political origins are obscured by the seeming importance of a money object. But how do these monetary networks develop over time? How does the use of money evolve?

Social conventions of money can be understood in parallel to the rules of a game that people play (Ganssmann, 2002: 25). While rules of games *can* be known explicitly as long as they show themselves in the conformity of action and regularity, they do not *need* to be known explicitly. Games and conventions can be learned through imitation without making all rules explicitly known in the process. Explicit and implicit rules nonetheless define obligations and duties, sanctioned and forbidden moves in relation to a particular game. Rules are iterative. They require repetition, which creates continuity, but also room for change. Heiner Ganssmann builds on Ludwig Wittgenstein to promote a third solution to our original money paradox, neither committing to ideas of commodity money, nor to circular explanations of utility:

> [...]. The pawn in chess neither has meaning in the sense of representing something, of being a sign of something, nor is it just the piece carved out of wood. What the pawn is, is determined by the rules of chess.
>
> (Wittgenstein, 1984a: 150, in Ganssmann, 2012a: 20)

In this view, money is defined by the money game that is being played. To know more about money, we then must ask how a particular game is being played. Money games can widely differ depending on how money is used, accessed, validated, controlled, what goods it can mobilize, and who is excluded. Narratives of money are important in building trust in a particular money game (e.g., narratives of commodity-backed money can build trust), but they are not the hidden ground of functioning money.

Some general assumptions about money can nonetheless be made. On the individual level, money does not come about as an ad hoc insight. In contemporary capitalist societies, money games are learned over time, mostly from an early age onwards, building routines and cognitive capacities that allow people to handle and recognize money. Beyond the taken-for-granted use of money lies a continuous training process in which the use of money is learned. This helps explain how there can be both general knowledge about money and also specific monetary practices affected by categories of race, gender, class, and so on (Zelizer, 1997). On the institutional level, a money game must have a nominal unit of account distinct from other commodities, an orderly minting process through which funds become available to agents, and there must be a settlement of balances to maintain monetary constraints (Cartelier, 2013).

In addition, money games are always politically charged because decisions are being made as to whom gets what and how (Carruthers and Babb, 1996). Money games are also strongly connected to political power, and the predominant money games of the present prevailed because they did "fit" with state structures and political forces constituting their players in particular constellations (Helleiner, 2003: 224). Bitcoin was built to challenge the predominant money game, so we must ask two questions: what is the dominant money game, and how does Bitcoin want to be different?

A slingshot full of (virtual) coins

Bitcoin was initially positioned as a clear criticism of the two-level money system consisting of central banks and commercial banks (Paul, 2016: 9; Nakamoto, 2008). With such criticism, this cryptocurrency (CC) points to a dominant money game that must be understood as a source of discontent. What can be said about the dominant money game? Even after the emergence of the modern nation-state, public money and private money have existed side by side, and the now dominant money game must be understood as a co-evolution of both forms of money (Keynes, 1971). On the one hand, there is public money (Knapp, 1924), which has value because it is accepted to discharge tax debts. Such money is based in the coercive power of the sovereign to tax. Such money commonly is accepted because and insofar successful states monopolize the coercive power to define what counts as abstract value capable of discharging tax debts (Ingham, 2007: 269). On the other hand, there is private bank money, which can be understood as an IOU issued by a bank, which is accepted because there is some form of private collateral backing it. What makes both money games problematic is that the upsides of each also cause their inherent weaknesses. For public money, the power of the state to make the rules can be abused in the state's favor when it decides to default on debt obligations. For private money, the power of private money to expand the money supply for economic growth can create inflation and instability, and, in the worst case, bank runs. The downsides of both money games were only curbed when they united and hybridized into state-backed credit money in 1694 with the creation of the Bank of England (Ingham, 2004).

Central banks combined the public backing of the public money (the taxation power of the then king) with the flexibility of private money. This generated institutional control over the conduct of the sovereign, predominantly over war expenditures, generating the constitutional monarchy of "the king in parliament" (Ingham, 2004). Under this arrangement, the stability of public money and the flexibility of private money could coexist, forming the minting process of this money game. What was central to this money game was that the central bank provided a lender of last resort function for the private banking system and the money it issued (Ingham, 2006, 2007). What occurred was an evolutionary process of building vertical trust (Aglietta, 2002) while curbing the dangers of despotic excesses undermining this trust.

Emerging nation states could not dispense with the need for banking money, yet had to use the power of lender of last resort sparingly. Further measures to stabilize this money game emerged, creating the growing area of banking regulation (Chick, 2013; Knafo, 2013). Over the twentieth century, a dominant type of money game closely tied to territorial states became so thoroughly entrenched that it became widely perceived as the "natural" monetary order. Nevertheless, this type of money game is a contingent historical development (Helleiner, 2003: 218). Built over this period were governance arrangements forming the institutional foundation of our current state-backed credit money that is guarded and strictly regulated by the state.

What brought stability to this public–private hybrid money game could once again destabilize it, specifically the power of the lender of last resort to suspend monetary constraints could act as an inflationary scourge (Aglietta and Orléan, 1984). In the financial crisis of 2008, with central banks acting as quasi-sovereigns, fears of despotic abuse of power debasing money and subsequent instability re-emerged. Bitcoin emerged as a criticism of this development. As a mode of governance, Bitcoin mobilizes two popular approaches to limiting political power: commodity backing and market competition. Bitcoin was meant to promote both approaches, not through a community deliberating on governance standards, but instead by embedding techno-libertarian beliefs into the coding of the underlying protocol. Bitcoin was built as a supposedly "trustless" and decentralized payment network. Users are meant to become independent of a trusted third party processing and watching over transactions, and instead rely on an algorithm facilitating a sort of race that rewards a distributed network of computers for remaining honest and including any transaction that is technically valid.

Bitcoin provides the institutional preconditions for money exemplified by Jean Cartelier: funds are denominated in a unique number of account (BTC/Satoshis), the minting process is integrated with the code distributing funds to those who maintain the network, and accounts are settled with the network functioning as a decentralized clearing house. By eliminating dependency on a third party, users are meant to be empowered insofar as they are granted full control of their money. It is this central characteristic that has led to Bitcoin being lauded as a libertarian watershed freeing its users from governmental oppression (Cox, 2013).

Bitcoin can thereby be understood as a political experiment promoting a radically different money game. It has much in common with activist-initiated local currencies in which activists seek to promote reform of the monetary system by building and pioneering alternative money games. The social utopianism that is central to its monetary theory is seeking to change economic reality and society as a whole (Dodd, 2015: 79ff.). There are thus two money games at play with Bitcoin: the dominant money game backed by the coercive power of the sovereign and extensive institutional underpinning, and the alternative proposed money game that originally lacked coercive power and institutional underpinning beyond what the coding provides. How could Bitcoin ever establish itself side by side with such dominant existing money games, lacking everything that seems fundamental to the making of money?

The evolution of the Bitcoin money game

In this section, we examine the development of the Bitcoin money game over time to understand how Bitcoin could prevail despite starting off without any institutional underpinning or political backing. We analyze how Bitcoin acts *in vivo*, so to say, in order to understand this puzzle and draw further conclusions on its implications for the future of the Bitcoin money game and its impact on the dominant money game. We evaluate recent journalistic publications on

Bitcoin (e.g., Vigna and Casey, 2015; Popper, 2015), as well as publications by central banks and government agencies from the US and Europe (e.g., European Central Bank, 2012, 2015; Lo and Wang, 2014; Brainard, 2016) and other scholars in the emerging field (e.g., Böhme et al., 2015; Weber, 2016) to develop a periodization of the development of Bitcoin. We identify three phases of the Bitcoin money game: a phase of initial confrontation (Phase I), a phase of attempted horizontal integration (Phase II), and finally a phase of likely vertical integration (Phase III). While phases overlap and actors of one phase remain relevant throughout other phases, we argue that the development within each phase can best be characterized by attributing it to the interaction with a particular set of key actors shaping decisive aspects of the development of the Bitcoin money game.

The confrontation phase (2009–14)

Introducing a new money game is anything but easy, as proponents of a new money game are confronted with the basic problem of gaining traction in a two-sided market, consisting of merchants and customers. For both sides, a new money game becomes interesting because their counterpart joins in and vice versa. Nonetheless Bitcoin developers did utilize the financial crisis of 2008 to promote an alternative money game supposedly removed from political intervention and "disruptive" state and central bank monetary policy (Nakamoto, 2008). However, most decisive for the early development of Bitcoin was that the proposal provided a "fit" with long-held political beliefs and libertarian visions of stateless money. The technology also spoke to "cypherpunk" dreams of bringing cash more thoroughly into the digital age (Popper, 2016: 16). Entry costs had become low because of technological advancements and design decisions that required no upfront payment beyond committing the time to look into this novel proposal. Bitcoin quite literally began as one person's proposal to another, with someone or some group using the pseudonym Satoshi Nakamoto proposing it, and computer scientist Hal Finney giving the proposal a trial as a monetary experiment (Popper, 2016: 25).

Attempts to build money based on cryptography are not unprecedented. There have been other money games based on cryptography, such as DigiCash which failed to become stable for one reason or another and were unable to build a critical mass of consumers (Tumine, 2002: 75). While heavily technical, this crypto-community was no stranger to explicit political activism. Efforts to bring encryption to the civil society have created severe political conflicts, including frequently re-emerging calls for banning secure encryption for civilians altogether (Ludlow, 2001). Some of the early advocates of Bitcoin such as Roger Ver and Ross Ulbricht were very much driven by strong political ideals and were intrigued by the idea of circumventing the state and building an anarchist society organized only by the market (Popper, 2016). Such techno-utopianism often has been dubbed the "Californian ideology" (Barbrook and Cameron, 1996). At this early phase shortly after the inception of Bitcoin, its development resembled the "communitarian spirit of an open source project" (Wallace, 2011). With nothing to purchase and hardly any exchanges operational, hoarding and tinkering were what were largely done with Bitcoin. As the still unknown creator Satoshi Nakamoto put it, users should get some Bitcoin "just in case it catches on" (cited in Vigna and Casey, 2015: 46).

While early advocates viewed Bitcoin as a permanent challenge to territorial state-backed currencies, the initial CC exhibited parallels with other local currencies. Local currencies, such as the Chiemgauer (Thiel, 2011) or the Brixton Pound (Dodd, 2014: 380), predominantly focus on the role of money in facilitating exchange, while seeking ways to discourage hoarding. Bitcoin's emergence as money began from hoarding, which helped Bitcoin to overcome the problem of users having to participate in an unproven payment network and allowed for gradually building confidence in the network. The predominance of hoarding and the importance of the specific ideological vision is echoed by the first institution, the Electronic Frontier Foundation, an international NGO advocating digital rights, have joined the money game of Bitcoin by accepting donations in Bitcoin. When the global digital money transfer firm PayPal was pressured into ceasing to process donations to WikiLeaks in 2010, demonstrating the salience of the interconnection of finance and government (Popper, 2016: 57), members of the Bitcoin community called for WikiLeaks to accept donations through Bitcoin. In 2011, Wikileaks began accepting donations through Bitcoin (Redman, 2016). Circumventing state limitations regarding particular transactions illustrates both the iterative character of the money game of Bitcoin and how it was positioned as an alternative to established money games, insofar as the Bitcoin money game was visibly operating outside of established legal frameworks and institutions were influencing how this money game is played and what moves are viable. The Bitcoin money game is iterative insofar as the game becomes more confrontational at this point, not just avoiding state regulation, but actively defying it and eventually alienating the creator of Bitcoin. WikiLeaks joining the Bitcoin money game contributed to the departure of Satoshi Nakamoto, who seemingly did not foresee how rapidly the uptake of Bitcoin would progress (Wallace, 2011).

Following the first adopters, non-state institutions emerged that were tightly linked to the functioning of Bitcoin, actively developing business models that were based on Bitcoin's status as a money game at the margins of the dominant system and in turn building the foundation of the Bitcoin ecosystem. Various Bitcoin-specific financial intermediaries began to emerge, such as currency exchanges, mining pools, digital wallets, and transaction anonymizers (Böhme et al., 2015). Throughout this early phase, Bitcoin was hardly integrated with the formal economy. Instead, it almost functioned as a catalyst for those inspired by the political vision of Bitcoin to build institutions that are strongly integrated with the functions of Bitcoin. The biggest representatives of this development were Mt.Gox, SilkRoad, and SatoshiDice, all of which provided a service unique to this money game as well as the first broad institutional underpinning of Bitcoin.

Mt.Gox[4] allowed for the exchange of national currencies into units of Bitcoin. This exchange was one of the first to build standardized interfaces with other money games, contributing to an increase in speculative activities in the process by allowing users to buy and sell units of Bitcoin more rapidly. While there were other exchanges in existence at the time, at its peak Mt.Gox handled almost 90 percent of the traffic occurring on all exchanges combined (Wallace, 2011). Its attractiveness stemmed partly from the fact that it avoided financial regulation of both the jurisdiction in which it was located and the regions in which its customers resided, including anti-money-laundering regulations and "know your customer" requirements. However, Mt.Gox reintroduced third-party intermediation and concentration to a degree that the exchange began acting as de facto bank for Bitcoin users, marking the first notable departure from the initial vision of Bitcoin that had insisted on a lack of third-party intermediation. The risks of such intermediation became evident when eventually Mt.Gox filed for bankruptcy with Japanese authorities in 2014, causing the loss of 850,000 BTC and thereby demonstrating the inherent risks in the money game of Bitcoin at that time (Dierksmeier and Steele, 2016).

The importance of Mt.Gox for this phase was rivaled only by the emergence of the black market vendor SilkRoad. Originally founded in 2011 by Ross Ulbricht, the service was quick to gain traction by allowing users and vendors to predominantly exchange various narcotics for BTC (Bearman, 2015). SilkRoad was a truly unique advance from the mailing of narcotics around the globe to individual customers that was previously hampered by the lack of a reliable and anonymous payment channel. Furthermore, Ulbricht explicitly identified strongly as a libertarian who was intrigued by the Bitcoin proposal. SilkRoad was incentivized by the prospect of Bitcoin circumventing existing regulations of financial transactions. Once again, the Bitcoin money game shifted in a novel direction, furthering access to services conflicting with rules outlined in other money games and bolstering a particular confrontational interpretation of the Bitcoin money game. Eventually, the FBI caught up with the creator of SilkRoad, which led to the arrest of Ulbricht in 2013 and the subsequent closure of the original SilkRoad.

At the time of SilkRoad's closure, other illicit and legitimate services had begun to flourish in the Bitcoin ecosystem. SatoshiDice emerged as a popular gambling service in 2012, harnessing the technological benefits of Bitcoin and the underlying blockchain.[5] SatoshiDice utilizes the fact that the maintenance of the public ledger of Bitcoin continuously produces randomized numbers, allowing users to place reliable online bets without having to trust in the soundness of a third-party code. At the time, SatoshiDice was responsible for about 50 percent of the volume occurring in Bitcoin transactions (Matonis, 2013). Other vendors offered access to games such as blackjack or roulette where BTC was used as wager. Partially attracted by the weak formal regulation of Bitcoin, these vendors built on the key properties of Bitcoin, predominantly privacy, payment irreversibility, and cost savings, rendering it the *ideal* digital casino chip (Matonis, 2013).

While once thousands of BTC could be bought for a few dollars, or even cents, the price of the leading CC skyrocketed in the two years following the inception of SilkRoad and Mt.Gox. The development emphasized the dual nature of Bitcoin as both a payment network and a speculative asset (Glaser et al., 2014). This phase also illustrated the importance of ideological convictions in participating in a particular alternative money game. Why would anyone place trust in the Bitcoin money game? We find continuous references to Bitcoin as finally allowing people to switch over to what they believe "good" money looks like (e.g., Popper, 2016: 53ff.). As a concept of money, Bitcoin resembles "free banking" ideas previously popular in the pre-1914 era allowing for any bank to issue money and have market forces control its value (Helleiner, 2003: 4), as well as ideas of commodity money or commodity-backed money, such as an idealized gold standard removing money supply from governmental control. Bitcoin could also benefit from existing interest in privacy in ownership through cryptography, while not requiring a firm commitment of resources or any noteworthy initial investment to participate beyond having access to a computer with an internet connection.

Bitcoin also built on the (re-)emerging distrust in other money games. With the proposal of a decentralized and hard-capped money game, Bitcoin positioned itself in stark contrast to established money games at the time. Events such as the Cyprus crisis of 2012/13 made citizens painfully aware of the previously invisible political dimensions of the dominant money games. This crisis led to a steep rise of interest in Bitcoin-related apps, especially in countries suspected to have a troubled banking sector (Luther and Olson, 2013: 25ff.). However, spikes in interest do not necessarily produce spikes of adoption.

Throughout this early adoption period, moves in the Bitcoin money game were often transactions strongly regulated or outright forbidden in other money games, such as gambling and the purchase of illicit goods. The Bitcoin money game was a money game emerging at the margins of current regulatory frameworks and legal spaces of legitimate money use. Yet, while notions of empowerment and self-determination are common amongst advocates, Bitcoin was never a project developed by the financially vulnerable or excluded. Instead, Bitcoin has been driven by a tech-savvy predominantly male elite, or, more generally, by groups otherwise understood as privileged, not marginalized.

Furthermore, the motive of financial speculation has been present from the very beginning of Bitcoin. The emerging institutional underpinning changed the money game of the original CC, causing shifts in the governance of Bitcoin without altering the base computer code. Various institutions ended up re-introducing the very third-party intermediation Bitcoin was meant to displace. While this allowed for the Bitcoin money game to interface with other money games (predominantly through unregulated exchanges), this re-intermediation softened the initial political vision of Bitcoin. A niche market emerged within the Bitcoin money game driven by overlapping normative (crypto-anarchism, libertarians, gold bugs) and strategic (profits, law avoidance, cost savings) considerations. Bitcoin's followers were "fighting the good fight" against perceived oppression and restrictions of the dominant money game.[6]

The horizontal integration phase (2012–15)

The second phase of the Bitcoin money, which can be described as the "horizontal integration phase," can be characterized by two main currents. The horizontal integration phase was marked by a notable departure from the more confrontational tone of the earlier phase as well as a steep increase in strategic motives for taking part in the Bitcoin money game, which was often combined with only a secondary interest in the actual usage of Bitcoin. Most notably, there was an increasingly publicly announced interest in Bitcoin by key incumbents in the global IT sector. Firms such as Baidu and eBay, and the acceptance of Bitcoin through Overstock.com, among other companies, represented the development of Bitcoin throughout this phase. We look at the position-taking of each in turn.

One of the first big companies to accept Bitcoin was Baidu, a Chinese internet search giant and the Chinese equivalent to Google. Contrasting the start-ups marking the first phase located at the fringes or in the shadows of the formal economy, Baidu was anything but unheard of. With Baidu having a market capitalization of $53 billion, recognition of Bitcoin came from a giant of the internet industry. Baidu Jiasule, a subdivision of Baidu selling cloud storage, allowed customers to make BTC payments for this service. In its public announcement, Baidu addressed Bitcoin as a "trendy" technology with which they wanted to associate and less as a political proposal that could challenge government authority and control of the money supply.[7] Baidu's support hence stands in stark contrast to the strong anti-government sentiment prevalent among the libertarians and crypto-anarchists of the initial phase. Instead, Baidu is known for its willing compliance with requests from Chinese censors and has been at the center of other scandals fueling calls for boycott by Chinese citizens (Huang, 2016).[8] Nonetheless, its position-taking towards Bitcoin seemed to indicate a possible mainstream adoption of the Bitcoin money game.

Another strong signal of support came from then eBay president John Donahoe, who argued that Bitcoin would become a "very powerful thing" that the firm was closely monitoring. While he made clear that there were no immediate plans for integrating Bitcoin with either eBay or its subsidiary PayPal, Donahoe's interest in Bitcoin signaled that Bitcoin was a viable technological innovation with possibly disruptive consequences. This heightened exposure of Bitcoin also fueled the speculative interests of incumbents of the IT industry and greatly increased the visibility of the Bitcoin money game. Yet this came with a severe shift in the framing of Bitcoin.

Instead of (explicitly) endorsing Bitcoin as a political experiment, incumbent firms drew on the less confrontational framing of Bitcoin as a borderless payment network. They endorsed a disruptive innovation, not a political movement. Previous research indicates that signals from high-status actors are key for driving the adoption of a new technology (Podolny, 2008). The reciprocal relationship allows for incumbent firms to signal that they sense developing trends by associating with Bitcoin. Nonetheless, it is very notable that the incumbent endorsement was much more driven by strategic than explicitly normative considerations. Furthermore, contrasting the start-ups of Phase I, this time around adoption was superficial and no commitments to "fighting the good fight" were made, other than overhauling the dated IT infrastructure of existing payment channels. This openness also has been a fundamental characteristic of Bitcoin, setting it apart from other, more strictly regional currencies. While Bitcoin started from strong normative demands regarding privacy, disintermediation, and self-determination of money users, almost no commitment or changes in conduct honoring these demands are required from firms that began to accept BTC payments.[9]

A more mixed endorsement reminiscent of Phase I came from Overstock.com adopting Bitcoin. Overstock.com was the first major retailer to accept payments in BTC for its entire range of goods. Overstock.com CEO and Chairman Patrick Byrne supported Bitcoin not only as a technological innovation but also as a political cause (Metz, 2014). Others to join the Bitcoin money game by allowing customers to pay in BTC for a limited range of goods and services were OkCupid, Virgin Galactic, and TigerDirect. Mike Maxim, chief technology officer of OkCupid, described Bitcoin as a way to "differentiate their product from other dating sites." Judd Bagley, director of communications for Overstock.com, also stressed how their Bitcoin adoption not only generated press coverage, but also led to members of the Bitcoin community advertising Overstock.com to other users (Bogle, 2014). Other companies in this second phase of the evolution to accept Bitcoin were Dell, Expedia, Shopify, Wordpress, Reddit, and Mega (Dodd, 2014: 365).

Once again we can return to the question of why anyone would place trust into Bitcoin. While government agencies began to crack down on the more deviant organizations of Phase I, incumbent firms began to take an interest in Bitcoin, furthering the institutional underpinning of Bitcoin by linking it with sections of the formal economy and fueling hopes of mainstream adoption and building methodical trust. Strong initial political demands (full anonymity, freedom from government, rule avoidance) were toned down by these incumbent corporations in favor of more moderate voices. The early involvement of many institutions in Bitcoin was a taxing learning experience leading to arrests or freezing of funds. Conflicts with prosecutors gave the impression of severe lack of understanding the existing political and legal dimension of the financial system on the side of Bitcoin advocates and developers, leading for example to Mt.Gox having its US accounts frozen. A growing focus on Bitcoin as an efficient borderless payment network and increasing media coverage, as well as hopes for mainstream adoption, empowered more moderate voices in the Bitcoin community.

Consequently (moderate) Bitcoin advocates were able to strike loose alliances with powerful incumbent actors, the latter seeking to set themselves apart from their competitors. This division in the existing money game between unwelcome criminal actors and welcome innovation was also echoed within the community of Bitcoin users. This was most strikingly illustrated by the creation of the

Bitcoin Foundation, a non-profit that sought to develop standardization and unity in the community, while departing from the more radical politics associated with the initial phase of Bitcoin (Popper, 2016: 138ff.; Weber, 2016). Frequently, the integration of Bitcoin as a payment option was superficial, and real-life adoption as a means of payment has been stagnating ever since.[10] With an eye on mainstream adoption, other more practical concerns moved to the forefront, such as how to properly tax Bitcoin earning without risking fallout with financial regulators.

While Bitcoin as a technology is heavily imbued with political convictions (Golumbia, 2015), many advocates of Bitcoin began to perform a cognitive split, setting apart Bitcoin as a radical and conflict-laden political experiment from Bitcoin as a disruptive borderless payment network. Once the latter framing became more pronounced, incumbent firms could more easily interface with Bitcoin, thereby watering down the political proposal of Bitcoin and alienating some early supporters in the process. Early experiences with exchanges moving into the focus of prosecutors also led to attempts by some exchanges to become more compliant by gathering data on customers and by, for example, registering with the US Financial Crimes Enforcement Network (Popper, 2016: 138). Beyond first attempts of fending off Bitcoin as an illegitimate and law-avoiding internet curiosity, incumbent firms also became involved in an alternative strategy of "pacification" (Oliver, 1991, in Bernstein and Cashore, 2007) by creating new initiatives (e.g., the R3 consortium of 70 major banks in 2014 exploring how to harness blockchain technology) seeking to adopt the technology through cooptation, while at the same time seeking to avoid its explicitly political normative demands. The cognitive differentiation between the controversial political experiment and welcome technological innovation that underlie this engagement would find its counterpart in the reception of Bitcoin in the regulatory community and lay the foundation for its legitimate integration with other money games.

Vertical integration phase (since 2013)

Regulatory responses to Bitcoin have always been more ambivalent than one might have expected, considering its early framings as internet drug money (Chen, 2011). Regulators found themselves in a position where they were to curb the downsides of an unregulated and anonymous payment network without scaring off emerging fintech benefits. As Lael Brainard, member of the Board of Governors of the Federal Reserve System, stated, "We will work together to foster socially beneficial innovation, while insisting that risks are thoroughly understood, managed, and controlled" (Brainard, 2016). The early proposal of the Bitcoin money game was grossly at odds with existing regulation, either ignoring it because of naivety and a lack of knowledge, or outright breaching it to facilitate illegal transactions. Nonetheless, when the first widely received public hearing on Bitcoin was held by the US Senate Committee on Homeland Security and Governmental Affairs in November 2013, the American regulatory environment proved generally flexible. While concerns about drug trafficking and other prohibited activities were prominent, it became clear that Bitcoin was also considered a viable technological innovation by US officials (Raskin, 2013).

This began the onset of a normalization process that separated Bitcoin transactions into cases of legitimate use and those of deviant conduct. Firms and merchants in the Bitcoin ecosystem increasingly voiced their desire for stringent regulation of Bitcoin. This group of actors was faced with the problem that even when they wanted to comply with regulation, it was unclear what exactly was required from them. As a pre-eminent American technology commentator put it:

> Bitcoin businesses – particularly those involved in trading bitcoins for dollars – sometimes complain that they operate in a grey area, where it's not entirely clear how or if they are in compliance with a patchwork of state and federal regulations.
>
> (McMillan, 2013)

Reoccurring experiences with theft and fraud had also left many users more willing to consider the upsides of more stringent regulation. However, the Bitcoin money game was also stuck in an odd spot. While broader sets of individuals and firms took an interest in Bitcoin throughout Phase II, horizontal integration was stagnating as Bitcoin did not seem to move towards building a critical mass when it came to actual adoption. Yet, excitement about the underlying technology, the blockchain, was nonetheless building:

> Nevertheless, there is growing recognition that the lasting legacy of Bitcoin most likely lies in the technological advances made possible by its protocol for computation and communication that facilitates payments and transfers.
>
> (Lo and Wang, 2014)

State regulatory responses are closely tied to the second cognitive split occurring with Bitcoin during this phase. On the one hand, Bitcoin had been associated with crime, money laundering, and scandal. On the other hand, blockchain intrigued incumbents of the financial industry and government agencies (Maurer, 2016: 85ff.). In contrast with the more controversial Bitcoin, blockchain technology has seen a steep increase in legitimacy and uptake (for a more detailed depiction, see Campbell-Verduyn, 2017). Nonetheless, because blockchain is the technology underpinning Bitcoin, separating the policy response from the Bitcoin has been virtually impossible. Instead, government agencies both in Europe and in the US seem to be willing to consider a trade-off where they avoid outright prohibition in favor of pushing for a normalization of the Bitcoin money game. Furthermore, overtly strict regulation would risk quickly driving Bitcoin activity elsewhere, weakening the grip of regulators on the institutions and intermediaries developing in this ecosystem (Böhme et al., 2015).

There has yet to be a stringent international regulation on Bitcoin. Regulation generally varies on a country-to-country basis.[11] Often some sort of legal definition as money of Bitcoin is acknowledged. This is not so much a scholastic debate as a question of taxation. For example, based on Sweden's tax office challenging a court decision, the Court of Justice of the European Union ruled that Bitcoins are exempt from value-added tax, rendering Bitcoin to be currency instead of a commodity (Clinch, 2015). However, Bitcoin's wider recognition as a currency by state authorities has been limited and commonly accompanied by steep warnings about the volatility and risks of virtual currencies, as well as concerns about central banks' authority on monetary policy. Generally, government agencies demand compliance with anti-money-laundering and know your customer regulations (see Campbell-Verduyn and Goguen, this volume).

On occasion, payments in BTC have been accepted by government agencies. For example, in the Swiss city of Zug, citizens were allowed to pay government services of up to 200 Swiss francs in BTC. However, this development is mostly owed to Switzerland seeking to foster a sort of blockchain Silicon Valley, or crypto valley, and has limited implications for the general acceptance of Bitcoin by state agencies.[12] On occasion, Bitcoin has also been endorsed by hedge fund managers as something that should be included in modern portfolios, and Cameron and Tyler Winkelvoss sought to get a Bitcoin exchange trading fund (ETF) approved by the US Securities and Exchange Commission (Roberts, 2017). While the filing for the ETF was rejected on the grounds of finding the Bitcoin market still insufficiently regulated, it was also indicated that this ruling might change in the future as Bitcoin markets become more regulated (Shin, 2017). What should be emphasized here is the productive site of regulatory power. As with many previous conflict-laden financial practices, it is political authority that creates moral and legal space for financial markets to operate and consolidates and legalizes a professional domain for particular financial practices (De Goede, 2005: 124).

The creation of such a moral and legal framework does not only concern private enterprises. Bitcoin has been increasingly identified with the long-held dreams of central bank control tied to the abandonment of cash altogether. The European Central Bank (2015: 27) pointed to the possibility that a major failure of an established virtual currency could harm the trust in e-money altogether. Bitcoin greatly contributed to "destigmatizing" the concept of a cashless society by making digital money cash-like (Kaminska, in Smith, 2014). As central banks contemplate the idea of issuing their own central bank-backed CCs, they might need to shape the regulatory framework that sets the ground for a lasting vertical integration of Bitcoin and other CCs as well.

Moneys at the margins

What we also have witnessed more widely in the last decade is the prevalence of three unique trends: *first*, an increased interest in free banking and frictionless e-commerce payments; *second*, increased interest in communitarian regional currencies as permanent reform movements (Helleiner, 2003; Ingham, 2002); *third*, the vast spread of special purpose moneys issued by private enterprises, such as air miles and supermarket loyalty schemes (Dodd, 2015: 391), or companies such as

Amazon, Google, Apple, Alipay, Groupon, and others issuing their own payment options to increase consumer loyalty and market share (Mariotto and Verdier, 2015: 15).

The Bitcoin money game has benefited from all three of these trends in its growth and diffusion. Bitcoin's evolution has been building on the increased interest in free banking and a permanent reform movement creating a *better* form of money. It has been exploited as a form of special purpose money by companies seeking free advertising, and it has been promoted as a frictionless e-commerce payment network. Therefore, it is decisive to look at how Bitcoin developed over time and what developments it set in motion that reach beyond the CC (Table 2.1).

Originally, Bitcoin started off as a strong political experiment gaining support from activists, "believers," and an emerging shadow economy providing first-use cases for this money game. Actors displayed both normative and strategic convictions, and Bitcoin was challenging established (national and supranational) money games. The weaker second phase of the horizontal integration of Bitcoin amongst firms closer to the formal economy followed. Incumbent firms with an IT affinity positioned themselves towards the emergent money game. However, while Bitcoin resonates with crypto-anarchist ideals (Ludlow, 2001), political goals became less pronounced and focus on borderless payments and technological innovation decreased. Voices in favor of circumventing regulation have become less vocal. Furthermore, incumbent firms show much less commitment to Bitcoin than the start-ups of Phase I in only superficially integrating Bitcoin as one payment option among many for a limited range of (often virtual) goods. Adoptions as a medium of exchange and the subsequent horizontal integration have largely stagnated. Instead, state actors have become more prominently involved.

Further formal regulatory action must be taken considering the shadow economy of Bitcoin. Regulators must curb the downsides of Bitcoin to harness the emerging greater blockchain environment. The evolution of the Bitcoin money game parallels the development of the blockchain as an emergent technology, but it is not synonymous with it. Rather, private and state actors seem to be building an infrastructure that benefits Bitcoin as they move towards developing a framework that allows them to harness the emerging technology (Rotolo et al., 2015) in general. Yet, commitment by state actors in the US and Europe has been predominantly provisional in the sense described by Jacqueline Best (2014), which allows regulators to embrace the emergence of blockchain technologies while revising or revoking should negative future events occur or new dangers become apparent.

The Bitcoin money game started from confrontation, but then showed signs of cooptation when incumbent firms reframed the meaning of Bitcoin. Even more important in shaping this money game is the prospective normalization through powerful state actors starting to build a legal framework for cryptocurrencies. Bitcoin was caught in a trade-off where it had to forgo some explicit normative demands to interface with other money games and the formal

Table 2.1 Evolution of the Bitcoin money game

Phase	Motivation of key institutions	Key institutions	Positioning of the Bitcoin money game	Bitcoin framing by key institutions	Commitment to Bitcoin by key institutions
Introduction (2009–14)	Normative + strategic	Shadow economy	Confrontation	Political challenge	Strong
Horizontal integration (2012–15)	Strategic	Incumbent merchants	Cooptation	Borderless payment network	Weak
Vertical integration (since 2013)	Strategic	Government agencies	Normalization	Distributed ledger technology	Provisional

Source: the authors.

economy. From then on, explicit normative demands did not vanish, but decreased in favor of broader adoption and regulatory compliance. This is not to say that there are not plenty of Bitcoin "believers" still looking to Bitcoin as a political experiment allowing them to put their money where their political beliefs stand. However, in actuality, Bitcoin does not seem to have delivered on the aspects that fuel this enthusiasm. Instead, the Bitcoin environment has been highly centralized in terms of funds, expertise, and authority (Atzori, 2017), and has even bred what some call a "Bitcoin aristocracy" (Varoufakis, 2013).

Bitcoin has been a continuous exercise of building an institutional underpinning. *First*, we find a shadow economy rendering Bitcoin almost as a special purpose money, allowing for transactions that are otherwise sanctioned or not possible in other money games. In this process, Bitcoin empowers marginal figures of society and marginalized ideologies and activities insofar as they were technologically proficient enough to participate in the money game. *Second*, Bitcoin was used by incumbent firms for a limited range of goods, raising hopes of horizontal integration with a broad set of merchants. In this phase, marginal figures and ideologies are pushed aside for an ideology more fitting with legitimate commerce and the mainstream belief in technological progress (trendy technology). *Third*, Bitcoin is becoming increasingly integrated with the regulatory frameworks, for example in Europe and the US. Here, the cooptation of Bitcoin becomes nearly complete, seeking to eradicate both illicit activities as well as illicit ideologies.

The development of Bitcoin is paralleled by the ever-present role of it as a speculative asset rather than as a medium of exchange, and each step in the evolution of Bitcoin as a money game leads to the appreciation of Bitcoin as an object of speculation (Glaser et al., 2014). Once again, why would someone trust Bitcoin based on this phase of the money game? One simple answer is that stagnant real-life adoption has been offset by a lasting speculative interest in Bitcoin, in particular now that we have seen almost a decade of a lingering financial crisis. Another answer is that government agencies might drag Bitcoin along while they make their way to harbor coming financial technology (fintech) innovations. Adoption of Bitcoin could be driven by states stepping in as the great equalizer, bestowing (some) political authority upon Bitcoin.

Considering our focus on money games, the third phase strongly links Bitcoin to the dominant money games. One of Bitcoin's most lasting achievements has been how it has shaped the wider debate surrounding virtual moneys. More than any other form of electronic money, Bitcoin has sparked debates on the *materiality* of virtual money (e.g., Selgin, 2015; Maurer et al., 2013). Central bank interest now goes beyond the question of how to properly regulate CCs like Bitcoin. Instead, central banks actively explore the possibility of making the transition to central-bank-issued "digital currency" (Mersch, 2016). Bitcoin has become a primer for a cashless society, opening up a debate that might transform the dominant money game it was meant to challenge while at the same time providing the technology that could become the foundation of this transition. The future of digital currency connects with long-held dreams of phasing out paper money altogether (Rogoff, 2014). Despite claims about decentralization and anonymity, Bitcoin has introduced a tremendously auditable and transparent digital payment system. Increasingly, research output from central banks and other monetary institutions such as the International Monetary Fund explore how the end of cash can be effected and how blockchains could take a role in achieving this end (Barrdear and Kumhof, 2016; Kireyev, 2017). Bitcoin could end up greatly empowering the central banks already located at the apex of power, significantly expanding their capacity to administer (unconventional) monetary policy. Eventually, Bitcoin could contribute towards fortifying the dominant money game it was meant to challenge and transforming the global governance of money flows in a manner far removed from its original vision.

Acknowledgments

We would like to thank Malcolm Campbell-Verduyn for his insightful comments and his invaluable work putting this volume together. We would also like to thank the participants of the "Bitcoin and Beyond" workshop at the Balsillie School of International Affairs for their comments and discussion on an earlier draft. This chapter benefited from a EURIAS fellowship at the Paris Institute for Advanced Studies (France), co-funded by Marie Skłodowska-Curie Actions, under the European Union's 7th Framework Programme for research, and from funding from the French State managed by the Agence Nationale de la Recherche, programme "Investissements d'avenir" (ANR-11-LABX-0027–01 Labex RFIEA+).

Notes

1 https://99bitcoins.com/bitcoinobituaries/ (retrieved on March 4, 2017).
2 BTC is common shorthand for units of Bitcoin and will be used as such throughout the chapter.
3 http://coinmarketcap.com/ (retrieved on March 4, 2017).
4 The domain Mtgox.com was originally registered by an American, Jed McCaleb, in 2007 with the intention of creating an online exchange for Magic: The Gathering game cards; however, it was never used for that purpose. In 2010, McCaleb turned the website into a Bitcoin online exchange where buyers and sellers of Bitcoins could be matched. Confronted with the tremendously fast growth of his platform, McCaleb decided he was "in over his head" (McMillan, 2014) and sold the platform.
5 SatoshiDice reported first-year earnings of 33,310 BTC. During the year, players bet a total of 1,787,470 in 2,349,882 individual bets at an average monthly growth rate of 78 percent. Earnings were calculated from eight months of data covering May to December 2012 (Matonis, 2013).
6 The development of the Bitcoin money game insofar can be compared with the broader theme of the establishment of non-state-marked driven governance standards, which has also inspired our analysis of the Bitcoin money game (Bernstein and Cashore, 2007).
7 For a translation of the announcement by Baidu, see: www.coindesk.com/chinese-internet-giant-baidu-starts-accepting-bitcoin/
8 Baidu stopped accepting Bitcoin only two months later when Chinese regulators restricted financial institutions from handling Bitcoin transactions.

9 Martin Gauss of Air Baltic addressed this issue most explicitly when he justified his company's acceptance of payments in Bitcoin as driven by the outlook of the resulting press coverage, granting an advertisement a company of this size could otherwise not afford. The commitment was therefore superficial insofar as all incoming payments were immediately exchanged into euro currency by a third party handling the transactions (see Koenen, 2015).

10 Websites such as coinmap.org still only list about 8,700 venues worldwide at the time of writing, often including small and local businesses offering a very limited range of products.

11 www.loc.gov/law/help/bitcoin-survey/

12 www.coindesk.com/blockchain-innovation-switzerland-crypto-valley-new-york/

Bibliography

Aglietta, M. (2002). Whence and wither money? In OECD (ed.) *The future of money* (pp. 123–45). Paris: OECD.

Aglietta, M., and Orléan, A. (1984). *La violence de la monnaie*. Paris: Presses Univ. de France.

Atzori, M. (2017). Blockchain technology and decentralized governance: Is the state still necessary? *Journal of Governance and Regulation, 6*(1), 45–62.

Barbrook, R., and Cameron, A. (1996). Californian ideology. In P. Ludlow (ed.) *Crypto anarchy, cyberstates, and pirate utopias*. Boston: MIT Press.

Barrdear, J., and Kumhof, M. (2016). *The macroeconomics of central bank issued digital currencies*. BoE Staff Working Paper 605.

Bearman, J. (2015). *The rise and fall of Silkroad. Part 1*. Retrieved October 6, 2015, from www.wired.com/2015/04/silk-road-1/

Bell, S. (2001). The role of the state and the hierarchy of money. *Cambridge Journal of Economics, 25*(2), 149–63.

Bernstein, S., and Cashore, B. (2007). Can non-state global governance be legitimate? An analytical framework. *Regulation and Governance, 1*(4), 347–71.

Best, J. (2014) *Governing failure: Provisional expertise and the transformation of global development finance*. New York: Cambridge University Press.

Bogle, A. (2014). *Is accepting Bitcoin just a publicity stunt for companies?* Retrieved May 8, 2017, from www.slate.com/blogs/future_tense/2014/02/05/overstock_virgin_galactic_tiger_direct_and_others_help_make_bitcoin_mainstream.html

Böhme, R., Christin, N., Edelman, B., and Moore, T. (2015). Bitcoin: Economics, technology, and governance. *Journal of Economic Perspectives, 29*(2), 213–38.

Brainard, L. (2016, October 7). *Distributed ledger technology: Implications for payments, clearing, and settlement*. Speech at the Institute of International Finance Annual Meeting Panel on Blockchain, Washington, D.C.

Campbell-Verduyn, M. (2017, February 24). *Technology, authority, and global governance*. Paper presented to annual conference of the International Studies Association, Baltimore, USA.

Carruthers, B.G., and Babb, S. (1996). The color of money and the nature of value: Greenbacks and gold in postbellum America. *American Journal of Sociology, 101*(6), 1556–91.

Cartelier, J. (2013). Beyond modern academic theory of money. In F. Ulgen, R. Tortajada, M. Meaulle, and R. Stellian (eds.) *New contributions to monetary analysis: The foundations of an alternative economic paradigm*. London: Routledge.

Chen, A. (2011). *The underground website where you can buy any drug imaginable.*

Retrieved May 8, 2017, from http://gawker.com/the-underground-website-where-you-can-buy-any-drug-imag-30818160

Chick, V. (2013). The current banking crisis in the UK: An evolutionary view. In J. Pixley and G. Harcourt (eds.) *Financial crises and the nature of capitalist money: Mutual developments from the work of Geoffrey Ingham* (pp. 148–61). London: Palgrave Macmillan.

Clinch, M. (2015). *Bitcoin now tax-free in Europe after court ruling*. Retrieved May 8, 2017, from www.cnbc.com/2015/10/22/bitcoin-now-tax-free-in-europe-after-court-ruling.html

Cox, J. (2013). *Bitcoin and digital currencies: The new world of money and freedom*. New York: Laissez Faire Books.

De Goede, M. (2005). *Virtue, fortune, and faith: A geneaology of finance*. Minneapolis: University of Minnesota Press.

Dierksmeier, C., and Seele, P. (2016). Cryptocurrencies and business ethics. *Journal of Business Ethics*, pp. 1–14.

Dodd, N. (1994). *The sociology of money: Economics, reason and contemporary society*. Cambridge: Polity Press.

Dodd, N. (2014). *The social life of money*. Princeton, NJ: Princeton University Press.

Dodd, N. (2015). Utopianism and the future of money. In P. Aspers, and N. Dodd (eds.) *Re-imagining economic sociology*. Oxford: Oxford University Press.

European Central Bank. (2012). *Virtual currency schemes*. Frankfurt: Author.

European Central Bank. (2015). *Virtual currency schemes – a further analysis*. Frankfurt: Author.

Ganssmann, H. (2002). Das Geldspiel. In C. Deutschmann (ed.) *Die gesellschaftliche macht des geldes*. Wiesbaden: VS Verlag für Sozialwissenschaften.

Ganssmann, H. (2012a). *Doing money: Elementary monetary theory from a sociological standpoint*. London: Routledge.

Ganssmann, H. (2012b). Geld und die rationalität wirtschaftlichen handelns. In A. Engels, and L. Knoll (eds.) *Wirtschaftliche rationalität* (pp. 221–39). Wiesbaden: VS Verlag für Sozialwissenschaften.

Glaser, F., Zimmermann, K., Haferkorn, M., Weber, M.C., and Siering, M. (2014). *Bitcoin – asset or currency? Revealing users' hidden intentions*. London: ECIS.

Golumbia, D. (2015). Bitcoin as politics: Distributed right-wing extremism. In G. Lovink, N. Tkacz, and P. De Vries (eds.) *MoneyLab reader: An intervention in digital economy*. Amsterdam: Institute of Network Cultures.

Graeber, D. (2011). *Debt: The first 5000 years*. Vienna: Eurozine.

Helleiner, E. (2003). *The making of national money: Territorial currencies in historical perspective*. Ithaca, NY: Cornell University Press.

Huang, Z. (2016). Chinese citizens are boycotting search engine Baidu – and praying for Google to come back. *Quartz*. Retrieved May 8, 2017, from https://qz.com/593120/chinese-citizens-are-boycotting-search-engine-baidu-and-praying-for-google-to-come-back/

Ingham, G. (2002). New monetary spaces? In OECD. (ed.) *The future of money* (pp. 123–45). Paris: OECD.

Ingham, G. (2004). *The nature of money*. Cambridge: Polity Press.

Ingham, G. (2006). Further reflections on the ontology of money: Responses to Lapavitsas and Dodd. *Economy and Society, 35*(2), 259–78.

Ingham, G. (2007). The specificity of money. *European Journal of Sociology, 48*(2), 265–72.

Jeong, S. (2013). The Bitcoin protocol as law, and the politics of a stateless currency. Available at SSRN: https://ssrn.com/abstract=2294124 or http://dx.doi.org/10.2139/ssrn.2294124

Keynes, J.M. (1971). *Treatise on money: Pure theory of money, Vol. I.* Cambridge: Cambridge University Press.

Kireyev, A.P. (2017). *The macroeconomics of de-cashing.* IMF Working Paper No. 17/71.

Knafo, S. (2013). *The making of modern finance: Liberal governance and the gold standard.* Abingdon: Routledge.

Knapp, G.F. (1924). *The state theory of money.* London: Routledge.

Koenen, J. (2015, February 17). Allein über den Wolken. Air Baltic zeigt, dass auch kleine Fluggesellschaften überleben können – zumindest eine Zeit lang. In. *Handelsblatt.*

Lo, S., and Wang, C.J. (2014). Bitcoin as money? *Current Policy Perspectives,* No. 14–4. Federal Reserve Bank of Boston, Boston, MA.

Ludlow, P. (2001). *Crypto anarchy, cyberstates, and pirate utopias.* Boston: MIT Press.

Luther, W.J., and Olson, J. (2013). Bitcoin is memory. *Journal of Prices and Markets, 3*(3), 22–33.

Mariotto, C., and Verdier, M. (2015). Innovation and competition in internet and mobile banking: An industrial organization perspective. *Communication and Strategies, 99,* 129–46.

Matonis, J. (2013). Bitcoin casinos release 2012 earnings. *Forbes.* Retrieved May 8, 2017, from www.forbes.com/sites/jonmatonis/2013/01/22/bitcoin-casinos-release-2012-earnings/

Maurer, B. (2016). Re-risking in realtime. On possible futures for finance after the blockchain. *Behemonth – A Journal on Civilisation, 9*(2), 82–96.

Maurer, B., Nelms, T.C., and Swartz, L. (2013). "When perhaps the real problem is money itself!": The practical materiality of Bitcoin. *Social Semiotics, 23*(2), 261–77.

McMillan, R. (2013). Feds reveal what they really think about Bitcoin. *Wired.* Retrieved May 8, 2017, from www.wired.com/2013/11/bitcoin_feds/

McMillan, R. (2014). The inside story of Mt.Gox, Bitcoin's $460 million disaster. *Wired.* Retrieved May 8, 2017, from www.wired.com/2014/03/bitcoin-exchange/

Mehrling, P. (2013). The inherent hierarchy of money. In L. Taylor, A. Rezai, and T. Michl (eds.) *Social fairness and economics: Economic essays in the spirit of Duncan Foley* (pp. 394–404). London: Routledge.

Menger, K. (1892). On the origin of money. *Economic Journal, 2*(6), 239–55.

Mersch, Y. (2016). *Distributed ledger technology: Role and relevance of the ECB.* Retrieved May 8, 2017, from www.ecb.europa.eu/press/key/date/2016/html/sp161206.en.html

Metz, C. (2014). The grand experiment goes live: Overstock.com is now accepting Bitcoins. *Wired.* Retrieved May 8, 2017, from www.wired.com/2014/01/overstock-bitcoin-live/

Mirowski, P. (1991). Postmodernism and the social theory of value. *Journal of Post Keynesian Economics, 13*(4), 565–82.

Nakamoto, S. (2008). *Bitcoin: A peer-to-peer electronic cash system.* Retrieved August 18, 2017, from https://bitcoin.org/bitcoin.pdf

Paul, A.T. (2012). *Die gesellschaft des geldes: Entwurf einer monetären theorie der modern.* Wiesbaden: VS Verlag für Sozialwissenschaften.

Paul, A.T. (2016). Bitcoin vs. sovereign money: On the lure and limits of monetary reforms. *Behemoth – A Journal on Civilisation, 9*(2), 8–21.

Podolny, J.M. (2008). *Status signals: A sociological study of market competition.* Princeton, NJ: Princeton University Press.

Popper, N. (2015). *Digital gold: The untold story of Bitcoin.* London: Penguin Books.

Raskin, M. (2013). U.S. agencies to say Bitcoins offer legitimate benefits. *Bloomberg.* Retrieved May 8, 2017, from www.bloomberg.com/news/articles/2013-11-18/ u-s-agencies-to-say-bitcoins-offer-legitimate-benefits

Redman, J. (2016). *WikiLeaks has raised 4,000 BTC since 2011.* Retrieved May 8, 2017, from https://news.bitcoin.com/wikileaks-raised-4000-btc-since-2011/

Roberts, J.J. (2017). Bitcoin may go boom: A guide to this week's big SEC decision (update). *Fortune.* Retrieved May 8, 2017, from http://fortune.com/2017/03/09/bitcoin-sec-etf/

Rogoff, K. (2014, April 11). *Costs and benefits to phasing out paper currency.* Presented at NBER Macroeconomics Annual Conference, Harvard University.

Rotolo, D., Hicks, D. and Martin, B. (2015). What is an emerging technology? *Research Policy, 44*(10), 1827–43.

Selgin, G. (2015). Synthetic commodity money. *Journal of Financial Stability, 17,* 92–9.

Shin, L. (2017). SEC rejects Winklevoss Bitcoin ETF, sending price tumbling. *Forbes.* Retrieved May 8, 2017, from www.forbes.com/sites/laurashin/2017/03/10/sec-rejects-winklevoss-bitcoin-etf-sending-price-tumbling/

Smith, Y. (2014). How Bitcoin plays into the hands of central bankers and will facilitate the use of negative interest rates. *Naked Capitalism.* Retrieved May 8, 2017, from www.nakedcapitalism.com/2014/01/bitcoin-plays-hands-central-bankers-will-facilitate-use-negative-interest-rates.html

Swan, M. (2015). *Blockchain: Blueprint for a new economy.* Farnham: O'Reilly Media.

Thiel, C. (2011). *Das ‚bessere' Geld: Eine ethnographische Studie über Regionalwährungen.* Berlin: Springer-Verlag.

Tumine, Z. (2002). The future technology of money. In OECD. (ed.) *The future of money* (pp. 123–45). Paris: OECD.

Varoufakis, Y. (2013). *Bitcoin and the dangerous fantasy of apolitical money: Thoughts for the post-2008 world.* Retrieved May 8, 2017, from www.yanisvaroufakis.eu/2013/04/22/bitcoin-and-the-dangerous-fantasy-of-apolitical-money/

Vigna, P., and Casey, M.J. (2015). *The age of cryptocurrency: How Bitcoin and the blockchain are challenging the global economic order.* New York: Macmillan USA.

Wallace, B. (2011). The rise and fall of Bitcoin. *Wired.* Retrieved May 8, 2017, from www.wired.com/2011/11/mf_bitcoin/

Weber, B. (2016). Bitcoin and the legitimacy crisis of money. *Cambridge Journal of Economics, 40*(1), 17–41.

Zelizer, V.A. (1997). *The social meaning of money: Pin money, paychecks, poor relief and other currencies.* Princeton, NJ: Princeton University Press.

3 The internal and external governance of blockchain-based organizations

Evidence from cryptocurrencies

Ying-Ying Hsieh, Jean-Philippe (JP) Vergne, and Sha Wang

Introduction

Blockchain technology proposes to create value by decentralizing the creation, verification, validation, and secure storage of economic transactions, both within and between organizations. Since 2015, central banks across the world are exploring the possibility of issuing money on a blockchain (Del Castillo, 2017). This could streamline monetary policy implementation at a global level, help combat counterfeiting and tax evasion, and potentially affect the business models of retail banks.

While the changes that would result from implementing large-scale block-chain solutions are worth studying in themselves, we also need to gain a deeper understanding of how these blockchain solutions would be operated and by whom. Put simply, we need to ask: How does blockchain governance work, and what are the implications? To answer these questions, we look at the cryptocurrency setting and argue that cryptocurrencies represent the first real-world instances of blockchain-based *organizations*. In this chapter, we thus shift the level of analysis from the global economy level to the organizational level. Theorists define organizations as "collectivities oriented to the pursuit of relatively specific goals and exhibiting relatively highly formalized social structures" (Scott and Davis, 2007: 29), and in the following we use theory on organizational and corporate governance to unpack how blockchain-based organizations operate.

In the organizational literature, corporate governance is defined as "the study of power and influence over decision making within the corporation," which defines the "rights and responsibilities of [...] different stakeholders toward the firm" (Aguilera and Jackson, 2010: 490). Since cryptocurrencies reside to a large extent in cyberspace, they are not embedded in the specific institutions of any one country in particular. As such, for the purpose of this study we treat them as global organizations (Lee, 2015: 380). We anchor our arguments on the notion that blockchain represents a new "institutional governance technology of decentralization" (MacDonald et al., 2016: 5) that can be implemented in various ways across blockchain-based organizations. We then link these various implementations to a measure of organizational value-creation in order to assess their effectiveness for governance.

Cryptocurrencies differ in terms of software design, ownership structure, decision rights, and degree of decentralization. These variations in governance design features could have profound implications on investors' evaluation of a cryptocurrency's value, as reflected in cryptocurrencies' returns on investment. Indeed, prior research suggests that cryptocurrency returns are driven by much more than media hype and speculative behavior. Wang and Vergne (2017) show that the continuous improvement of the technology behind a cryptocurrency is the primary predictor of price increases (as captured by weekly returns). Thus, treating cryptocurrencies as traditional currencies or as commodities is misleading, since behind each cryptocurrency, there is a team of people who work hard to develop the technology. For instance, whereas developers such as programmers and technologists write the blockchain software program, miners validate and update transactions by devoting computing power to the network. In other words, cryptocurrencies are best conceived of as a new kind of transnational organization. Understanding how these organizations then are governed is essential and will help devise formal policy recommendations at a macro level (Wright and De Filippi, 2015).

Blockchain governance is about determining who has authority (internal and external actors); how these actors are endowed (e.g., ownership rights vs. decision authority), in what form (formal and informal governance forms/structures), and at which level (Narayanan et al., 2016). In the context of cryptocurrencies, whose success relative to one another is captured by superior market returns (a relative price increase from one period to the next), little is known about how internal governance (at the blockchain and protocol levels) and external governance (by the broader cryptocurrency community) affect cryptocurrency returns. Drawing on the corporate governance literature in organizational and management studies, we thus examine the relationship between internal and external governance design features and cryptocurrency returns.

To shed light on this relationship empirically, we collected weekly panel data on five cryptocurrencies with varying degrees of decentralization and predict weekly returns in regression models using a number of governance-level indicators. In line with corporate governance research (Hambrick et al., 2008; Yermack, 2017), we look at several internal governance design choices: at the blockchain level, direct control by cryptocurrency owners over the consensus schemes; at the protocol level, the existence of formal voting mechanisms for miners to participate in decision-making; at the organizational level, the existence of centralized funding backing the cryptocurrency creators. In addition, in line with the idea that the media act as agents of external governance for corporations (Aguilera et al., 2015; Walsh and Seward, 1990), we also study the effects of both social (e.g., Reddit, Twitter, and Facebook) and traditional media (i.e., mainstream newspapers) governance on cryptocurrency returns, after controlling for a number of factors such as cryptocurrency supply and liquidity.

Our findings reveal a paradoxical pattern, namely, decentralization at the blockchain level affects returns positively – as one would expect, since the promise of blockchain is decentralization as a way to create value – but we also find that decentralization at both the protocol and organizational levels affects returns negatively. This is to say, while decentralization stands as an important value proposition that provides opportunities for the cryptocurrency community, this very feature can present challenges for investors. Investors generally value commercialization opportunities managed by centralized organizations. They also have more confidence in financing coordinated through centralized funding as a reliable source to motivate innovations. In this regard, decentralization brings about different opportunities and challenges for various stakeholders. Not unlike open source software projects, blockchain-based organizations can also be governed by decentralized communities, by centralized corporations, or jointly by both as hybrids. Our findings imply a wide range of blockchain-based organizational governance design options, which address various implementation settings. This study also highlights the need to investigate novel organizational forms, including "decentralized autonomous organizations" (DAO; DuPont, this volume). In the following, we review the corporate governance literature, introduce cryptocurrency and our methodology, describe our analyses, and finally, we discuss our findings and contributions to the governance literature.

Corporate governance: what we know

To understand how cryptocurrencies redefine organizational governance, we need to revisit the literature on corporate governance, which is concerned with organizational goals and the control of organizational stakeholders on collective outcomes (Aguilera et al., 2015; Aguilera et al., 2008; Moore and Kraatz, 2011; Williamson, 1996). Corporate governance concerns "who rules" and "how the organization is ruled" (Moore and Kraatz, 2011; Fama and Jensen, 1983; Hambrick et al., 2008). Similar to any governance issues, corporate governance is generally about the allocation of power and control. Historically, corporate governance has its economics roots in agency theory (Jensen and Meckling, 1976), which is concerned with mitigating opportunistic behavior. This is to say, owners and managers of a corporation can have very different risk attitudes and preferences. While owners attend to profit maximization, managers are assumed to be self-interested and can engage in misconducts that benefit their own career advancement or compensation at the expense of owners' benefits (Dalton et al., 2007). In other words, for managers, individual benefits can significantly outweigh the concern of the organization's profitability. Therefore, the main objective for governance is to design contracts with incentive mechanisms that optimally allocate ownership rights, design ownership structures, and define control such that interests are aligned between owners (principals) and managers (agents) (Connelly et al., 2010; Fama and Jensen, 1983; Jensen and Meckling, 1976; Walsh and Seward, 1990).

Recent developments in the governance literature begin to embrace a broader range of roles for both internal and external organizational actors. While internal actors include owners, shareholders, and managers, external actors include customers, the media, government, and the broader community. These internal and external stakeholders can exert influence over the organization through not just economic but also social, behavioral, cultural, and political means (e.g., Aguilera et al., 2015; Dyck and Zingales, 2002; Dyck et al., 2008; Bednar et al., 2013; Hambrick et al., 2008). In this view, organizational objectives are no longer tied with financial indicators capturing shareholder value such as stock returns, but take into account other stakeholders as alternative forces of control (Aguilera et al., 2008; Aguilera et al., 2015). When internal and external actors interact jointly, shareholder value maximization may not prevail anymore as the primary purpose of the corporation. Instead, corporations can also attend to corporate social performance, stakeholder orientations, restructuring, or asset redeployment as alternative objectives (Aguilera et al., 2015).

Cryptocurrency governance

Blockchain-based organizations such as cryptocurrencies compete with traditional economic institutions by proposing alternative forms of organizational governance (Davidson et al., 2016a, 2016b; Narayanan et al., 2016). Specifically, they upset the traditional principal–agent relationships by placing machines (i.e., the blockchain software program) at the core of organizational governance, and human actors (i.e., stakeholders) at the edges (Buterin, 2014). Although humans are still involved in the creation, modification, and decision-making about the code, now formal organizational rules and routines are written directly in the software program. Instead of CEOs or top managers, it is core developers who write the organizational rulebook of cryptocurrencies in the software code, in a decentralized fashion. It is miners (or validators), rather than employees, who verify the validity of economic transactions and maintain a digitally shared, distributed ledger recording their history. Incentives are not defined by employment contracts, but written in the code. There are no headquarters or subsidiaries, but a network distributed in cyberspace that is inherently global and borderless. Coordination between stakeholders is lubricated by the exchange of cryptocurrency tokens, whose value is determined by supply and demand, among other things (Wang and Vergne, 2017). Finally, each cryptocurrency is embedded in a digital community that plays an important external governance role. All these stakeholders have power and govern the cryptocurrency at varying levels in different ways (Narayanan et al., 2016; Yermack, 2017). In short, blockchain-based governance in the context of cryptocurrencies calls for a revised understanding about power and control within the organizations.

In the context of cryptocurrencies, not only is governance borderless, but also decentralized, albeit to various extents (Atzori, 2017; Yermack, 2017). Anyone can decide to "join" a public cryptocurrency organization, maintain and update the open ledger based on "competitive bookkeeping" such as mining or other consensus mechanisms (Yermack, 2017). Admittedly, *decentralization* distinguishes blockchain-based corporate governance from the traditional model based on hierarchies. It is important to note that cryptocurrency governance models can exist in different degrees of decentralization. Decentralization, on the one hand, creates value for cryptocurrencies as a peer-to-peer payment system that does not rely on centralized financial intermediaries such as banks or payment companies (Nakamoto, 2008). On the other hand, decentralization can create excessive inefficiencies as governance decisions are made without centralized authorities, but through consensus mechanisms in a non-hierarchical fashion. It is generally believed in economics that there is a trade-off between decentralization and efficiency. For this reason, we think it is appropriate to think about blockchain-based corporate governance forms in terms of their degrees of decentralization. We will follow this logic throughout our reasoning and analysis.

Returns as a measure for cryptocurrency investors' value

Demand for cryptocurrencies mainly stems from two sources: first, consumers and merchants using cryptocurrencies as a means of payment; and second, investors holding a cryptocurrency as an investment, hoping that the price will rise (Narayanan et al., 2016: 100, 173). Here we focus on the latter, as the former, during our period of study, typically do not hold the cryptocurrency after the transaction has occurred, and tend to use it mostly as a payment rail (i.e., as a channel for fast and efficient fiat currency transfers; Hileman and Rauchs, 2017). Just like corporate shareholders multiply a firm's stock price by the number of shares outstanding to determine market capitalization, cryptocurrency *investors* multiply a cryptocurrency's price by the number of crypto-tokens in circulation to determine its market value (Narayanan et al., 2016). According to agency theory, the main objective of shareholders is their *return on investment*. Yet why do some cryptocurrencies generate more returns for investors than others? Since the overarching value proposition of cryptocurrencies is decentralization, we examine how different governance design features imply varying degrees of decentralization across cryptocurrencies, and how they end up affecting returns.

Cryptocurrency governance: internal and external

Following the corporate governance literature, we distinguish between the internal and external governance features of cryptocurrencies. While the effectiveness of internal governance is typically rooted in the design of incentives, the effectiveness of external governance depends on the influence exerted by the community, the media, and the general public over the organization. In line with the theme of this book, for each level, we think in terms of (1) who has power (empowerment), and (2) how these are actors empowered. Considering how cryptocurrencies are structured, we distinguish, internally, between the blockchain, the protocol, and the organizational levels, and externally between the community, media, and social levels. Below we discuss each level of analysis in detail.

Internal governance

Here we identify three internal governance forms: *owner control at the block-chain level, formal voting at the protocol level*, and *centralized funding at the organizational level.*

The blockchain level. At the blockchain level, *miners* (or *validators* in general), whose behavior is guided by the rules and incentives encoded in the cryptocurrency's software, constitute the key stakeholder group. On the one hand, miners/validators work by the software's rulebook and are incentivized accordingly. In this regard, miners/validators work like "employees" who are governed by predetermined incentive mechanisms. On the other hand, miners/validators have the power to decide which transactions to accept into a block, as well as to agree or disagree on the "longest chain" that will constitute the trusted version of the distributed ledger that all users will follow going forward (Nakamoto, 2008). However, there are different ways to tie transaction validation to cryptocurrency ownership. For instance, while a proof-of-work (PoW) miner does not have to own the cryptocurrency to mine, on proof-of-stake (PoS) blockchains, validators are incentivized in proportion to the amount of cryptocurrency tokens they hold. Owner control can thus increase centralization in governance by concentrating validation tasks in the hands of a small percentage of wealthy cryptocurrency owners. Similarly, if a cryptocurrency is "pre-mined" (i.e., a number of tokens are pre-attributed by design to the cryptocurrency founders), ownership will be more concentrated. In addition, some cryptocurrencies allow miners/validators to nominate other network nodes they consider more trustworthy to converge more rapidly to a common decision. In sum, there are three governance design features at the blockchain level associated with more centralization: the use of PoS, the use of pre-mining, and the use of nomination.

The protocol level. Developers who specialize in programming blockchain applications constitute the key stakeholder at the protocol level as they are the people who "write the rulebook" (Narayanan et al., 2016: 173). For most cryptocurrencies including Bitcoin, developers work on a voluntary basis and are not hired or funded by any centralized organization. The code that they work on is typically open source, meaning that any developer can contribute to the code using online repositories such as Github.com (which acts as the Wikipedia of software development). Still, a small group of very dedicated "core" developers can be formed and governance decisions may thus become more centralized. However, major changes to the underlying code can be contested by the wider community of miners/validators or users, who can voice divergent views on online forums or at conferences. Some cryptocurrency organizations formalize this process by requiring formal voting by the miners/validators before developers can roll out code changes across the network in the form of software updates. For example, Bitcoin requires voting backed by miners' computing power on Bitcoin Improvement Proposals, or BIPs, before they get implemented. A cryptocurrency with a *formal voting* procedure in place is considered more decentralized in terms of the governance of its protocol, since developers are then unable to unilaterally impose code changes to the rest of the organizational stakeholders.

The organizational level. In theory, the formative ideology behind Bitcoin and many subsequent cryptocurrencies is rooted in the ideas of decentralized control over token distribution, network participation, and openness. However, there are still substantial differences in how cryptocurrencies are governed in practice. For example, unlike Bitcoin, Ripple has its network and tokens centrally managed by the Ripple company, a venture capital-backed start-up with offices based in five locations: San Francisco (headquarters), New York, London, Luxembourg, and Sydney. While the Ripple blockchain is decentralized across approved nodes, like any other centralized company, it has top managers who make decisions on resource allocation and control the direction for code development. Developers are hired as formal employees; "trusted nodes" are selected into the network based on approval, along with other business functions such as product design, marketing, and business development. Under this more centralized model, management strategies not only are prevalent but necessary for the cryptocurrency-as-company to attract external funding and grow. The presence of such *centralized funding* reflects a more centralized form of governance.

External governance

External governance mechanisms influence organizations less through formal mechanisms such as control over decision rights or ownership rights, than through informal social mechanisms such as social evaluations, reputation effects, informal voting, or public image (Aguilera et al., 2015; Dyck and Zingales, 2002; Walsh and Seward, 1990). Often times, external mechanisms are triggered by failures in internal organizational governance (Walsh and Seward, 1990). However, as noted, for most cryptocurrencies, the stakeholder structure is very different from that of traditional organizations. For example, there are no CEOs or top management teams to be held accountable for the decline of performance, hence the absence of external market for corporate control and potentially weaker reputation effects (Walsh and Seward, 1990; Dyck and Zingales, 2002). In addition, at the center of the organization is the self-validating blockchain, which defines the internal governance rules. Arguably there is very little room for external forces to exert formal and direct influence over the blockchain, even through developers and miners. Further, external actors attempting to make alterations to technical features can create controversy. Does informal and indirect governance by external stakeholders such as media or the general public matter to investors in the same way as for traditional corporations? The Bitcoin blockchain scalability debate provides an interesting illustration. Whereas many users and developers in the community believe there is a clear need to expand the current limit of the Bitcoin block size (1MB) to accommodate the growing number of transactions by allowing for more transactions per block, making changes to the block size appears to be implausible to others. For example, many community enthusiasts firmly believe in the preservation of Bitcoin's core value rooted in the ideology of immutability and decentralization, even if it means Bitcoin will not scale as rapidly. As a result, the debate has been inconclusive since 2015 as of the time of writing (March 2017). In the following, we identify three specific external governance forms: *community governance at the community level, negative publicity at the media level,* and *public interest at the social level.*

Community level. Many cryptocurrencies were created from the open-source Bitcoin software code, and follow the same open-source development model. Like many open-source software projects, initial participation is usually driven by the need for software-related improvements, but later evolves with developers becoming hobbyists (O'Mahony, 2007; Shah, 2006). However, compared with open-source software communities, cryptocurrency communities generally consist of a much more diverse base of stakeholders, including: developers, miners, start-ups, enthusiasts, and users. Community governance involves forum discussions and sometimes informal online voting over decisions. The most used forums for cryptocurrency discussions include cryptocurrencies' official forums, specific cryptocurrency sub-groups within forums such as bitcointalk.org, Reddit.com, and social media such as Facebook and Twitter. Not unlike internal stakeholders, community members self-select into the roles driven by needs, beliefs in the ideologies or technologies, and business opportunities. These external stakeholders take on an "active and possibly democratic role in the management and operation of the organization" (Van Valkenburgh et al., 2015; Dietz et al., no date). It is reasonable then to expect a greater level of participation (as observed in the online forums) to be associated with a more decentralized governance of cryptocurrency organizations by the digital community.

Media level. Recent developments in the corporate governance literature have treated media as an important source of external governance (Aguilera et al., 2015; Bednar et al., 2013; Dyck et al., 2008). Different from controlling through ownership and decision rights, the media can influence key stakeholders of an organization by serving as an information intermediary that plays a governance role through informing, monitoring, and reputation effects (Bushee et al., 2010; Dyck and Zingales, 2002). In particular, scholars have demonstrated that *negative publicity* conveyed in the media is especially effective in influencing organizations. Durand and Vergne (2015), for instance, show that negative publicity targeting weapons manufacturers is associated with a higher probability of asset divestment. Since the early days of the cryptocurrency industry, when Bitcoin transactions were often associated with illegal exchanges on the Dark Web (Campbell-Verduyn and Goguen, this volume), there has been a lot of negative media coverage around blockchain-based organizations on issues related to fraud and various hacking scandals. While many expect that such negative attention should scare away investors and negatively affect returns, prior research failed to find a significant association between the two (Wang and Vergne, 2017).

Social level. The third source of external corporate governance mechanism is rooted in *public interest* from the broader society. Public interest pertains to aggregated search activities motivated by curiosity, attempts to learn or under-stand the technology, and cryptocurrency-related affairs. Arguably, crypto-currencies that receive greater public interest are also subject to more decentralized monitoring and scrutiny regardless of the nature of search and inten-tion. Similar to the way market stakeholders (i.e., suppliers, customers, and share-holders) can exert pressure to corporate decision-making (Stevens et al., 2005), for cryptocurrencies, social pressure comes from a broader range of external stake-holder groups such as merchants, regulators, and service providers. Therefore, public interest captures the aggregate external governance at the social level.

Methodology

To shed light on how internal and external governance affects cryptocurrency returns, in this study we focus on decentralization as the key dimension by which organizational governance forms vary. As the ideology that underpins the very notion of cryptocurrency, decentralization represents a continuum along which one can effectively distinguish between various forms of internal governance. At one end of the spectrum, one finds cryptocurrencies such as Bitcoin, Litecoin, and Peercoin, which strive to retain the self-organized transaction system allow-ing for pseudonymity, decentralization, and disintermediation (Nakamoto, 2008). At the other end of the spectrum, one finds the less decentralized cryptocurrency organizations such as Ripple, built on a blockchain that is permissioned and wherein the nodes are known, trusted participants (e.g., financial institutions and organizations in the remittances industry). Following the method and analysis proposed by Wang and Vergne (2017), we sampled five cryptocurrencies corre-sponding to five different waves of blockchain innovation, and to various degrees of decentralization, in order to capture variance across several attributes of their external and internal governance.

Sampling

We collected data on Bitcoin (BTC), Litecoin (LTC), Peercoin (PPC), Ripple (XRP), and Stellar (XLM). These cryptocurrencies vary in terms of their tech-nology, applications, and most importantly, degree of decentralization. Bitcoin is included in our sample because it represents the first and most established cryptocurrency. At the organizational level, Bitcoin is not centrally funded, and its core developers are not employed by the Bitcoin Foundation or other centralized entities associated with Bitcoin. Building on proof-of-work (PoW) consensus mechanism, Bitcoin distributes governance among miners who allocate external resource to mining (Narayanan et al., 2016: ch7.3). At the protocol level, miners can also have influence over code changes through formal voting mechanisms such as the Bitcoin Improvement Proposals (BIPs), wherein proposals for code improvement are being reviewed, published, and voted for (or against) by miners (for more details, see https://github.com/bitcoin/bips).

Since Bitcoin's creation in 2009, new cryptocurrencies have been created to embrace new ideas, such as faster transaction verification using Scrypt hashing algorithm (e.g., Litecoin). Introduced in 2011, Litecoin was built on the Bitcoin source code as a proof-of-work cryptocurrency but using a different hashing algorithm. It was created as "a lite version of Bitcoin," which improves the transaction processing speed and security (Lee, 2011). In contrast to Bitcoin, the identity of the Litecoin founder, Charles Lee, is known. Also, a small amount (150 units) of Litecoin was pre-mined.

We also included Peercoin because of its ability to achieve greater energy efficiency by incorporating a proof-of-stake (PoS) consensus mechanism. In contrast to PoW mining, PoS validators' voting power is in proportion to the amount of cryptocurrency one holds. Founded in 2012, Peercoin combines both PoW and PoS, and grants more decision-making power and control to current owners of the cryptocurrency.

Since 2013, blockchain-based implementations extended beyond strictly decentralized participation. For instance, centrally funded blockchain organizations emerged as a solution for the financial industry. Some are permissioned, such as Ripple (founded in 2013), whose membership is set by a central authority. Ripple took on a distinct governance approach not only for the cryptographic consensus, but also regarding how participants need to be approved before joining the network. As noted above, Ripple is funded and managed by a centralized, for-profit organization called Ripple Labs. All Ripple coins (the cryptocurrency tokens) were pre-mined at founding.

Finally, we chose to include Stellar (founded in 2014), which incorporates further improvements on Ripple's model by using the Federated Byzantine Agreement (FBA) to make participation open, while ensuring that the cryptocurrency is adoptable by financial institutions for instantaneous processing of transactions (Mazières, 2016). Similar to Ripple, Stellar is not minable, that is, most of it was pre-mined before launch. Despite being permission-less, Stellar is also centrally funded by a non-profit foundation to facilitate certain social objectives such as open financial accessibility and financial inclusion. Figure 3.1 summarizes where each cryptocurrency in our sample is located on the decentralization spectrum.

Data

We acquired panel data from CoinGecko.com, a leading scholarly project that collects daily and weekly data at both the market and community level (Wang and Vergne, 2017; Ong et al., 2015). CoinGecko.com is an independent data source compiled by two cryptocurrency academic researchers, Bobby Ong and Teik Ming Lee, at Singapore Management University's Sim Kee Boon Institute for Financial Economics. The CoinGecko database consists of information extracted and scraped from cryptocurrency specialist websites (such as Coinmarketcap.com), code repositories (e.g., Github.com), community forums (such as Reddit.com), social media (e.g., Twitter and Facebook), and search

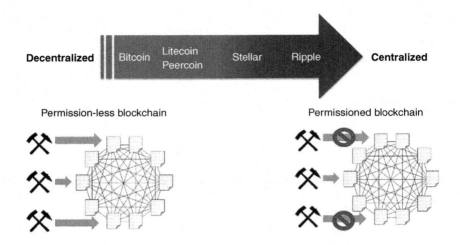

Figure 3.1 Variation of the five cryptocurrencies in our sample along the decentralization spectrum.

Source for graphs of permission-less vs. permissioned blockchains: www.linkedin.com/pulse/making-blockchain-safe-government-merged-mining-chains-tori-adams.

engines (e.g., Bing or Alexa). In addition to information on price, volume, and market capitalization, CoinGecko.com also contains indexes measuring liquidity, protocol development, community activities, and public interests using composite scores. This database has been drawn upon in other scholarly analyses, including the book chapter co-authored by the two founders, "Evaluating the potential of alternative cryptocurrencies" (Ong et al., 2015) in *The Handbook of Digital Currency* (Lee, 2015).

We complemented CoinGecko data with weekly data from Factiva for media coverage, and manually coded several governance indicators such as the association with fraud, hacks, and Ponzi schemes. We did not make a distinction between the financial and the generalist media. Instead, we focused on mainstream media that follows closely the blockchain industry, such as the *Financial Times*, the *Wall Street Journal*, and *The Economist* as they are generally more objective and neutral in commenting on the disruptive nature of cryptocurrencies and blockchains than pro-industry sources, who tend to act as cheerleaders.

Observation period

We study the five cryptocurrencies on a weekly basis between September 2014 and August 2015 (when we first began to collect the data). This is a period when the cryptocurrency market has become more established and stabilized in contrast to the earlier period in which only a handful of cryptocurrencies existed. More variations in cryptocurrencies were present in this period, with the introduction of Stellar at the start of our observation period. All crypto-currencies in our sample existed throughout the period, forming a balanced panel data for analysis. The final dataset contains weekly data for 255 observations.

Measures

Dependent variable: weekly returns

Supply and demand (by investors) determine cryptocurrency value (Narayanan et al., 2016). Financial returns are a common measure used to evaluate the performance of organizational governance. For example, stock returns have been used to measure the performance of internal (Ittner et al., 2003) and external governance (Daines et al., 2010). We model returns using multivariate linear regression, where returns are a linear combination of various governance-related variables. In particular, we identified factors pertaining to multiple levels of internal and external governance that may directly or indirectly drive investment decisions. For example, whereas cryptocurrencies governed by highly decentralized blockchains may be more attractive as an investment target because of the value propositions rooted in security of the network and transactions, a centrally funded blockchain organization can be more appealing to investors who believe in managerial strategic planning.

Following Wang and Vergne (2017), we measured weekly returns as $[\text{Price}_{t+1} - \text{Price}_t] / \text{Price}_t$, whereby price is the cryptocurrency's weekly average price weighted by trading volume. We build on Wang and Vergne's (2017) sample statistics, which indicate that the distribution for returns is close to normal.

Independent variables

Internal governance. As previously explained, we coded three internal governance variables at three different levels: *owner control, formal voting*, and *centralized funding* at the blockchain, the protocol, and organizational levels, respectively. We measured *owner control* using three binary indicators: "PoS," "nomination," and "pre-mined." We first studied in detail the white papers of the cryptocurrencies in our sample and identified blockchain design elements that are related to governance. "PoS" was coded as a 1 if the consensus mechanism contains proof-of-stake and 0 otherwise. We assigned the value 1 (and 0 otherwise) to "nomination" if the cryptocurrency allows the network participants to select a subset of nodes as trusted validators. Finally, we coded "pre-mined" as 1 if the cryptocurrency allocated a certain amount of coins to the core developers or their closed loop before launch and 0 otherwise. We then added up scores of these three indicators and assigned the sums as scores for *owner control*. This aggregated score thus takes on higher values when cryptocurrency accumulation by owners is associated with more centralized control over the cryptocurrency.

We measured *formal voting* by coding the presence of formal procedures for miners to vote on protocol changes, using a binary variable. We coded 1 for the presence of formal voting, which indicates a democratic governance mechanism at the protocol level, and 0 for the absence of such a mechanism.

We measured *centralized funding* as a binary variable by assigning 1 to the cryptocurrency if it is centrally funded by an organization and 0 if otherwise. For example, the Bitcoin Core projects (and the core developers) are funded through a "Sponsorship Program" by several organizations such as the MIT Media Lab, and start-ups such as Blockstream, Chaincode Labs, and BTCC (van Wirdum, 2016). Therefore, Bitcoin is coded 0 for centralized funding. Conversely, Stellar have their platforms and developers funded centrally by the Stellar Foundation. Stellar tokens are centrally allocated toward salaries, Stellar grants for participants in the direct sign-up program, and other strategic planning. Therefore, Stellar was assigned a score of 1 for centralized funding.

External governance. We capture external governance of blockchain organizations by looking at *community governance*, *negative publicity*, and *public interest* using data from social media, traditional news media, and search engines, respectively. For social media, we adopted the composite score, "community governance," developed by CoinGecko to capture the degree of community participation in social media forum discussions. CoinGecko weighted indicators for each cryptocurrency consisting of: the number of Reddit subscribers, the number of Reddit active users, the number of Reddit new posts in 48 hours, the number of Reddit new comments in new posts in 48 hours, the number of Facebook likes, and the number of Twitter followers. Because of our non-disclosure agreement with CoinGecko, we are unable to reveal the exact weightings for each indicator.

For news media, we adopted the measure *negative publicity* developed in Wang and Vergne (2017). The authors counted the weekly number of negative news articles using content analysis by keywords associated misconducts such as criminal or underground activities with the name of the cryptocurrency. A research assistant was hired to search in Factiva by keywords such as ["Bitcoin" AND ("fraud*" OR "hacked" OR "Ponzi" OR "theft")] or ["ripple" near7 ("bitcoin" OR "crypto*" OR "altcoin)] AND ("fraud*" OR "hacked" OR "Pomzi" OR "scam" OR "theft"). The results for coding were randomly cross-verified and validated by one of the authors. The final numbers of article counts plus one were logged for the regression model estimation.

Finally, we measure *public interest* from search engine data using the indicator developed by CoinGecko. It is a composite measure consisting of a weighted average of the number of web search results for each specific cryptocurrency on Bing and the Alexa web traffic ranking for the cryptocurrency website. This measure captures the interest that the public pays to particular cryptocurrencies, whether it is for general inquiries, searches for specific information, or technical details. Conceptualized as "buzz" around a cryptocurrency (Wang and Vergne, 2017), public interest serves as an indicator for external governance which influences investors' decisions. CoinGecko computes the *public interest* variable by normalizing the raw value against the Bitcoin value as a benchmark.

Control variables

We control for cryptocurrencies' *supply growth, liquidity*, and *technological development* for the analysis. Although the coin *supply growth* rate based on the speed of new block generation time is usually predefined in the protocol, variation exists when there is a surge or rapid decline in network activities, such as mining power for PoW cryptocurrencies. New coins can also be distributed unexpectedly to the network in the case of non-minable cryptocurrencies such as Ripple and Stellar. Despite the fact that coin issuance self-adjusts to account for network changes, temporary deviation in supply from the targeted average is still present, affecting returns in the short term. Therefore, we control for supply growth computed as $(\text{Supply}_{t+1} - \text{Supply}_t)/\text{Supply}_t$.

We also control for *liquidity* using the CoinGecko liquidity score obtained from major cryptocurrency exchanges such as Bitfinex and Okcoin. Finally, we control for *technological development* to capture the innovation potential enabled by cryptocurrencies' underlying software. Our previous research indicates that the extent to which the code base is maintained and the level of collaborated problem-solving by developers is positively and significantly related to returns (Wang and Vergne, 2017). We adopted the technological development measure developed by CoinGecko, which weighted the number of unique code collaborators, the number of proposals merged in the code repository, the number of issues raised and fixed, and the number of forks as indicators. We are unable to reveal the exact weightings for the composite measure because of a confidentiality agreement with CoinGecko. We lagged all external governance predictors except *liquidity* as in Wang and Vergne (2017) to avoid the problems of contemporaneous feedback from return to community, media, and other internet activities.

A detailed list of variables and their definitions are presented in Table 3.1.

Analyses

We conducted three model estimations. Model 1 contains only the control variables, Model 2 includes the external governance variables, and Model 3 is the full model with both internal and external governance variables. Following Wang and Vergne (2017), we used fixed effect (FE) estimations for Model 1 and Model 2 to account for unobserved individual group-level heterogeneity. However, for Model 3, FE are inappropriate since internal governance variables such as owner control, formal voting, and centralized funding are coded as cryptocurrency-level time-invariant variables (they would be dropped from the FE estimates). Random effect estimation, on the other hand, can yield unbiased, consistent, and efficient estimation on the condition that group-level variables are independent of the regressors. We conducted a Hausman test, which failed to reject the null hypothesis. Therefore, we ran random effect estimations for Model 3.

Table 3.1 List of variables

Variable	Level	Definition
Dependent variable Returns [Price$_{t+1}$ − Price$_t$]/Price$_t$	Organization	Weekly weighted returns of the cryptocurrency
Internal governance Owner control	Blockchain	The sum of three binary variables below: PoS: 1 if the blockchain consensus is proof-of-stake, else 0. Pre-mined: 1 if all or part of the cryptocurrency was issued to core developers or their closed loops before launch, else 0. Nomination: 1 if participants have the power to nominate their trusted nodes, else 0.
Formal voting	Protocol	1 if there exist formal voting mechanisms (e.g., BIPS) for miners to vote for protocol change, else 0.
Centralized funding	Organization	1 if the cryptocurrency core development activities and core developers are centrally funded directly by a firm or foundation, else 0.
External governance Community governance (t−1)	Community	A composite score consisting of social media data: the number of Reddit subscribers, the number of Reddit active users, the number of Reddit new posts in 48 hours, the number of Reddit new comments in new posts in 48 hours, the number of Facebook likes, and the number of Twitter followers.
Negative publicity (t−1)	Social	Log (the number of negative media news articles in the previous period).
Public interest (t−1)	Social	A composite score consisting of the weighted average of web searches on Bing, and the Alexia web traffic ranking of the cryptocurrency's website in the previous period.
Control variables Supply growth since t−1		[Supply$_{t+1}$ − Supply$_t$]/Supply$_t$
Liquidity		Liquidity measured and supplied by CoinGecko.
Technological development (t−1)		A composite score including: the number of unique code collaborators, the number of proposals merged in the code repository, the number of issues raised and fixed, and the number of forks in the previous period.

Results

Table 3.2 displays the regression results. Model 1 includes control variables, crypto-currency fixed effects, and the time trend. Model 2 adds the external governance variables, and Model 3 the internal governance variables. All models are estimated using Huber-White standard errors which are robust to heteroscedasticity.

Interpretation of the findings

Internal governance. Model 3 indicates that *owner control* at the blockchain level has a negative and significant ($p < 0.001$) effect on returns. For a one standard deviation increase in owner control (0.6330), returns decrease by 19

Table 3.2 Regression results

	Model 1 (FE)	Model 2 (FE)	Model 3 (RE)
External governance effects			
Public interest (t−1)		−5.85***	−5.49***
		(1.543)	(1.110)
Negative publicity (t−1)		0.052	0.057
		(0.066)	(0.072)
Community governance (t−1)		−3.88	−3.15**
		(3.401)	(1.506)
Internal governance design choices			
Owner control			−0.30***
			(0.053)
Formal voting			−0.16***
			(0.021)
Centralized funding			0.10***
			(0.030)
Control variables			
Liquidity	2.12***	2.34***	2.41***
	(0.564)	(0.617)	(0.667)
Supply growth since (t−1)	0.87*	0.21***	0.20***
	(0.046)	(0.072)	(0.072)
Technological development (t−1)	1.40***	2.60***	2.53***
	(0.296)	(0.616)	(0.523)
Cryptocurrency fixed effects	included	included	n/a
Weekly trend	−0.000228	−0.00144	−0.00139
	(0.0007)	(0.001)	(0.0009)
Constant	−0.52***	0.20	0.40*
	(0.088)	(0.526)	(0.263)
N	250	250	250
Within- or adjusted R^2	0.060	0.109	0.108

Notes
1 All models instrument liquidity (not lagged) using all regressors.
* $p < 0.10$;
** $p < 0.05$;
*** $p < 0.01$.

percent (i.e., $0.6330 \times (-0.30) = (-0.190)$). In other words, blockchain-level routines governed in a more centralized form yield lower returns. If decentralization is precisely what investors value in blockchain organizations, they should indeed evaluate more highly the more decentralized blockchains.

Surprisingly, though, at the protocol level, the existence of decentralized formal voting mechanisms is negatively and significantly ($p < 0.001$) related to returns. When formal voting increases by one standard deviation (0.49029), returns drops by 7.8 percent (i.e., $0.49029 \times (-0.16) = (-0.078)$). It could be that investors perceive decentralization at the protocol level as a source of governance inefficiency. Indeed, voting on protocol changes is time-consuming and does not allow for quick decision-making, as illustrated by the lingering debates in the Bitcoin community around increasing block size.

Finally, at the organizational level, *centralized funding* is positively and significantly ($p < 0.001$) associated with returns as shown in Model 3. For a one standard deviation increase in centralized funding (0.4903), returns increase by 4.9 percent ($0.4903 \times 0.10 = 0.049$). A centrally funded blockchain-based organization may appeal more to investors by demonstrating clear strategic directions and organizational mandates which lead to better efficiency and returns. Overall, our findings reveal that more decentralization adds value for investors only at the lower (blockchain) level of the governance hierarchy; when it comes to higher-level protocol changes or the overall strategic direction of the cryptocurrency organization, more centralization is preferred.

External governance. Public interest is negatively and significantly ($p < 0.001$) associated with returns. In other words, the "buzz effect" does a disservice to returns. According to Model 3, for a one standard deviation (0.02146) increase in public interest, returns drop by 11.8 percent (i.e., $0.02146 \times (-5.49) = -0.118$; see Wang and Vergne, 2017, for a discussion). Furthermore, *negative publicity* is not significantly associated with returns. As such, unlike in prior studies of the media as agents of external corporate governance (e.g., Dyck et al., 2008), here we do not find that negative media coverage decreases returns. This could be explained by the fact that most cryptocurrencies do not have a central authority to which blame can be attributed, such as a top management team. In turn, the absence of a central authority could make negative publicity a lot less effective than in the context of traditional corporations. Finally, community governance is negatively and significantly ($p < 0.05$) associated with returns. For a one standard deviation increase in community governance (0.58625), returns decrease by 18.5 percent (i.e., $0.05862 \times (-3.15) = (-0.185)$). We do not find increased community governance to be beneficial for the market returns of blockchain-based organizations. This could be because community involvement becomes more intense in periods of intense criticism (that is not captured by negative publicity), as was the case around the time of the attack against the decentralized, Ethereum-powered investment vehicle called "The DAO" (Breitman, 2017; DuPont, this volume). To explore further the relationship between community governance and cryptocurrency returns, future studies should not only capture the centralization and intensity of community governance, as we do here, but also the overall sentiment (positive or negative) of the community.

Conclusion

Our findings point to interesting effects of governance on returns. Internally, while centralized governance design choices at the blockchain level decrease returns, centralized governance design choices at the protocol and the organizational levels appear to be more beneficial for returns. The results correspond to the idea that, on the one hand, investors value cryptocurrencies' core value proposition, rooted in decentralization; but on the other hand, they are suspicious of decentralized governance at higher levels in the organization because they could slow down strategic decision-making (e.g., regarding the introduction of new innovations) or create information asymmetries between investors and technologists.

Since March 2017, the cryptocurrency market has become increasingly competitive – Bitcoin's market dominance is reduced significantly, indicating the growth of a more diverse range of blockchain-based governance models, which entail additional complexity relative to traditional corporate governance. These new forms of governance, which place computer code at the center of the system, emphasize the need for new research on organizational governance accounting for the interdependence of various levels within blockchain-based organizations (i.e., the blockchain, protocol, and organizational levels). This study paves the way for crafting new theories about the governance with, and by, "decentralized autonomous organizations" (DuPont, this volume) such as cryptocurrencies.

In terms of global governance, these new and open blockchain organizations embody more inclusive solutions to governance problems that could alter the balance of power between incumbent firms and start-ups. As noted at the beginning of the chapter, blockchain technology has attracted considerable attention from central banks and multinational retail banks. Today, many of these financial institutions turn to financial technology start-ups (e.g., Ripple) to leverage blockchain technology. Foreseeably, this collaboration between centralized financial institutions and decentralized blockchain organizations will also foster the emergence of hybrid governance forms across organizational boundaries, as was previously observed in the context of open-source software communities (O'Mahony, 2007; Shah, 2006). It is therefore urgent for scholars in the social sciences to address the rise of blockchain with solid empirical research and fresh theory on these new forms of organization.

Acknowledgments

This work was supported by a Social Sciences and Humanities Research Council of Canada (SSHRC) grant (no. 430-2015-0670); by the Ontario Government's Early Researcher Award (no. R4905A06); and by the Scotiabank Digital

Banking Lab at Ivey Business School. The funders had no role in study design, analysis, decision to publish, or preparation of the manuscript.

Bibliography

Aguilera, R.V., Filatotchev, I., Gospel, H., and Jackson, G. (2008). An organizational approach to comparative corporate governance: Costs, contingencies, and complementarities. *Organization Science, 19*(3): 475–92.

Aguilera, R.V., and Jackson, G. (2010). Comparative and international corporate governance. *Academy of Management Annals, 4*(1): 485–556.

Aguilera, R.V., Desender, K., Bednar, M.K., and Lee, J. (2015). Connecting the dots: Bringing external corporate governance into the corporate governance puzzle. *Academy of Management Annals, 9*(1): 483–573.

Atzori, M. (2017). Blockchain technology and decentralized governance: Is the state still necessary? *Journal of Governance and Regulation, 6*(1): 45–62.

Bednar, M.K., Boivie, S., and Prince, N.R. (2013). Burr under the saddle: How media coverage influences strategic change. *Organization Science, 24*(3): 910–25.

Breitman, K. (2017). Op ed: Why Ethereum's hard fork will cause problems in the coming year. *Bitcoin Magazine*. Retrieved March 30, 2017, from https://bitcoinmagazine.com/articles/op-ed-why-ethereums-hard-fork-will-cause-problems-coming-year/

Bushee, B J., Core, J.E., Guay, W., and Hamm, S.J.W. (2010). The role of the business press as an information intermediary. *Journal of Accounting Research, 48*(1):1–19.

Buterin, V. (2014). *Ethereum Blog*. Retrieved February 21, 2017, from https://blog.ethereum.org/2014/05/06/daos-dacs-das-and-more-an-incomplete-terminology-guide/

Connelly, B.L., Hoskisson, R.E., Tihanyi, L., and Certo, S.T. (2010). Ownership as a form of corporate governance. *Journal of Management Studies, 47*(8):1561–89.

Daines, R.M., Gow, I.D., and Larcker, D.F. (2010). Rating the ratings: How good are commercial governance ratings? *Journal of Financial Economics, 98*(3): 439–61.

Dalton, D.R., Hitt, M.A., Certo, S.T., and Dalton, C.M. (2007). 1 The fundamental agency problem and its mitigation: Independence, equity, and the market for corporate control. *Academy of Management Annals, 1*(1): 1–64.

Davidson, S., De Filippi, P., and Potts, J. (2016a). Disrupting governance: The new institutional economics of distributed ledger technology. SSRN: http://ssrn.com/abstract=2811995

Davidson, S., De Filippi, P., and Potts, J. (2016b). Economics of blockchain. SSRN: http://ssrn.com/abstract=2744751 or http://dx.doi.org/10.2139/ssrn.2744751

Del Castillo, M. (2017). Decentralizing central banks: How R3 envisions the future of fiat. *Coindesk*. Retrieved April 5, 2017, from www.coindesk.com/decentralizing-central-banks-how-r3-envisions-the-future-of-fiat/

Dietz, J., Xethalis, G., De Filippi, P., and Hazard, J. (no date) Model distributed collaborative organizations. *Stanford Working Group*. Retrieved August 21, 2017, from https://fair.coop/?get_group_doc=50/1430309418-SWARMSTANFORDModelDCOTemplate.pdf

Durand, R., and Vergne, J.P. (2015). Asset divestment as a response to media attacks in stigmatized industries. *Strategic Management Journal, 36*(8): 1205–23.

Dyck, A., and Zingales, L. (2002). *The corporate governance role of the media*. Unpublished working paper. Harvard University.

Dyck, A., Volchkova, N., and Zingales, L. (2008). The corporate governance role of the media: Evidence from Russia. *Journal of Finance, 63*(3): 1093–1135.

Fama, E.F., and Jensen, M.C. (1983). Separation of ownership and control. *Journal of Law and Economics, 26*(2): 301–25.

Hambrick, D.C., Werder, A.V., and Zajac, E.J. (2008). New directions in corporate governance research. *Organization Science, 19*(3): 381–85.

Hileman, G., and Rauchs, M. (2017). *Global cryptocurrency benchmarking study*. Research by Cambridge Centre of Alternative Finance.

Ittner, C.D., Lambert, R.A., and Larcker, D.F. (2003). The structure and performance consequences of equity grants to employees of new economy firms. *Journal of Accounting and Economics, 34*(1): 89–127.

Jensen, M.C., and Meckling, W.H. (1976). Theory of the firm: Managerial behavior, agency costs and ownership structure. *Journal of Financial Economics, 3*(4): 305–60.

Lee, C. (2011). *Bitcointalk*. Retrieved February 23, 2017, from https://bitcointalk.org/index.php?topic=47417.0

Lee, D.K.C. (2015). *Handbook of digital currency*. Amsterdam: Elsevier.

MacDonald, T.J., Allen, D.W.E., and Potts, J. (2016). Blockchains and the boundaries of self-organized economies: Predictions for the future of banking. https://ssrn.com/abstract=2749514.

Mazières, D. (2016). *The Stellar consensus protocol: A federated model for internet-level consensus.* Stellar White Paper. Retrieved August 21, 2017, from www.stellar.org/papers/stellar-consensus-protocol.pdf

Moore, J.H., and Kraatz, M.S. (2011). Governance form and organizational adaptation: Lessons from the savings and loan industry in the 1980s. *Organization Science, 22*(4): 850–68.

Nakamoto, S. (2008). *Bitcoin: A peer-to-peer electronic cash system*. Retrieved August 21, 2017, from https://bitcoin.org/bitcoin.pdf

Narayanan, A., Bonneau, J., Felten, E., Miller, A., and Goldfeder, S. (2016). *Bitcoin and cryptocurrency technologies: A comprehensive introduction*. Princeton, NJ: Princeton University Press.

O'Mahony, S. (2007). The governance of open source initiatives: What does it mean to be community managed? *Journal of Management and Governance, 11*: 139–50.

Ong, B., Lee, T.M., Li, B., and Lee, D.K.C. (2015). Evaluating the potential of alternative cryptocurrencies. In D.K.C. Lee (ed.) *Handbook of digital currency* (pp. 81–135). Amsterdam: Elsevier.

Scott, W.R., and Davis, G.F. (2007). *Organizations and organizing: Rational, natural, and open systems perspectives*. Upper Saddle River, NJ: Prentice Hall.

Shah, S.K. (2006). Motivation, governance, and the viability of hybrid forms in open source software development. *Management Science, 52*(7): 1000–14.

Stevens, J.M., Steensma, K.H., Harrison, D.A., and Cochran, P.L. (2005). Symbolic or substantive document? The influence of ethics codes on financial executives' decisions. *Strategic Management Journal, 26*(2): 181–95.

Van Valkenburgh, P., Dietz, J., De Filippi, P., Shadab, H., Xethalis, G., and Bollier, D. (2015). *Distributed collaborative organisations: Distributed networks and regulatory frameworks*. Harvard Working Paper.

Van Wirdum, A. (2016). Who funds Bitcoin core development? How the industry supports Bitcoin's 'reference client'. *Bitcoin Magazine*. Retrieved August 21, 2017, from https://bitcoinmagazine.com/articles/who-funds-bitcoin-core-development-how-the-industry-supports-bitcoin-s-reference-client-1459967859/

Walsh, J., and Seward, J. (1990). On the efficiency of internal and external corporate control mechanisms. *Academy of Management Review, 15*(3): 421–58.

Wang, S., and Vergne, J-P. (2017). Buzz factor or innovation potential: What explains cryptocurrencies' returns? *PLoS One, 12*(1): e0169556. http://journals.plos.org/plosone/article?id=10.1371/journal.pone.0169556

Williamson, O.E. (1996). *The mechanisms of governance.* New York: Oxford University Press.

Wright, A., and De Filippi, P. (2015). Decentralized blockchain technology and the rise of Lex Cryptographia. SSRN: http://ssrn.com/abstract=2580664.

Yermack, D. (2017). Corporate governance and blockchains. *Review of Finance,* p.rfw074.

4 The mutual constitution of technology and global governance

Bitcoin, blockchains, and the international anti-money-laundering regime

Malcolm Campbell-Verduyn and Marcel Goguen

How do blockchain applications affect global anti-money-laundering (AML) governance and how does global governance affect the evolution of blockchain applications? This chapter navigates between technological and social determinism in highlighting the mutually constitutive relationships between blockchains and global anti-money-laundering governance. We question both directions of "loss of control" (Shields, 2005b: 497) perspectives that consider global governance as subjected to the predetermined trajectories of technological change as well as the interactions between key actors operating separately from their wider socio-technical environment. Drawing on constructivist global political economy (GPE) studies emphasising the roles of technologies in international regimes, as well as media reports and the budding interdisciplinary literature on blockchains, we stress the unexpected and often underappreciated manners in which even applications of novel sets of knowledge impact governance practices that in turn impact the evolution of emergent technologies.

This argument is elaborated in two steps. First, we reveal how the technical features of blockchain technologies shape and constrain governance in the international anti-money-laundering regime. In a second step, we illustrate how the responses of this regime in turn shape and constrain the evolution of this set of emergent technologies. Taken together, these arguments provide a nuanced understanding of the mutual constitution of emergent technologies and global governance that can also be understood as 'dialectical'. Both terms consider how socio-technical environments condition the interactions underpinning global governance yet are also influenced by the specific relations of competition, collaboration, and conflict amongst state and non-state actors in international regimes.

This chapter develops these arguments over three sections. The first section begins by situating our analysis within GPE literatures on international regimes that tend to underappreciate the mutually constitutive relationship between technologies and global governance. The second section empirically illustrates the co-evolution of technology and global governance in the relationships between the international AML regime and blockchain technologies. We focus on how the specific responses to the money laundering implications of these technologies by a leading actor in this regime, the Financial Action Task Force, are constituted by the technical features of blockchains. We also illustrate how global governance responses in turn influence the evolution of applications of this emerging technology in unexpected but important manners. The concluding section summarises and points to further considerations for improving understanding of the co-evolution of technologies and governance in the global political economy.

International regimes and the socio-technical environment of global governance

GPE as well as International Relations (IR) scholarship understand international regimes in varying manners. Despite overlapping in some respects, their conceptions can generally be grouped in two broadly diverging categories. On the one hand, rationalist approaches regard international regimes in principle–agent terms as formal rule-based organisations that reflect either the common or the individual interests of their members, who tend to largely be nation-states. Liberal approaches, for example, stress how international regimes benefit common interests, whilst realist approaches understand international regimes as advancing the particular interests of the most powerful 'hegemonic' state(s) (Gilpin, 2011; Keohane, 1983; Krasner, 1983). On the other hand, constructivist accounts move beyond rational utility-maximising models in stressing how international regimes influence the perception of actor interests, even those of the most dominant state(s). Here international regimes are considered not merely as formal organisations but as also consisting of less formalised intersubjective norms, conventions, and standards of practice. The latter can shape state identities, interests, and ultimately international interactions in particular manners (Onuf, 1989; Reus-Smit, 1997; Wendt, 1992). As Hasenclever, Mayer, and Rittberger (1997: 155) succinctly put it, regimes "prescribe certain actions in defined circumstances, they also serve as commonly used points of reference for the determination and the assessment of individual behavior."

Rationalist and constructivist understandings of international regimes overlap in foregrounding the roles of states. Yet these state-centric analyses tend to overlook relationships between international regimes and non-state actors as well as material applications of knowledge imbued in technologies. States and regimes interact less in abstract voids than within particular socio-technical environments shaped, yet not wholly determined, by technologies and their applications by non-state actors. International interactions at the United Nations or the European Union, for example, are enabled and structured by the translation services offered by firms mobilising applications of particular information communication technologies (ICTs). The specific nature and composition of the socio-technical environments characterised by state as well as non-state actors and technologies influence the character of international regimes and global governance more generally. This influence can be causally determined by revealing how specific actors in international regimes perceive technologies as posing implications "to which changes in the regimes were designed to respond, and if they had the ability to bring about these changes" (Porter, 1993: 148). GPE scholars have for instance revealed how the highly technocratic and depoliticised international regime overseeing financial governance reflects the specific socio-technical characteristics of global finance itself (Best, 2003; Porter, 2003).

The relationships between technologies and non-state actors in the broader socio-technical environment in which international regimes operate are not merely one-way or uni-directional. Rather, technologies and socio-technical environments are themselves also shaped and influenced by international regimes. More specifically, the responses of international regimes to the implications raised by applications of novel technologies in turn influence the development and evolution of technologies and the actors applying them in particular manners. Whether technologies are perceived as challenges or as opportunities by key actors in international regimes can entail different types of responses. A technology regarded as a threat to a regime may instigate much different responses from those regarded as providing opportunities for global governance. In either instance, governance responses are neither wholly determined by the specific features and applications of technology, nor are they completely socially determined. Rather, responses to technological change are shaped and constrained by the particular set of state and non-state actors involved, as well as their perceptions of the specific implications posed by technological changes. Governance responses then tend to shape and constrain the evolution of technologies and their applications by state and non-state actors. The interactive or 'dialectical' relationship between international regimes and technologies can also be understood as 'mutually constitutive', as Figure 4.1 illustrates in a simplified manner.

Blockchains and the international AML regime[1]

This section illustrates the mutual constitution of technology and global governance through an examination of relationships between blockchain technologies and the international anti-money-laundering (AML) regime. After a brief overview of what precisely money laundering entails, we proceed to scrutinise the character of the international AML regime and blockchain technologies in turn. The mutual constitution of the former and latter are then elaborated in detailing how key actors in the international AML regime perceived blockchain-influenced changes as challenges. The responses to such challenges are shown to have been integrally influenced, yet not wholly determined, by key features of blockchain

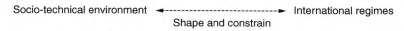

Socio-technical environment ◄---------------------------► International regimes
Shape and constrain

Figure 4.1 The mutually constitutive relationship between technologies and international regimes.

technologies. A final subsection reveals how the responses of key actors in the AML regime in turn shaped and constrained the particular evolution that applications of this emerging technology has undertaken.

What exactly is money laundering?

Money laundering, simply put, is the 'mainstreaming' of proceeds from illicit activities into the legitimate financial system in ways that conceal their illegitimate origins. Scholars scrutinising these activities tend to analytically sub-divide money laundering into three distinct stages: placement, layering, and integration (Straub, 2001: 518–19; Shields, 2005b: 486). Placement is the process of taking direct proceeds of crime and transferring them into less suspicious forms, which can then be 'slipped' into the financial system. Layering then involves attempts to conceal the origins and ownerships of funds in shifting them to and from multiple different institutions in order for their origins to become indecipherable. Finally, integration is the stage when the proceeds of crime are ultimately masked as part of the legitimate financial system.

Several types of money laundering exist. These can involve the physical smuggling of large quantities of paper money, the siphoning of aid funds, the use of front businesses, tax evasion, bribery, prepaid cards, insurance claims, international trade, and real estate transactions, as well as 'non-bank payment services providers' such as PayPal (Levi and Reuter, 2006: 312; Tropina, 2014: 74; Unger, 2013: 359; Choo, 2009: 12; Isa *et al.*, 2015: 8; Hett, 2008: 1–6; Zdanowicz, 2004: 54; Stokes, 2012: 222). Despite this wide array of possibilities, money laundering activities tend to involve specific financial intermediaries (Ping, 2004: 48; Zdanowicz, 2004: 53). Banks and other financial institutions have long served as the main trusted third parties between two or more parties seeking to engage in money laundering. Because of their central roles within global finance and specifically in international payment and settlement systems, these centralised institutions have been considered the main 'choke points' (Shields, 2005b: 488) that the AML regime has long targeted and relied upon (Chong and Lopez-de-Silanes, 2015: 79; Isa *et al.*, 2015: 9).

The international anti-money-laundering regime

Money laundering did not originate with the application of blockchain technologies to Bitcoin and other CCs (Bjerg, 2016: 10). Rather it is a longstanding practice (Chong and Lopez-de-Silanes, 2015: 78) that formally became criminalised with the 1986 passage of the Money Laundering Control Act in the United States (Shields, 2005b: 499). By 2008 over 170 countries had formally criminalised the activity.

Studies by GPE scholars and social scientists from a variety of disciplines have detailed the origins and expansion of the international AML regime. Rationalist analyses stress how the security interests of the world's hegemon, the US, were central to the development of an international regime targeting money launderers initially as part of the 'war on drugs' and then later as part of the 'war on terror' (Reynolds, 2002; Kingah and Zwartjes, 2015).[2] These analyses emphasise the key roles of the US in the creation and expansion of the Financial Action Task Force (FATF), the Paris-based intergovernmental organisation formally comprising 35 member states and two regional organisations. Through its associate and observer members, as well as members of regional bodies, however, the FATF is linked to nearly every country in the world.[3] The FATF issued 40 recommendations following its 1989 founding and a further nine recommendations after the 11 September 2001 attacks. Its 40+9 recommendations are widely regarded as central to the international AML regime (Stringer, 2011: 110; Isa *et al.*, 2015: 8). Constructivist accounts of the international AML regime, meanwhile, tend to stress how the informal and non-legally binding recommendations of the FATF have been adopted by a majority of the world's countries through informal forms of governance. The use of 'blacklisting', for example, has been regarded as inducing recalcitrant states to comply with AML recommendations through forms of peer pressure, both from within the wider international community of states, as well from the wider set of banks and financial institutions in seeking to avoid being identified with non-compliant jurisdictions (Wessel, 2006: 174). Together, rationalist and constructivist accounts have insightfully illustrated the key role of hegemonic power in developing the international AML regime, as well as the roles of informal standards and practices in compliance with its key recommendations (Sharman, 2008: 636).

Interdisciplinary studies of the international AML regime stress the roles of key non-state actors in general and banks in particular. These centralised institutions are considered crucial for investigating the 'audit trail' (Shields, 2005b: 492) left behind by international financial transfers. Banks in particular have been tasked to 'follow the money' in helping regulators to identify criminal money launderers (Levi, 2015: 276). These non-state actors play key roles in the international AML regime by providing access to wire transfer records. Individual bank employees are effectively deputised as AML enforcers (Shields, 2005b: 490; Masciandaro, 2004: 22; Ping, 2004) as they fulfil currency transaction reports (CTRs) for deposits/transactions of $10,000 or more, suspicious activity reports (SARs) when there is a 'reasonable' basis for suspecting that money laundering might be occurring, and make profiles on clients whose sources of money seem likely to be associated with criminal activities following know your customer (KYC) requirements (Boles, 2015: 379; Donahue, 2006: 396; Gruber, 2013: 191; Hett, 2008: 3; Shields, 2005b: 489, 2005a: 19). Though usefully recognising the important roles played by non-state actors such as banks, existing accounts nevertheless tend to overlook or simply assume in passing the specific technologies banks and regulators rely upon, as well as how the wider socio-technical environment shapes the international AML regime (e.g. Shields, 2005b: 495; Stokes, 2012: 223).

Blockchains and international money laundering in theory and in practice

Two specific features of blockchain technologies pose novel implications for international money laundering: the decentralisation and quasi-anonymity of transactions on global networks. This subsection details how these implications pose *theoretical* rather than *actual* challenges for the centralised actors charged with identifying suspicious transactions and for the verification of the individuals involved in suspicious transactions by the international AML regime.

First, by enabling transactions directly between users in decentralised networks spread worldwide, blockchains bypass the trusted third parties such as banks that have long been central to the international AML regime. Rather than trusting traditional centralised institutions such as banks to verify and police the exchange of funds, blockchain transactions rely both on complex algorithms and on decentralised networks of users to continuously verify the validity of exchanges.[4] In other words, cryptocurrencies (CCs) such as Bitcoin and other blockchain applications enable users to exchange directly between themselves without going through traditional trusted third parties. Since, theoretically at least, there are no centralised institutions to 'deputise' in ensuring that transactions meet international AML requirements, blockchain applications such as CCs "neatly sidestep the plethora of anti-money laundering regulations developed over the past 25 years" (Stokes, 2013: 3). American government analyst Andrew Macurak (2014: 3) succinctly summarises this first implication posed by the technical design of blockchains for the international AML regime: "[w]ith digital exchanges of real currency, financial intermediaries collect a fee to verify that value has actually changed hands [...] Bitcoin makes files change hands like physical cash".

The second technical feature of blockchains posing implications for the international AML regime is the quasi-anonymity provided to users. The tension between the desire for transparency and anonymity is a central issue confronting digital technologies more widely (DeNardis, 2014: 57–9) that plays out in particular ways with blockchain applications. Identifying real-world individuals based on user addresses is rendered difficult – but not impossible[5] – by the complexity of cryptographic methods underpinning blockchains (Kostakis and Giotitsas, 2014: 31). The central implication for the international AML regime is that, as Deloitte principal Fred Curry states, regulators "can't monitor transactions if [they] don't know who the parties are" (cited in Rubenfeld, 2015). For employees of financial institutions whose job it is to recognise "evasive or defensive answers to questions", it becomes difficult to identify whom exactly to question (Stokes, 2013). A related implication is for financiers and regulators alike to develop an understanding of what 'atypical' and what 'normal' blockchain transactions are. As the legal scholar Robert Stokes (2013) puts it, this is the issue of knowing exactly "what a suspicious BTC [Bitcoin] transfer would 'look' like". Put differently, how can suspicious blockchain-based transactions be identified without any standard reference of their typical use?

Together, the decentralised and quasi-anonymous features of blockchains present important implications for the international AML regime. Blockchain-based transactions in applications such as CCs do not rely on centralised banks and financial institutions as 'choke points' to undertake exchange. Meanwhile, the ability to identify the parties involved in blockchain-based transactions is significantly diminished. The most prominent real-world example of the money laundering potential of blockchain technology was the online exchange Silk Road, which exclusively accepted Bitcoin in its 'dark net' market for illicit goods and services and whose alleged creator was sentenced to life in prison for money laundering and other charges.[6] Some research has identified a correlation between interests in CCs and illegal activity, more generally, by analysing American search engine data (Yelowitz and Wilson, 2015). Yet beyond this, little evidence has directly linked blockchain applications to actual money laundering operations. The 2015 British National Risk Assessment concluded that "[t]here are a limited number of case studies upon which any solid conclusions could be drawn that digital currencies are used for money laundering" and that "[t]he money laundering risk associated with digital currencies is low" (Her Majesty's Treasury and Home Office, 2015). Despite sensationalistic media claims, there is also little evidence to suggest that blockchain applications are used in terrorist financing (Fernholz, 2015: 32, 33). Initial suggestions that the perpetrators of the November 2015 Paris terrorist attacks had utilised CCs turned out to be unfounded (Perez, 2015). While a theoretical risk of enabling terrorists and "money launderers to move illicit funds faster, cheaper, and more discretely than ever before" (Bryans, 2014: 447), blockchain applications such as CCs have yet to be shown as concretely used to such ends. Indeed, legal scholars have warned that blockchain-based money "laundering opportunities may well be more *perceived than real*" (Stokes, 2013: 5, emphasis added; see also Brown, 2016: 332). Similarly, many technologists claim that the risk of CCs being used for money laundering are "inflated" (Eddy Travia, cited in Nicholls, 2016a). Nevertheless, as the following subsection shows, key actors in the international AML regime have perceived applications of blockchain technologies as fundamentally challenging their efforts.

International responses shaped by the properties of blockchain technologies

Key actors in the international AML regime have stressed the illegitimate nature of blockchain applications to CCs. The Bank of International Settlements (BIS) stressed that because of their distributed global networks and 'pseudonymity', CCs "are *potentially* vulnerable to illicit use" (Committee on Payments and Market Infrastructures, 2015, emphasis added). The SWIFT Institute, the advisory body to the Society for Worldwide Interbank Financial Telecommunication, regarded CCs as a particularly lucrative "target of those engaged in drug trafficking and money laundering" (Valcke *et al.*, 2015: 7). The International Monetary Fund (IMF) emphasised how CCs "can be used to conceal or disguise the illicit origin or sanctioned destination of funds, thus facilitating the money laundering [*sic*]" (He *et al.*, 2016: 27). These warnings were echoed by intergovernmental police organisations such as Europol (2015b), who maintained, without offering evidence, that CCs "are being used as an instrument to facilitate crime, particularly in regard to the laundering of illicit profits".[7] CCs were also recognised as a challenge in an initial report issued by the FATF (Financial Action Task Force, 2013), although subsequent reports acknowledged the potential legitimate usages of CCs (Financial Action Task Force, 2014: 8–9), such as for remittances (see Rodima-Taylor and Grimes, this volume).

The widespread perception that blockchains and their applications constituted challenges to the international AML regime informed the particular character of governance response. The United Nations Office on Drugs and Crime produced a detailed manual for detecting and seizing CCs implicated in money laundering. Together with the Organization for Security and Cooperation in Europe (OSCE), the UNODC began training officials to investigate money laundering through CCs (United Nations Office on Drugs and Crime, 2017). Interpol and Europol established a joint partnership coordinating police activities "against the abuse of virtual currencies for criminal transactions and money laundering" (Europol, 2015a).

Similarly, the two key features of blockchain technologies – decentralisation and quasi-anonymity – shaped the response of the main intergovernmental organisation at the heart of the international AML regime. First, the FATF recognised the difficulties of tracing and identifying decentralised transactions by quasi-anonymity CC users. As a 2015 report put it, the lack of "central location or entity" to "target … for investigative purposes" effectively "undermines countries' ability to employ effective, dissuasive sanctions" and "presents a significant challenge to law enforcement's ability to trace illicit proceeds that are laundered" (Financial Action Task Force, 2015: 8–11). Rather than targeting CC users, the FATF recommended a focus on CC-to-fiat money exchanges and other 'nodes' in decentralised blockchain-based systems. These are the key institutions whose activities intersect in important manners with what the FATF described as "the regulated fiat currency financial system" (ibid.). The FATF thereby directed the focus of international AML efforts towards the centralised institutions that "send, receive, and store" CCs (Financial Action Task Force, 2015: 6) once they are transferred from state-backed national currencies of the "upperworlds" to the "underworlds" of the global economy (van Duyne *et al.*, 2002).

Second, the FATF guidance recommended a flexible set of informal and formal responses to the perceived challenges presented by blockchain applications to global AML governance. On the one hand, the FATF called for CC-to-state-backed-currency exchanges to be formally registered and monitored in order to encourage the voluntary enactment of "customer identification/verification and recordkeeping requirements" (Financial Action Task Force, 2015: 11). The FATF suggested that in order to formally register these 'nodes' might also be obligated to "undertake customer due diligence when establishing business relations or when carrying out (non-wire) occasional transactions using reliable, independent source documents, data or information" (ibid.: 12). FATF advanced a decentralised approach in recommending that CC exchanges *themselves* identify users through a reliance on government social insurance numbers, internet protocol (IP) addresses, and even use Internet searches in "corroborating activity information consistent with the customer's transaction profile" (ibid.: 13). Only when money laundering practices might be suspected did the FATF call for "enhanced due diligence measures" by governments (ibid.: 8). Nevertheless, the FATF recommended state actors remain sensitive to the potential "impact(s) a prohibition would have on the local and global level of [money laundering/terrorist finance] ML/TF risks, including whether prohibiting [virtual currency] VC payments activities could drive them underground, where they will continue to operate without AML/CFT controls or oversight" (ibid.: 9). Like other key actors in the international AML regime who stressed how "the decentralised nature of these digital currency schemes means that it is difficult to impose such restrictions on transactions" (Committee on Payments and Market Infrastructure, 2015), the FATF recognised how exchanges and other "easily identifiable institutions with readily detectable headquarters" (Singh, 2015: 58) are able to relocate to jurisdictions with more relaxed AML requirements. Since exchanges specifically, and blockchain-based activities more generally, operate in a distributed environment, they are able to shift their activities around the world with a fair degree of ease. The FATF therefore stressed the need for less coercive "coordination mechanisms" between state and non-state actors (Financial Action Task Force, 2015: 9). Such measures include sharing of information and knowledge (ibid.: 8), efforts to formulate and adopt "similar AML/CFT treatment for similar products and services having similar risk profiles" (ibid.), and mutual legal assistance between countries in either seizing assets or potentially extraditing individuals charged with money laundering crimes (ibid.: 11). Once again, though, only when such measures prove to be insufficient does the FATF recommend more coercive strategies be considered, including a "range of effective, proportionate and dissuasive sanctions" that include outright prohibition of blockchain-based activities (ibid.: 9).

The response of the intergovernmental organisation at the heart of the international AML regime was shaped and constrained by the particular technical characteristics of blockchains. The digital, decentralised and quasi-anonymous features of applications of this emergent technology influenced – yet in no way wholly determined – FATF suggestions for a plethora of decentralised initiatives that provided room for both coercive and flexible responses. That blockchain applications like CCs were regarded as challenges to the international AML regime was not inevitable. Yet the responses proceed as such and in turn shaped and constrained the evolution of this emergent technology.

Blockchain activities shaped by the responses of the international AML regime

Responses by the international AML regime to the perceived challenge of blockchain applications influenced the evolution of this emergent technology most centrally by encouraging the bifurcation of blockchain-based activities. On the one hand, the decentralised response of the international AML regime to the perceived challenge of blockchains encouraged AML-compliance by some non-state actors whose blockchain-based activities became 'mainstreamed' into the 'upperworld' of the global economy. On the other hand, this flexible response also permitted for state strategies that, by harnessing blockchain applications to track and trace users, have induced other activities further into the 'underworld' of the global political economy.

Voluntary AML compliance and the mainstreaming of blockchain applications

The decentralised and flexible international response to the perceived challenge of blockchain applications encouraged the development of varying AML-compliant activities by state and non-state actors. On the one hand, jurisdictions in several regions of the world sought to distinguish themselves as legitimate centres for AML-compliant blockchain activities. Most prominently, New York State developed a 'Bitlicense', which is granted to actors undertaking "initial and annual risk assessments, ten-year records of all transactions, suspicious activity reports, a customer identification program, checks and compliance, annual internal or external audits, and no structuring to evade reporting, or obfuscating identity" (Kiviat, 2015: 601–2, fn 229). Competing jurisdictions such as Singapore also sought to attract AML-compliant blockchain-based activities. The Suspicious Transaction Reporting Office of the city-state actively verifies user identities and monitors suspicious transactions (Townend, 2015). The English Channel island of Alderney promotes itself as an AML-compliant blockchain hub (Connell, 2014) in competing for the title of 'Bitcoin Isle' with the likes of the Isle of Man (Nicholls, 2016b).

Meanwhile, several fiat-money-to-CC exchanges have 'mainstreamed' their operations to become compliant with informal global AML recommendations. The Hong Kong firm BitFinex (n.d.), for example, undertook "a comprehensive and thorough KYC and AML compliance implementation" involving certified customer identification documents and valid proof of address. Hong Kong-based competitor Gatecoin (n.d.), as well as the British exchanges Bitstamp (n.d.) and its rival CEX.IO (n.d.) all enforced AML standards in requiring customers to provide copies of their passports in verifying their identities. Although 'mainstreaming' blockchain-based activities, these voluntary AML efforts varied considerably. For instance, user identification is only required for account holders that HitBTC (n.d.) and other CC exchanges deem to be 'suspicious'.

The variance between voluntary industry AML compliance efforts led a set of common industry guidelines to be proposed by a self-regulatory body called the Digital Asset Transfer Authority (DATA). In seeking to formulate "common risk management and compliance standards" (Digital Asset Transfer Authority, 2015: 834), this Delaware-based organisation released a draft set of 'global AML guidelines' for public comment in 2015. Stressing the balance of AML efforts with "fundamental rights and values, including civil liberties, financial privacy and inclusion, transparency and accountability", the draft guidelines advised firms operating with CCs to each implement "a basic AML Compliance Program *whether or not required by law*" (ibid.: 2, emphasis in original). The DATA recommended implementing written internal procedures and annual employee training on risk-based due diligence assessments overseen by independent chief compliance officers. These draft guidelines suggested firms collect customer names and addresses as well as "consider implementing more in-depth customer identification and verification procedures – especially for customers and products identified in the risk assessment as high risk" (ibid.: 4). Examples of 'in-depth' procedures involved "everything from simply 'googling' the person or company involved or checking the appropriate government agency for corporate registration, to requesting banking and other references, to obtaining credit or business reports, and even obtaining a criminal background check" (ibid.: 5). Finally, the draft DATA guidelines[8] urged firms to monitor the potential for AML through the "entire cycle of a relationship".

Such industry- and firm-led efforts to develop AML standards and mainstream blockchain-based activities were encouraged by the flexible, decentralised response of the international AML regime. The 2015 FATF guidance specifically suggested industry-level associations "develop policies and practices for members that allow them to identify specific transactions as coming from a member that has applied appropriate CDD and is conducting appropriate transaction monitoring" (Financial Action Task Force, 2015: 14). However, the flexibility provided by the decentralised response of the international AML regime also provided space for other strategies that alternatively encouraged blockchain activities to shift deeper into the 'underworlds' of the global political economy.

Going (further) underground

The flexibility of the response by the international AML regime to the perceived challenges of blockchains also provided state and quasi-state actors room to experiment with bans and other governance strategies to discourage specific blockchain applications, namely CCs. States such as Bangladesh, Bolivia, and Ecuador, for example, banned the use of CCs outright. Other countries, including China and Vietnam, applied CC bans more selectively on financial services firms operating in their jurisdictions (Smart, 2015; see Jia and Zhang, this volume). A number of central banks have also sought to discourage the use of CCs. In Iceland the purchase of CCs was regarded by its central bank as a violation of the Foreign Exchange Act, while in Indonesia the central bank announced that "Bitcoin and other virtual currency are not currency or legal payment" (Bank Indonesia, 2014). Looser discouragements emanated from the European Central Bank (2016: 2), which warned financial authorities in the European Union to "take care not to appear to promote the use of privately established digital currencies". Similarly, the European Banking Authority (2014) suggested that regional authorities "discourage" credit institutions from dealing in CCs.[9]

Together, these varying governance strategies directly encouraged blockchain activities to shift or remain in the 'underworld' rather than enter the mainstream 'upperworlds' of the global economy.

The flexibility provided by the international AML regime also provided state and non-state actors space to harness blockchain technologies for identifying users that have further prompted blockchain-based activities to shift underground. Companies such as BlockTrail and Coinalytics have provided services enhancing the ability of intergovernmental police organisations such as Europol and Interpol to match CC transactions with individual profiles by locating particular patterns of use (Basquill, 2015). Transaction flows associated with specific user identities have been developed with the help of 'forensic' computer scientists (Luu and Imwinkelried, 2016). While encouraging the mainstreaming of some blockchain activities, efforts to identify specific users for AML purposes sparked countervailing anonymisation services seeking to frustrate the possibilities of AML regulators identifying CC users. So-called 'anonymisers' transfer CCs in and out of state-backed currencies using different identities. Meanwhile, other 'mixer' or 'tumbler' services with names such as BitLaundry and Bitcoin Fog were developed to allow CC users to pool together in order to prevent identity tracking by 'mixing' and joining transactions together into unpredictable combinations (Böhme *et al.*, 2015; Scafuro and Shipman, 2017).[10] In a final instance, new CCs such as Zcash (n.d.) and Zerocoin (n.d.) as well as Dash (n.d.), formerly known as Darkcoin, were developed to ostensibly provide users complete anonymity in transactions. These new CCs, along with anonymisers and 'mixing services', can all be understood principally as counter-reactions to concerns that Bitcoin and blockchain-based transactions more generally are no longer as anonymous as initially believed (Heilman *et al.*, 2017: 1). Efforts to effectively 'follow the money' in identifying blockchain users, permitted by the flexibility of the AML regime, have thereby pushed blockchain activities further into the 'underworlds' of the global economy.

The development of services seeking to frustrate state AML efforts illustrates how the response of the international AML regime to the perceived challenge of blockchains has in turn shaped blockchain-based activities in manners that were initially difficult to predict. While bans and other state and quasi-state efforts to discourage the use of blockchain technologies can be expected to push such activities further into the 'underworlds' of the global economy, other ostensibly more permissive state activities have also had similar effects. The New York State Bitlicense, for instance, was considered by many industry participants as "very innovation unfriendly" and resulted in an "exodus" (del Castillo, 2015) of CC operators in less AML-compliant jurisdictions (Van Valkenburgh, 2015).[11] Just like efforts to find the identities of blockchain users by drawing on the emergent technology itself, seemingly well-meaning state activities instigated a shift of blockchain-based activities in the 'underworlds' of the global economy.

Technologies and global governance: a mutually constitutive relationship

Technological change can pose varying challenges and opportunities for global governance. The case of blockchain applications since 2008 stresses how key actors in the international AML regime regarded applications of the emergent technology primarily as challenges. Their responses in turn influenced the development of activities enabled by the emergent technology. Some non-state actors sought to alter their practices in order to remain beyond government surveillance, while others sought to comply with key stipulations of the international regime. Such bifurcated technological development is, of course, not solely the result of responses by the international AML regime. Neither technology nor international regimes have 'complete control' over one another. Yet neither is 'out of control'. The relationships between technology and key actors underpinning global governance do not merely flow one-way. Both influence and mutually constitute one another in particular manners that are often surprising and unexpected.

Conclusion

By investigating relationships between blockchain technologies and the international anti-money-laundering (AML) regime, this chapter has illustrated an underappreciated element of global governance: the mutual constitution of international regimes and emergent technologies. Our analysis highlighted this mutually constitutive relationship in two steps. First, the decentralised and quasi-anonymous features of blockchain technologies were shown to have shaped and constrained the responses of the leading actor in the international AML regime, the Financial Action Task Force (FATF). The FATF emphasised a decentralised approach to the perceived challenges of blockchains. Rather than the users of CCs, specific institutions at the nexus of blockchain-based activities and the mainstream economy were targeted and encouraged to pursue their own, at times divergent, approaches to AML compliance. States were also encouraged to experiment with both flexible and coercive approaches in achieving a shared overarching goal: ensuring that blockchain activities occur in a financial 'upperworld' rather than disappear into the financial 'underworld'.

In a second step this chapter illustrated how the particular governance responses of the international AML regime shaped and constrained the evolution of blockchain applications. Decentralised and flexible response to the perceived challenges of this emergent technology influenced the evolution of blockchain-based activities. Blockchain applications became increasingly bifurcated into an 'upperworld' compliant with international AML efforts and an 'underworld' that sought to maintain the very features of the technology that were perceived to challenge AML efforts. On the one hand, voluntary AML-compliant state and non-state activities contributed to the 'mainstreaming' of blockchain applications. On the other hand, official bans on the most prominent blockchain applications and the harnessing of the technology for identifying potential money launderers encouraged another segment of blockchain-based activities to shift further underground, into the 'underworlds' of the global political economy.

More generally, this chapter stressed how neither technologies nor international regimes exist in abstract voids. Global governance operates within socio-technical environments where specific features of technologies shape and constrain the activities of key actors in unexpected manners. It was certainly not predetermined that blockchain applications such as cryptocurrencies would be mainly perceived as challenges rather than opportunities for global AML governance efforts, although it certainly makes sense that they were. Key actors in the international AML regime, such as the FATF, acknowledged the important opportunities for tracking and tracing international financial transactions to be gained from blockchains. Similarly, it was not predetermined that the harnessing of these emergent technologies for state surveillance purposes would be negatively perceived by blockchain users and instigate a backlash that shifted some blockchain-based activities further into the 'underworlds' of the global political economy. Indeed, some non-state actors perceived state attempts to harness blockchain technologies as profit opportunities to market and sell their expertise. Overall, the predominantly negative perception of blockchain applications as challenges to existing forms of governance was shaped by the specific features of these emergent technologies and instigated responses that in turn have shaped the evolution of the emergent technology in particular manners.

Examining the co-evolution of technologies and governance provides opportunities for more nuanced understanding of the often-unexpected changes in the socio-technical environments in which international regimes operate. There is much to be gained from considering how emergent technologies such as blockhains and the international AML regime mutually evolve. Further research might investigate how and why state and non-state actors perceived regulatory and technological developments as challenges, as well as the normative implications arising from the responses to such perceptions. When the novel features of emergent technologies are regarded primarily as challenges, or as tools akin to nails, international responses can function as hammers whose coercive thrusts respond to one challenge yet undermine more beneficial possibilities that might also be afforded. It is highly unlikely that money laundering, whether in CCs or state-backed currencies, will ever be completely eradicated (Tsingou, 2010). Beyond Bitcoin and CC-to-national money exchanges, the laundering of money continues to occur in the 'upperworld' of global finance and involve mainstream financial institutions such as banks (e.g. Corkery and Protess, 2017). In attempting to combat this activity, other potentially beneficial innovations, such as improvements of payments to whistleblowers or the facilitation of remittances, may be hampered or even stamped out. Understanding how wider socio-technical environments and global governance mutually constitute one another helps foreground other possible responses to technological changes in the global political economy. Scholars, policy-makers, and citizens alike will benefit from a more nuanced understanding of both the potential benefits and risks accrued from a sensitivity to the co-evolution of technology and global governance.

Acknowledgements

The feedback and support of Mark Nance and Stephen J. Kay, as well as participants in the 'FATF @ 25' workshop at the Federal Reserve Bank of Atlanta in 2016 is gratefully acknowledged. Malcolm Campbell-Verduyn acknowledges research support from the Social Sciences and Humanities Research Council of Canada (award no. 756-2015-0474).

Notes

1 Material from this section draws on Campbell-Verduyn (forthcoming 2017).
2 Although it has become common to deal with terrorist financing and money laundering conjointly (Kingah and Zwartjes, 2015: 343), these activities pose fundamentally alternative problems for law enforcement (Abeyratne, 2011: 68; Donahue, 2006: 394) This chapter concentrates on the former.
3 For a list of full members, associate members, and observers of the FATF, see www.fatf-gafi.org/about/membersandobservers/
4 The problem of ensuring that money that is transferred over long distances and borders is not simultaneously retained and used by an individual to purchase goods more than once.
5 The record of individual transactions is publicly broadcast on blockchains, meaning that a digital trail can be traced in 'following the money'. The ledger of transactions provides a trail that can be followed in ways that the use of conventional bills and coins cannot. Yet, as we discuss further below, a range of further new techniques frustrate this identification.
6 The US Federal Bureau of Investigation (FBI) shut down the original Silk Road in 2013. Silk Road 2.0 subsequently appeared but was closed down in a 17-country operation by police agencies. Silk Road 3.0 opened in mid-2016 and remains open at the time of writing, though faces competition from other marketplaces such as Dream Market and Valhalla.
7 Europol (2015b: 46) also offers no supporting evidence for claims that Bitcoin has featured "heavily in many EU law enforcement investigations, accounting for over 40% of all identified criminal-to-criminal payments".
8 Which remain open for comment at the time of writing.
9 The money laundering potential of CCs had attracted formal attention in the European Union following the November 2015 Paris terrorist attacks as the European Commission proposed to amend the Fourth Anti-Money Laundering Directive to bring CC exchanges under existing AML laws and create a central database registering CC user identities.
10 See for instance the anonymisation method 'CoinJoin': https://en.bitcoin.it/wiki/CoinJoin
11 Though it should be noted that some two dozen firms, including the prominent exchange Coinbase, have remained in the state and applied for such a licence.

Bibliography

Abeyratne, R. (2011). Suppression of the financing of terrorism. *Journal of Transportation Security, 4*(1): 57–71.

Bank Indonesia. (2014, 6 February). Statement of Bank Indonesia related to Bitcoin and other virtual currency. Retrieved 27 August 2016 from www.bi.go.id/en/ruang-media/siaran-pers/Pages/SP_160614.aspx

Basquill, J. (2015, 12 October). Interpol reveals Bitcoin tracking research. *Blockchain Briefing.*

Best, J. (2003). From the top–down: The new financial architecture and the re-embedding of global finance. *New Political Economy, 8*(3): 363–84.

Bitfinex. (n.d.). *Terms of service.* Retrieved 27 August 2016 from www.bitfinex.com/terms

Bitstamp. (n.d.). *Bitstamp limited antimoney laundering ("AML") and counter terrorist financing ("CTF") policy.* Retrieved 27 August 2016 from www.bitstamp.net/aml-policy/

Bjerg, O. (2016). How is Bitcoin money? *Theory, Culture and Society, 33*(1): 53–72.

Böhme, R., Christin, N., Edelman, B., and Moore, T. (2015). Bitcoin: Economics, technology, and governance. *Journal of Economic Perspectives, 29*(2): 213–38.

Boles, J.R. (2015). Financial sector executives as targets for money laundering liability. *American Business Law Journal, 52*(3).

Brown, S.D. (2016). Cryptocurrency and criminality: The Bitcoin opportunity. *Police Journal, 89*(4): 327–39.

Bryans, D. (2014). Bitcoin and money laundering: Mining for an effective solution. *Indiana Law Journal, 89*, 441–72.

Campbell-Verduyn, M. (forthcoming, 2017). Bitcoin, crypto-coins, and global anti-money laundering governance. *Crime, Law, and Social Change.*

CEX.IO. (n.d.). *AML/KYC policy.* Retrieved 27 August 2016 from https://cex.io/aml-kyc

Chong, A., and Lopez-De-Silanes, F. (2015). Money laundering and its regulation. *Economics and Politics, 27*(1): 78–123.

Choo, K.-K.R. (2009). Money laundering and terrorism financing risks of prepaid cards instruments? *Asian Criminology,* (4): 11–30

Committee on Payments and Market Infrastructures. (2015). *Digital currencies.* Basel: Bank for International Settlements.

Commonwealth Working Group on Virtual Currencies. (2015). *Working group report.* Retrieved 24 November 2016 from http://thecommonwealth.org/sites/default/files/press-release/documents/P14195_ROL_Virtual_Currencies_D_Tait_V5_LoRes.pdf

Connell, J. (2014). Alderney: Gambling, Bitcoin and the art of unorthodoxy. *Island Studies Journal, 9*(1): 69–78.

Corkery, M., and Protess, B. (2017, 22 May). Citigroup agrees to $97.4 million settlement in money laundering inquiry. *New York Times.*

Dash. (n.d.). *What is Dash?* Retrieved 27 August 2016 from www.dash.org/

del Castillo, M. (2015, 12 August). The 'Great Bitcoin Exodus' has totally changed New York's Bitcoin ecosystem. *New York Business Journal.*

DeNardis, L. (2014). *The global war for internet governance.* New Haven, CT: Yale University Press.

Digital Asset Transfer Authority. (2015). *Draft anti-money laundering guidelines.* Retrieved 22 August 2017 from http://datauthority.org/blog/2015/07/01/global-aml-kyc-guidelines-data/

Donohue, L. (2006). Anti-terrorist finance in the United Kingdom and United States. *Michigan Journal of International Law, 27*(2): 303.

European Banking Authority. (2014). *Opinion on 'virtual currencies'.* Op/2014/08.

European Central Bank. (2016). *Opinion of the European Central Bank.* Retrieved 23 November 2016 from www.ecb.europa.eu/ecb/legal/pdf/en_con_2016_49_f_sign.pdf

Europol. (2015a, 2 October). *Europol Interpol Cybercrime Conference makes the case for multisector cooperation.* Retrieved 27 August 2016 from www.europol.europa.eu/latest_news/europol-%E2%80%93-interpol-cybercrime-conference-makes-case-greater-multisector-cooperation

Europol. (2015b). *The internet organised crime threat assessment.* Retrieved 16 August 2016 from www.europol.europa.eu/iocta/2015/

Fernholz, T. (2015). Terrorism finance trackers worry ISIS already using Bitcoin. *Defense One, 13.*

Financial Action Task Force. (2016). *International standards on combating money laundering and the financing of terrorism and proliferation: The FATF recommendations.* Retrieved 15 August 2016 from www.fatfgafi.org/media/fatf/documents/recommendations/pdfs/FATF_Recommendations.pdf

Financial Action Task Force. (2015). *Guidance for a risk-based approach: Virtual currencies.* Retrieved 15 August 2016 from www.coe.int/t/dghl/monitoring/moneyval/Publications/Guidance-RBA-Virtual-Currencies.pdf

Financial Action Task Force. (2014). *Virtual currencies: Key definitions and potential AML/CFT risks: FATF report.* Retrieved 15 August 2016 from www.fatf gafi.org/media/fatf/documents/reports/virtual-currency-key-definitions-and-potential-aml-cft-risks.pdf

Financial Action Task Force. (2013). *Guidance for a risk-based approach to prepaid cards, mobile payments and internet-based payment services.* Retrieved 15 August 2016 from www.fatf gafi.org/publications/fatfrecommendations/documents/rba-npps-2013.html

Gatecoin. (n.d.). *Anti-money laundering and counter-terrorist financing (AML/CFT) policy summary statement.* Retrieved 27 August 2016 from https://gatecoin.com/aml-policy

Gilpin, R. (2011). *Global political economy: Understanding the international economic order.* Princeton, NJ: Princeton University Press.

Gruber, S. (2013). Trust, identity and disclosure: Are Bitcoin exchanges the next virtual havens for money laundering and tax evasion. *Quinnipiac Law Review, 32*: 135.

Hasenclever, A., Mayer, P., and Rittberger, V. (1997). *Theories of international regimes.* Cambridge: Cambridge University Press.

He, D., Habermeier, K., Leckow, R., Haksar, V., Almeida, Y., Kashima, M., *et al.* (2016). Virtual currencies and beyond: Initial considerations. *IMF Staff Discussions Note* 16/03.

Heilman, E., AlShenibr, L., Baldimtsi, F., Scafuro, A., and Goldberg, S. (2017). *TumbleBit: An untrusted bitcoin-compatible anonymous payment hub.* Paper presented at the Network and Distributed System Security Symposium, 26 February–1 March. San Diego, California.

Her Majesty's Treasury and Home Office. (2015). *UK national risk assessment of money laundering and terrorist financing.* London: Stationery Office.

Hett, W. (2008). Digital currencies and the financing of terrorism. *Richmond Journal of Law and Technology, 15*: 1.

HitBTC. (n.d.). *HitBTC terms of use.* Retrieved 27 August 2016 from https://hitbtc.com/terms-of-use

Isa, Y.M., Sanusi, Z.M., Haniff, M.N., and Barnes, A. (2015). Money laundering risk: From the bankers' and regulators' perspectives. *Procedia Economics and Finance, 28*: 7–13.

Keohane, R.O. (1983). Theory of world politics: Structural realism and beyond. In A.W. Finifter (ed.) *Political science: The state of the discipline.* Washington: American Political Science Association.

Kingah, S., and Zwartjes, M. (2015). Regulating money laundering for terrorism financing: EU–US transnational policy networks and the financial action task force. *Contemporary Politics, 21*(3): 341–53.

Kiviat, T.I. (2015). Beyond Bitcoin: Issues in regulating blockchain transactions. *Duke Law Journal, 65*: 569–608.

Kostakis, V., and Giotitsas, C. (2014). The (A)political economy of bitcoin. tripleC: Communication, capitalism and critique. *Open Access Journal for a Global Sustainable Information Society, 12*(2): 431–40.

Krasner, S. (1983). Structural causes and regime consequences: Regimes as intervening variables. In S. Krasner (ed.) *International regimes.* Ithaca, NY: Cornell University Press.

Levi, M. (2015). Money for crime and money from crime: Financing crime and laundering crime proceeds. *European Journal on Criminal Policy and Research,* 1–23.

Levi, M., and Reuter, P. (2006). Money laundering. *Crime and Justice, 34*(1): 289–375.

Luu, J., and Imwinkelried, E.J. (2016). The challenge of Bitcoin pseudo-anonymity to computer forensics. *Criminal Law Bulletin.*

Macurak, A.B. (2014). *Regulating Bitcoin: Capstone strategic project for the American Bankers Association.* Stonier Graduate School of Banking. Retrieved 22 August 2017 from www.abastonier.com/stonier/wp-content/uploads/2014-Macurak-Andrew.pdf

Malkin, L., and Elizur, Y. (2002). Terrorism's money trail. *World Policy Journal, 19*(1): 60–70.

Masciandaro, D. (2004). Combating black money: Money laundering and terrorism finance, international cooperation and the G8 role. *International Cooperation and the G8 Role.* Universita di Lecce Economics Working Paper, 56/26.

Nicholls, J. (2016a, 8 January). Are decentralised currencies better at curing AML woes? Experts Split. *Blockchain Briefing.*

Nicholls, J. (2016b, 6 January). Isle of Man sees blockchain through prism of e-gaming triumphs. *Blockchain Briefing.*

Onuf, N. (1989). *World of our making.* Columbia, SC: University of South Carolina Press.

Perez, Y. (2015, 20 November). Bitcoin, Paris and terrorism: What the media got wrong. *Coindesk.*

Ping, H. (2004). Banking secrecy and money laundering. *Journal of Money Laundering Control, 7*(4): 376–82.

Porter, T. (2003). Technical collaboration and political conflict in the emerging regime for international financial regulation. *Review of International Political Economy, 10*: 520–51.

Porter, T. (1993). *States, markets, and regimes in global finance.* New York: St. Martins Press.

Reus-Smit, C. (1997). The constitutional structure of international society and the nature of fundamental institutions. *International Organization, 51*(4): 555–89.

Reynolds, J.A. (2002). The new US anti-money laundering offensive: Will it prove successful? *Cross Cultural Management: An International Journal, 9*(3): 3–31.

Rubenfeld, S. (2015, 2 July). FATF pushes risk-based approach toward virtual currencies, services. *Wall Street Journal.*

Scafuro, A., and Shipman, M. (2017, 8 February). New system makes it harder to track Bitcoin transactions. *NC State University News.* Retrieved 22 August 2017 from https://news.ncsu.edu/2017/02/tumblebit-bitcoin-2017/

Sharman, J.C. (2008). Power and discourse in policy diffusion: Anti-money laundering in developing states. *International Studies Quarterly, 52*(3): 635–56.

Singh, K. (2015). New Wild West: Preventing money laundering in the Bitcoin network. *NorthWestern Journal of Technology and Intellectual Property, 13*(1): 38–64.

Shields, P. (2005a). The 'information revolution', financial globalisation, state power and money-laundering. *Journal of International Communication, 11*(1): 15–39.

Shields, P. (2005b). When the 'information revolution' and the US security state collide: Money laundering and the proliferation of surveillance. *New Media and Society, 7*(4): 483–512.

Smart, E. (2015, 27 May). Top 10 countries in which Bitcoin is banned. *CryptoCoinNews.*

Stokes, R. (2013). Anti-money laundering regulation and emerging payment technologies. *Banking and Financial Services Policy Report, 32*(5): 1–10.

Stokes, R. (2012). Virtual money laundering: The case of Bitcoin and the Linden dollar. *Information and Communications Technology Law, 21*(3): 221–36.

Straub, J.P. (2001). The prevention of e-money laundering: Tracking the elusive audit trail. *Suffolk Transnational Law Revue, 25*, 515.

Stringer, K.D. (2011). Tackling threat finance: A labor for Hercules or Sisyphus? *Parameters, 41*(1): 101.

Townend, D. (2015, 19 November). Singapore PM makes blockchain leader case. *Blockchain Briefing.*

Tropina, T. (2014). Fighting money laundering in the age of online banking, virtual currencies and internet gambling. *ERA Forum, 15*(1): 69–84.

Tsingou, E. (2010). Global financial governance and the developing anti-money laundering regime: What lessons for international political economy? *International Politics, 47*(6): 617–37.

Unger, B. (2013). Can money laundering decrease? *Public Finance Review, 41*(5): 658–76.

Unger, B. (2009). Money laundering – A newly emerging topic on the international agenda. *Review of Law and Economics, 5*(2): 807–19.

United Nations Office on Drugs and Crime. (2017, 1 February). *UNODC helps tackle Bitcoin banking fraud and money laundering.* Retrieved 22 August 2017 from www.unodc.org/unodc/en/frontpage/2017/February/unodc-helps-tackle-bitcoin-banking-fraud-and-money-laundering.html

Valcke, P., Vandezande, N., and van de Velde, N. (2015). *The evolution of third party payment providers and cryptocurrencies under the EU's upcoming PSD2 and AMLD4.* SWIFT Institute, Working paper number 2015-001.

van Duyne, P.C., von Lampe, K., and Passas, N. (2002). *Upperworld and underworld in cross-border crime.* Nijmegen: Wolf Legal Publishers.

Van Valkenburgh, P. (2015, 2 June). Tracking Bitcoin regulation state by state. *CoinCentre.*

Wendt, A. (1992). Anarchy is what states make of it: The social construction of power politics. *International Organization, 46*(2): 391–425

Wessel, J. (2006). The financial action task force: A study in balancing sovereignty with equality in global administrative law. *Widener Law Revue, 13*: 169.

Yelowitz, A., and Wilson, M. (2015). Characteristics of Bitcoin users: An analysis of Google search data. *Applied Economics Letters, 22*(13): 1030–36.

Zcash. (n.d.). *About.* Retrieved 22 November 2016 from https://z.cash/

Zdanowicz, J.S. (2004). Money laundering and terrorist financing. *Communications of the ACM, 47*(5): 53.

Zerocoin Project. (n.d.). *What is Zerocoin?* Retrieved 27 August 2016 from http://zerocoin.org/

5 Between liberalization and prohibition

Prudent enthusiasm and the governance *of* Bitcoin/blockchain technology

Kai Jia and Falin Zhang

Introduction: bring the state back in

The implications of technology for global governance are generally classified into two conflicting narratives. On the one hand are tales of hope based on optimistic ideas that advances in technology will improve governance (Kurzweil, 2005; Pielke et al., 2008). On the other hand are tales of dystopia based on pessimistic ideas that new technologies have negative consequences for governance (Matthewman, 2011). The former assumes that technological developments lead to improvement of economic productivity and elevated human living conditions. The latter skeptical attitudes focus more on catastrophes and pending risks of annihilation caused by technological advancement such as nuclear weapons, toxic particles, etc.

Both tales are over-simplifications of a much more complex intertwined relationship between technology and governance (Mayer et al., 2014a, 2014b). They each consider technology as exogenous to rather than deeply implicated in the fabric of governance. Technology is embedded in the power structure of people's daily lives and is modified all the time. The limitation of "two tales" of technology leads us beyond superficial instrumentalism and to focus on the deeper relationship between technology and governments, enterprises, individuals, etc.

In the 1960s, the Organization for Economic Co-operation and Development (OECD) promoted the concept of "knowledge economy/society," which emphasized the development of technology as an indicator of state capacity (Singleton, 2008). Technology became recognized as a central battlefield for state power competition and was increasingly considered to be a decisive factor for not only economic growth but also social welfare. For instance, intellectual property (IP) rights quickly became the most controversial areas of rivaling interests among countries (May, 2013).

Yet, like in previous periods, states did not play the sole governance roles in the era of "knowledge economy/society." With the development of information and communication technologies (ICTs), especially the emergence and expansion of the Internet, technology empowered enterprises as well as individuals to communicate and transact across borders. This eroded, but did not eliminate, the controlling power of sovereign countries. States have adjusted to the networked global information society from more hierarchical structures. The Snowden leaks revealed the breadth and depth of digital surveillance of governments in partnership with private firms such as Apple, Microsoft, etc. (Foster and McChesney, 2014). Despite the intricate relationships with non-state actors around the globe, states are still located in the center of the power field. The policy responses of states to technology remain as important as ever, even if states are not the only actor determining their consequences.

The advent of Bitcoin and related blockchain technologies exemplify these power dynamics. On the one hand, the disintermediation they provide in enabling individuals to transact directly without centralized institutions empowers people against the control of governments or central banks. On the other hand, centralized institutions are not completely circumvented by such technology. To the contrary, the policy responses from governments influence the development path of Bitcoin specifically and blockchain technologies more generally.

This chapter explains the interactive relationship between blockchain technology and the corresponding policy responses of governments it has provoked. We examine two questions: what are the challenges that Bitcoin has brought to states? How have states responded to these challenges? We therefore bring the state back in the analysis of political dynamics evoked by technological change, illustrating how states influence the development of emergent technologies through their different policies.

We develop a model illustrating three types of policy responses that are exemplified by three states: the US, Russia, and China. The US is where most of the Bitcoin developer communities are located, while China is the largest Bitcoin market globally. Despite the relatively limited influence of Russia in the field of high-tech, it is a major state whose policies have implications regionally and even globally. We plot governance responses along a continuum, with laissez-faire at one end (US), prohibition (Russia) at the other end, to argue that a middle ground "prudent enthusiasm" (China) position provides the best balance between the risks and opportunities presented by blockchain technologies.

This argument has implications for countries in the Global South that are struggling to narrow the gap that seems to be widening because of the technology advancements in the Global North. Bitcoin may serve as yet another catalyst polarizing North–South developmental divides. As we elaborate, Global South countries tend to avoid emergent technology because of their incapability to bear and manage the accompanying uncertainties and risks that Global North countries are better able to bear because of first-mover advantages. We situate the alternative policy choices for the governance *of* Bitcoin globally to find a balanced middle path for benefiting from the technology while at the same time keeping risk at an acceptable level. We argue that with this approach countries in the Global South may be capable of navigating through the dilemma between technology adoption and uncontrollable risk.

The chapter proceeds in five sections. The proceeding section reviews existing global governance and global political economy literatures on the implications of technology change. The third section explores the origins of Bitcoin and the challenges it has brought for governance. The fourth section analyzes the policy responses of different countries, summarizing three distinct approaches. Finally, the concluding section extends our analysis to the discussion between the Global North and Global South, illustrating the policy alternatives that the former could learn and from which the latter may choose.

Literature review and methodology

Nearly a decade since its inception, the global popularity of Bitcoin reveals the increasingly established nature of the emergent technology (Young, 2016). Compared with earlier crypto-technologies, Bitcoin for the first time realizes decentralization and *quasi*-anonymity simultaneously. Blockchain technologies not only permit distributed peer-to-peer transactions, but also allow varying degrees of individual anonymity by way of digital encryption (Nakamoto, 2008). Similar to other technologies such as telegram or Internet, the potential influence of Bitcoin on society and the corresponding response from states go well beyond its technical achievements. Technological advancement not only provides individuals the capacity to do things once impossible, but also has the potential to reshuffle power relations (Feenberg, 2012). Bitcoin itself should be considered as the result of a political struggle, rather than merely a technological achievement. Therefore, it is critical to deliberate on the interactive relationship between Bitcoin and the political response from governments, especially the relevant regulatory policies.

The social implications of technology, especially the interactive relationship between technology and policy responses, is a long-standing GPE issue (Ruggie, 1975; Rosenau and Singh, 2002). Like any other technology innovation, the advent of Bitcoin, as well as the blockchain technologies, has attracted broad interests of state and non-state sectors alike. Blockchains have already been applied in numerous fields such as finance (Wharton, 2016), insurance (Wang and Safavi, 2016), accounting (Lazanis, 2015), ride-hailing (Buntinx, 2016), and even the legal profession (Raczynkski, 2016). The emergent technology is confronting power structures in manners that have significant socio-economic and political implications.

However, academic analysis of the governance challenges that Bitcoin invoked and the corresponding policy responses of the states remains insufficient. A small but growing literature has begun to consider the governance problems of Bitcoin and blockchain technology, focusing mainly on the self-governance of the Bitcoin community consisting of developers, miners, and other stakeholders (De Filippi and Loveluck, 2016; Gasser et al., 2015). The role of the state and its policy choices are largely ignored in existing academic analysis. This is important to analyse, however, as the policy response from states will not only affect the future development of Bitcoin in particular and blockchain technology in general, but also their implications on the global political economy.

The policy responses of sovereign countries can be classified into three categories: liberalization, prohibition, and prudent enthusiasm. These responses include the formal regulations developed by governments towards technology in the format of laws, statutes, or investigations. Although non-government actors such as enterprises and social groups also play an important part in regulations that would influence the development of Bitcoin, they are not the central concern of this chapter. We mainly focus on the policy responses of states, as they are not only critical to sustain the shocks caused by technology advancement, but also obligatory for stakeholders that would determine the future development of technology.

Methodologically, our analysis is based on three case studies of the US, Russia, and China. Bitcoin is confronted with different regulatory policies in different countries, which as a whole can be modeled across a spectrum. On the right of the spectrum, it is the liberalization approach, which is characterized by the US, where few formal regulations are imposed on Bitcoin other than some basic requirements such as anti-money-laundering (see Campbell-Verduyn and Goguen, this volume). On the left of the spectrum, Bitcoin is completely prohibited by authorities. Of the countries on the left of the spectrum, Russia is the most prominent, not only because it is one of the major players in global governance, but particularly because of its influence on the policy choices of Eastern European countries, such as Ukraine, where many core developers and main miners come from in the Bitcoin global network (Tillet and Lesser, 2014). China lies in the middle of the two ends of the spectrum. As the largest Bitcoin market and jurisdiction where the main miners are located, China is considered one of the two most important countries to blockchain governance besides the US (Coleman, 2016). Therefore, it is interesting to examine the regulatory responses of Chinese authorities to see whether it is truly possible to develop alternative policy choices besides the two polarized extremes. Our spectrum is illustrated in Figure 5.1.

The extant literature largely ignores the regulation of Bitcoin in China. We seldom see academic analysis of Chinese regulation in the Western world, while Chinese scholars are busy introducing Western ideas and institutions, overlooking the value of endogenous innovation in China (Li, 2013). This chapter examines a spectrum of regulation all over the world to highlight the novelty of the regulatory experiment in China. As an authoritative state, China is often considered as advancing a conservative approach to the emergence and development of emergent technologies (Abrami et al., 2014). From liberal perspectives, the planned economy would not be appropriate for technological innovation as

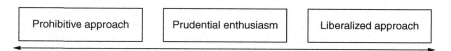

Figure 5.1 Spectrum of Bitcoin/blockchain governance.

the hierarchical administrative institutions of the state are understood to shackle the development of technology (Hayek, 1945).

In contrast, the argument we advance here is that Chinese policy is much more flexible than considered from conventional perspectives. China has balanced the risks and benefits of blockchain technology. As a result, China has grown to be the largest Bitcoin market globally. Despite the existing problems and uncertainties in the future, China provides both the Global South and the Global North an alternative between two other polarized extremes of either liberalization or prohibition.

Origins and governance challenges of Bitcoin

Political origins of Bitcoin

Although the Bitcoin White Paper issued on October 31, 2008, by Satoshi Nakamoto, the still unknown Bitcoin inventor, was filled with technical details and did not mention a word of its political origins, the inception of Bitcoin is still widely believed to be the result of political struggles and a political manifesto.[1] In the genesis block,[2] Satoshi wrote the following, which was the headline of *The Times* on January 3, 2009:

> Chancellor on brink of second bailout for banks.
>
> (Nakamoto, 2008)

Later on January 19, 2009, the British government announced the second-round bailouts for bankrupting banks, investing nearly $150 billion to buy bank shares and providing securities for troubled assets. Among the massive criticisms was that the government of a liberal market economy was using taxes to rescue commercial banks responsible for the global financial crisis. Bitcoin was then presented as an alternative to the centralized banking and finance system. Based on blockchain technologies, Bitcoin provided a decentralized peer-to-peer transaction network that ostensibly no longer relies on centralized institutions for clearing and endorsement, and has finally diminished the necessity of governments or central banks.

The political ideas of Satoshi are not only reflected in the obscure quotation buried in the blockchain, but are also exposed through their daily activities in the community (De Filippi and Loveluck, 2016). The activity records they left in the community show a clear connection with the ideology of the "cypherpunk movement." The White Paper on Bitcoin was issued in the online forum organized by a group of hackers, mathematicians, and activists called *cypherpunks*.

The cypherpunk movement originated from the political struggle against the US government that tried to suppress the development of cryptography in the 1990s (Hughes, 1993). Cypherpunks sought to build an anonymous society using cryptography as a means of achieving greater privacy and security in the face of massive government surveillance. Despite its focus on privacy, the ultimate goal of the cypherpunk movement could be summarized as enabling self-organized direct interactions between individuals without relying on external authority for coordination or coercion (De Filippi and Loveluck, 2016). In other words, the cypherpunk movement attempted to establish a decentralized society without centralized authority as leaders or controllers, a political pursuit that can also be found in an ancient and important political genre: anarchism (de Geus, 2014).

Despite widespread misunderstanding, the essence of anarchism is not "chaos without principle" but rather "an organized society without ruler" (Vodovnik, 2012; Wachhaus, 2014; de Geus, 2014). Centralized hierarchical authorities are seen as not only inefficient in an environment replete with uncertainty, but also detrimental to the autonomy and creativity of individuals who are ready for cooperation and mutual aid (Kropotkin and Baldwin, 1970). However, despite the heavy criticisms from anarchists, centralized authorities remain indispensable for many basic and functional necessities. Take the monetary system as an example. Banks work as clearinghouses and credit endorsement for all kinds of transactions, while central banks assume the responsibility as the lender of last resort to sustain stability. Although anarchists do not trust banks as protectors of collective goods, because of the many bank runs or financial crises that have occurred over history, it remains impossible to transact without these centralized institutions. Even traditional electronic coins such as e-cash had to rely on centralized banks to confirm transactions (Chaum, 1983). It was not until the inception of Bitcoin that a monetary system that ostensibly replaced centralized authorities with a peer-to-peer network was established.

There is a clear connection between Bitcoin and the political ideals of cypherpunks, as well as anarchists. The inception of Bitcoin should not be considered merely as a technical advancement, but rather a political reform with clear political goals to decentralize traditional monetary systems. Despite the benefits of the decentralized system that anarchists advocate, it is also accused of being highly unstable, unaccountable, and unsustainable (Wachhaus, 2014). The next section will discuss problems of Bitcoin and the governance challenges that it has brought.

Challenges for formal governance *of* Bitcoin

As it is still a rather niche market, it is not necessarily for states to directly regulate Bitcoin. However, as the Bitcoin market expands and its influence increases, the negative effects of the technology become prominent and the governance challenges *of* Bitcoin grow. These governance challenges could be classified into three categories: volatility, vulnerability, and illegal use.

Volatility

Bitcoin is exposed to market risks and volatile speculation. Investors have flooded into the market and pumped up Bitcoin prices. When a fiat currency is confronted with such speculation, central banks, or states, would usually

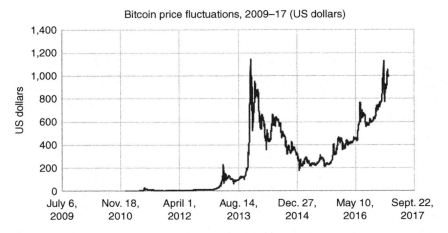

Figure 5.2 Bitcoin price fluctuations, 2009–17 (US dollars).

issue hedging policies to offset potential price fluctuations. However, as a decentralized peer-to-peer network, there is no centralized authority to carefully monitor the market changes and make corresponding adjustments. In other words, the price of Bitcoin is volatile because of the laissez-faire condition. Since 2011, Bitcoin has been through at least six significant price fluctuations (Salmon, 2013).

As a medium of exchange, merchants and customers pay more attention to the transaction costs of Bitcoin, rather than the exchange rates to fiat currencies. However, if Bitcoin is to be a store of value or unit of account, the price has to be stable to satisfy people's expectation. Therefore, the price volatility would fundamentally harm faith in Bitcoin and would probably end the future of Bitcoin (Farrell, 2013). Worse still, as the transaction volume of Bitcoin grows, the fluctuation of the Bitcoin market would affect other markets and even the global economy. This is especially serious for the Global South, where economies are fragile. When serious inflation occurs, residents' wealth in the Global South countries would possibly flee outside the borders through the Bitcoin network, despite the regulations on capital outflows, as has occurred in Latin America (Lahrichi, 2016).

Price volatility does not necessarily mean that Bitcoin and its market cannot grow. The market value of Bitcoin has already exceeded $10 billion despite the price fluctuations (Jonathan, 2013). One possible explanation is that mechanisms counteracting the volatility such as derivatives markets have gradually developed. Yet given their relatively small scale, these markets are insufficient to stabilize the price of Bitcoin. Therefore, government interventions become necessary when the price fluctuation of Bitcoin becomes detrimental to the whole economic system.

Vulnerability

Despite the relative simplicity of its source code, the Bitcoin protocol is virtually unhackable, as the computer science literature has shown. For example, Dan Kaminsky (2013), a famous computer security researcher, announced publicly that he was unable to hack Bitcoin protocol after several attempts. As long as the prevailing cryptographic methods that Bitcoin adopts remain secure, the Bitcoin protocol should be impervious to malicious attacks (Whittaker, 2015). However, this does not necessarily suggest that the *entire* global Bitcoin network is secure. Applications built on the Bitcoin protocol, including wallets or exchanges, are critically vulnerable to security risks, which can affect the stability of the whole system.

For example, in 2012 hackers successfully stole 24,000 Bitcoin (BTC) from Bitfloor (Coldewey, 2012), while in 2015, 19,000 BTC were stolen from Bitstamp (Whittaker, 2015). Although in these two cases the exchange operators repaid or committed to pay for the victims, the Mt.Gox scandal revealed a much different case. Mt.Gox was the first functional Bitcoin exchange to enjoy broad name recognition. By 2013, it had already taken up 70 percent of global Bitcoin transactions. In 2014, Mt.Gox suddenly filed for bankruptcy in Japan as it had lost 850,000 BTC in a suspected hack. Some evidence suggested that a Mt.Gox employee stole the Bitcoins. Mt.Gox's customers still had not been reimbursed by the end of 2014. The Mt.Gox scandal had a significant impact on the global Bitcoin market as its dollar price plummeted nearly 20 percent in one day. From this incident, we clearly see the vulnerability of the global Bitcoin network, not because of the weakness of the Bitcoin protocol itself, but because of the security risks of applications in its ecosystem.

The vulnerability of the global Bitcoin network, however, is not dissimilar to the security risks in traditional finance revolving around state-backed currencies. Fiat currencies can be counterfeited, banks can be robbed, and personal financial information can be hacked. In these conditions, banks should assume the responsibility for the loss of customers, and when banks went bankrupt, central banks and even states would be the last resort. However, as mentioned above, the decentralized structure of Bitcoin means that there is no centralized authority to be held accountable for customers who suffer from the vulnerability. Under the current laws, exchanges are generally considered to be "firms," which only assume limited liability rather than unlimited liability. Therefore, the vulnerability of the global Bitcoin network still exists and could harm the development and application of the emergent technology.

Illegal use

Because of the pseudonymous characteristics of Bitcoin, it is used for ill as well as for good. The two most common illegal uses of Bitcoin across jurisdictions are in digital black markets and for money laundering. Digital black markets enable the selling and buying of illicit goods or services. With the popularity of the Internet, online black markets have developed quickly all over the world. The centralized electronic payment systems limit the scale of black markets by tracking the money through banks or third party payment providers. The advent of Bitcoin provides new opportunities to the online black markets because of its quasi-anonymity, which makes it difficult to trace the identity of the operators and users. Silk Road, for example, provided an infamous black market exclusively using Bitcoin. From 2011 to 2013, Silk Road was where thousands of illegal goods were traded every day, with total monthly transactions amounting to $1.2 million (Christin, 2012). Although Silk Road was shut down in 2013, other online black markets such as Black Market Reloaded (Mac, 2013) and Sheep Marketplace (Bershidsky, 2013) have emerged quickly, both of which adopted Bitcoin as their alternative payment methods.

Another possible illegal use of Bitcoin is international money laundering. As a global network, it is easy to transmit ill-gotten money across borders. Theoretically speaking, Bitcoin is an option for those who attempt to move ill-gotten money secretly. However, this may not be as attractive as it seemed to be. First, the transaction scope of Bitcoin is limited. Second, all of the transaction records are open and accessible to the public. Although users' addresses and identities are protected by the encryption technology, it is still possible for law enforcement to confirm suspects, especially when Bitcoins are exchanged with certain fiat currencies, as we saw in the Silk Road case. Third, political regulations are gradually being imposed on Bitcoin exchanges, which are pressured to comply with anti-money-laundering record-keeping and reporting requirements, as we see in the European Union (van Wirdum, 2016).

When Bitcoin was only a niche market and its influence was limited in scope, these three negative effects were not sufficiently important to necessitate special regulatory responses by states. However, as Bitcoin has become increasingly accepted worldwide, its influence has increased as well. The price volatility, security vulnerability, and illegal use can affect the stability of financial systems and thus become the target of the regulatory departments of the state. Yet the question remains: how can states balance the risks and benefits of this emergent technology? In the following section, we further analyze different policy alternatives based on the case study of the US, Russia, and China.

Governance *of* technology: three models of the future

Just as Robert Gilpin (1975) predicted the future international economy in the 1970s, the future approaches of the governance *of* technology can be classified into "three models." An emerging technology, blockchains and their applications to cryptocurrencies such as Bitcoin largely exist in a legal "grey area" as they tend not to fit the statutory definitions of either currency or specific financial instruments. As we mentioned above, if left unchecked, the downsides of Bitcoin might not only demolish the cryptocurrency, but more widely affect social stability and harm the greater public good. Yet, if more regulatory burdens are imposed than can be sustained, the innovative potential of the technology might be impeded. Confronted with this dilemma, countries have reacted differently. Some have adopted more laissez-faire policies, while others have adopted more prohibitive ones. Besides this polarization, we argue, is a middle way characterized by prudent enthusiasm. In this section, we model three approaches based on the empirical examples of the US, Russia, and China.

Liberalized governance of technology in the United States

"Don't ask permission; ask forgiveness" is a well-known saying in Silicon Valley that represents a liberal understanding of state–market relations (Kenney and Zysman, 2016). The market is believed to be able to reach Pareto optimality spontaneously without interferences from exogenous actors, including the state. Following this belief, technological advancement is dealt with through a "liberalized governance" approach that relies less on the state to regulate the development of technology than the invisible hand of the market.

American history is replete with cases characterizing the "liberalized governance" approach to the development of technology. Take the VOIP (Voice over Internet Protocol) as an example (Cannon, 2004). When it first emerged, VoIP did not fit the Communications Act and Federal Communications Commission (FCC) regulations, which only covered voice communications over the traditional public switched telephone network. However, the US Congress and FCC charted a path for VoIP that clarified much of the legal ambiguity without overburdening the new technology. As a result, VoIP not only boomed, but also introduced competition to a previously stagnant market that had been monopolized by telephone companies (FCC, 2011).

Following a similar ideology, the US government also adopted this liberalized approach in the governance of Bitcoin and blockchain technology. The country not only allows the transactions using Bitcoin, but also permits and even encourages market actors, such as financial institutions, to conduct business based on the Bitcoin network.

However, Bitcoin, and participants in the blockchain ecosystem, are not completely free from regulation in this laissez-faire environment. The US, like nearly every country, has regulatory institutions and laws that do pertain to the governance of Bitcoin. Most existing American regulations concern the illegal use related to Bitcoin. For example, in March 2013, the Financial Crimes Enforcement Network (FinCen), the law enforcement department of the US Treasury Department, issued guidance on the application of the Bank Secrecy Act (BSA) to Bitcoin. The guidance clearly states that the Bitcoin exchanges are subject to regulations as money transmitters, meaning that they are required to register with FinCEN, implement anti-money-laundering programs, collect information of their customers, keep records of suspicious transactions, etc. (FinCen, 2013).

Besides the anti-money-laundering requirements and the regulations against illegal use in the black markets, however, there are little other formal restraints and regulations imposed on Bitcoin and its related players in the US and countries with similarly liberal political traditions. Although individual states are prohibited from coining money, privately issued currency, such as Bitcoin, is not forbidden under the US Constitution.[3] Furthermore, although both California and New York passed laws to require enterprises to apply for a license to conduct businesses related to Bitcoin, these regulations do not prohibit any entity from becoming involved in this industry.[4] Beyond the US, jurisdictions such as Hong Kong declared it to be unnecessary to regulate Bitcoin businesses or forbid people entering this industry as they considered the cryptocurrency not to be a significant threat to the financial system (Lombardo, 2015).

The liberalized approach tends to stimulate the rapid development of new technology-related businesses. Without the barriers set by the state to enter the market, there will be plenty of resources swarming into markets to promote the research and application of technology if it is truly useful and profitable. Without the distortions from the state, such resource allocation is considered to reach Pareto optimality. However, the liberalized approach has considerable flaws as well. For example, without proper regulations from the state, the price volatility of Bitcoin mentioned above can affect the confidence of investors and harm the development of the emergent technology. Additionally, the risks and uncertainties accompanying emergent technology are another concern for authorities, especially for the Global South, whose financial systems are vulnerable to capital outflows through Bitcoin. It is for these reasons that some countries choose another governance approach to emergent technologies, prohibiting them completely.

The prohibitory approach in Russia

The first two countries that banned Bitcoin domestically were Ecuador and Bolivia. In February 2014, Russia became the third and by far the largest, most important country to ban Bitcoin, resulting in chaos of the global Bitcoin market. The Russian Prosecutor General lamented that cybercurrencies had gained too large a circulation, becoming money substitutes, and thus were to be banned according to a federal law signed by President Putin in 2002 (Baczynska, 2014). The other official reason was to thwart the potential use of Bitcoin in funding terrorism, buying illicit goods and services, money laundering, etc.

Countries prohibiting Bitcoin completely tend to do so out of concern for the impacts to their domestic financial systems. They mainly fear that Bitcoin would weaken their capacity to regulate their financial system and that domestic wealth may flee abroad through the global Bitcoin network. The countries affected by rapid capital outflows are mainly located in the Global South, while the capital tends to flow to Global North countries. Thus, even though all countries are confronted with the same challenges of capital outflows using Bitcoin, different countries are positioned differently in global financial networks, contributing to different policy choices. The unbalanced power structure between the Global South and Global North underpins the fear of the former countries that emergent technology might be used as instruments of the latter to weaken their authority.

Russian officials forbid the circulation of Bitcoin completely because the invention of Bitcoin was regarded as a conspiracy plotted by foreign trouble-makers (Rizzo, 2015). Besides the three countries mentioned above, Vietnam also joined in banning the digital currency because of fears of foreign intervention in their economies.

The prohibitive approach can certainly help protect countries from risks and uncertainties accompanying emergent technologies such as blockchains. However, there are also flaws to this second governance approach. While reducing risk, hope and opportunities can be reduced at the same time. Countries are less able to benefit from the potential that emergent technology offers, harming their developmental potential. Thus, the question becomes how to balance the risks and benefits of emergent technology to escape the dilemma that unprivileged countries usually confront. A third approach is therefore valuable to assess.

A balanced middle ground approach to governance of technology: prudent enthusiasm of China

Between polarized global regulatory responses on Bitcoin exists a middle ground approach exemplified by China. Conventionally, China is usually considered to be slow to react to cutting-edge technology and a follower in the emerging global governance of Bitcoin (Abrami et al., 2014). However, closer analysis reveals that the Chinese government is more active than expected. The policy response of Chinese regulatory institutions is neither laissez-faire nor completely prohibitory. Rather, it is a middle way that is not only enthusiastic about technological change, but also prudent in controlling the scope of its impacts.

By the end of 2016, China occupied more than 50 percent of the computation power in the Bitcoin global network. Thousands mined Bitcoins all across the country. Chinese engineers first designed and used Application Specific Integrated Circuit (ASIC) to compute the SHA256 algorithm, which is 100 times faster than conventional computers (CCID, 2014). Besides the mining industry, China also occupies the largest market of Bitcoin transactions, with more than 70 percent of the global market share. The top two Chinese exchanges even occupied nearly 96 percent of the global exchange volume at the time of writing.[5] The rapid development of Bitcoin in China is based on the tolerance and enthusiasm of a Chinese government that is arguably more inclined to liberalization on the regulation of Bitcoin than the US. However, Chinese regulatory institutions also closely monitor the development of Bitcoin and are prudent about taking risks that may affect the stability of its domestic economic system. In other words, China adopted a middle way between laissez-faire and complete prohibition.

Prudent central bank enthusiasm

In September 2016, the vice-president of the People's Bank of China (PBC) declared publicly that "digital currency is the inevitable future and the Chinese

Central Bank needs to pay close attention to the development of crypto-currency that private sectors issued, like Bitcoin" (Fan, 2016). The PBC had already begun research on digital currency in 2014 (Liu, 2016). In contrast to countries such as Russia, which consider Bitcoin as a conspiracy plotted by hostile trouble-makers, China has embraced it with more enthusiasm. There are multiple reasons to explain such enthusiasm, such as the incentive to stimulate the economy, the professional capability of the PBC, and soon. Of these, perhaps the most important is the potential of Bitcoin, and the related blockchain technology, to be used to improve the efficiency of the Chinese financial system.

Although China had steadily conducted macro-economic reforms for more than three decades, during which its aggregate GDP rose to second worldwide, trailing only the US, there remain fundamental flaws in its financial system. For example, despite tight controls on money flows among banks and other formal institutions, the PBC has few data on the money flow outside the formal financial system. These outflows were exaggerated by the recent rapid development of Internet finance, which greatly amplifies the magnitude of liquidity outside the formal financial system. In addition, tax evasion is common in China, which encourages citizens to invest in Bitcoin to avoid taxes.

The advancement of digital currency, symbolized by the invention of Bitcoin, provides the Chinese government with opportunities to reform the financial system. The PBC regards digital currency as beneficial for decreasing the cost of issuance and circulation of paper money, for increasing convenience and transparency of the economy, and for combatting financial criminality such as tax evasion and money laundering (PBC, 2016). The PBC in 2016 declared its intention to issue its own digital currency based on blockchain technology as soon as possible (PBC, 2016). This is in stark contrast to other major countries or economies, including the US, the EU, and Japan, which chose to wait and see until the potential impacts of digital currency fully unfold. The PBC was enthusiastic about digital currencies despite their considerable potential downsides. However, this enthusiasm does not necessarily mean that the PBC followed its American counterparts in pursuing a liberalized approach. On the contrary, the Chinese government was prudent in seeking to avoid risks that may affect the stability of its domestic economic system.

Prudent government enthusiasm

The prudence of Chinese regulators is evidenced by the "Notice to Prepare for the Risks of Bitcoin" jointly issued in December 2013 by five departments, including the PBC, MIIT (Ministry of Industry and Information Technology), CBRC (China Banking Regulatory Commission), CSRC (China Securities Regulatory Commission), and CIRC (China Insurance Regulatory Commission). In the form of an administrative order, this notice is the first regulation in China that officially granted legal status to Bitcoin. In this notice, Bitcoin is therefore considered to be a virtual commodity asset rather than a form of currency.

Along with other stipulations concerning the illegal use of Bitcoin, the most important article in the 2013 notice was the ruling that all financial institutions are forbidden to undertake businesses related to Bitcoin. In addition, payment institutions were banned from providing services to companies conducting Bitcoin businesses. The purpose of this article is to prevent speculation risks in Bitcoin from spreading to financial institutions. As mentioned above, volatility is one of the three main downsides of Bitcoin, which would probably be leveraged and amplified if financial institutions were to become involved in speculation, resulting in chain reactions and even a crisis. Given the limited and restrained domestic capital markets of China, speculation poses risks higher than other Global North countries, where individuals can find other ways to allocate their capitals.

Countries adopting a more liberal governance approach are mainly concerned with the illicit use of Bitcoin, while underdeveloped countries that ban Bitcoin completely fear particularly the potential impacts of Bitcoin to their fragile financial systems. China goes beyond the liberal approach to actively restrain speculation activities of its financial institutions while avoiding a total ban on Bitcoin activities. It is for this reason that China is positioned in the middle along the global governance spectrum identified in Figure 5.1. These regulations are effective and played an important role in restraining the price vulnerability of Bitcoin (People's Bank of China, 2014).

The Chinese government retains multiple tools to restrain the speculation risks of Bitcoin. One of the most important in its regulatory toolkit is the possibility of implementing harsher regulations, or the background "shadow of regulation." Regulators may question key firms when the price of Bitcoin fluctuates sharply, and did so in early 2017 when it rose sharply to exceed $1,000 (Zhou, 2017). The PBC scheduled a meeting with the heads of several main exchanges about speculation risks. The news spread that more severe restrictive measures might be imposed on the Bitcoin market. The negative expectation pushed investors to sell Bitcoin and the price went down gradually on the expectation that the PBC might intervene in the operation of Bitcoin exchanges and investigate whether their transactions satisfy the regulation demands.

Table 5.1 lists the major regulation events and policies in China. Comparing Figure 5.1 and Table 5.1, we see that most of the regulatory interventions of the PBC into the Bitcoin industry in 2013 and 2017 occurred when the price rose quickly. After these interventions, the global price of Bitcoin decreased quickly.[6] On the one hand, these interventions and the resulting price declines of Bitcoin indicate the tremendous influence of China on the global Bitcoin market. On the other hand, these interventions illustrate how Chinese policy response are relatively effective in preventing the spread of volatility to other markets.

The Chinese regulatory policy provides an alternative to the polarized policy options discussed before. Although conventional understandings of China as an authoritarian state tend to expect a more conservative policy from the Chinese government to manage emergent technology in general and Bitcoin in particular, China has navigated a middle way between the two main existing approaches.

Table 5.1 Key events and policies in China

Date	Key events and policies in China
December 3, 2013	The PBC and four other ministries of China jointly release the "Notice of Preventing the Risk of Bitcoin," the first national regulation concerning the characteristics and transactions of Bitcoin. The notice identified Bitcoin as a virtual commodity rather than one kind of currency and banned any financial and payment institutions from involvement in Bitcoin.
December 16, 2013	The PBC officially demands third-party payment institutions to cease provision of payment and clearing services for Bitcoin exchange platforms.
March, 2014	The PBC releases the "Notice on Further Strengthening the Bitcoin Risk Prevention Work," demanding that commercial banks and payment institutions stop providing services to the Bitcoin industry immediately.
January 1, 2017	The PBC officials meet with managers of the three largest domestic Bitcoin exchange platforms, demanding them to check unusual fluctuations of Bitcoin and ensure that their operations satisfy the regulatory requirements.
January 11, 2017	The PBC officials investigate the operations of the two largest Bitcoin exchange platforms to check whether there are any illegal transactions on the platforms.
February 9, 2017	The PBC branches at Beijing meet with nine small Bitcoin exchange platforms, demanding them to ensure that their operations satisfy regulatory requirements.

Confronted with the potential benefits as well as the risks of Bitcoin, the Chinese government demonstrated prudent enthusiasm towards the challenges of vulnerability, volatility, and criminality. Rather than complete prohibition, the Chinese regulators, to a large extent, tolerate the vulnerability and volatility of Bitcoin. They ban the illegal use of Bitcoin. Yet, Chinese regulators prevent domestic financial institutions from conducting businesses related to Bitcoin, a clear divergence from the liberalization approach. Consequently, China cuts off the connections between domestic financial markets and Bitcoin, and thus seeks to reduce the potential risks for mainstream finance and investors at large.

The tolerance of vulnerability and volatility of Bitcoin does not mean that Chinese regulators never encounter problems. In early 2017, when the price of Bitcoin grew fast in a short time, the PBC actively warned major exchanges that the transactions on their platforms might be illegal, affecting confidence and suppressing the overheated market as a result. The Chinese government operates largely as an "invisible regulator" by functioning behind the scenes. Its actions are mostly in the background when the market functions well, yet intervenes directly when the market deviates from a stable development path. From this perspective, the Chinese regulatory policy is effective not solely because it is capable of suppressing Bitcoin price volatility, but also because it confines the scope of influence and prevents the risks of volatility from spreading to the rest of the financial system.

Conclusion

What are the challenges that Bitcoin has brought to states? How have states responded to these challenges? In the spirit of the cypherpunk movement to fend off governmental interference in individual privacy, digital currency was designed to encrypt transactions and enhance trust between individuals rather than centralized institutions. Through blockchain technology Bitcoin established a global decentralized transaction network that, for the first time, eliminated the necessity of any centralized institutions for currency issuance and settlement. After its inception in 2009, Bitcoin grew to a $10 billion global market. However, along with growth and other potential benefits, this emergent technology also brought about three challenges: price volatility, security vulnerability, and illegal usages.

How have states responded to the challenges and opportunities presented by Bitcoin and blockchain technology? One view is that the development of ICTs such as blockchain completely marginalize the governance capacities of governments and elevate those of non-state actors such as transnational enterprises, NGOs, and individuals. The decentralized characteristics of Bitcoin and blockchain technology more generally, for instance, entail that centralized institutions such as central banks are no longer essential in monetary systems. However, examining the regulatory responses of three major countries shows that centralized efforts still play important roles in the governance of the global Bitcoin network. Governments are not bystanders of the technology revolution, but active participants in the future of emergent technologies.

In this chapter we subdivided government policy responses into three categories: liberalization, prohibition, and prudent enthusiasm. Countries such as the US exemplified the liberalization path. Except regulations on illegal use of Bitcoin, the US mainly provides a laissez-faire environment for the development of Bitcoin. No one is entirely forbidden from conducting business in Bitcoin. Meanwhile, countries such as Russia choose to prohibit completely the circulation of Bitcoin for fear of negatively affecting their domestic financial systems. Between these two approaches, China adopts a middle way. It restrains only financial institutions from operating with Bitcoin and seeks to balance the potential benefits of the emergent technology with the possible risks of its downsides.

It is difficult to conclude which approach is ultimately best given the early phase of blockchain technology development. However, one provisional conclusion becomes clear: China's policy is more flexible than what is conventionally assumed. As an authoritarian state, the Chinese government is considered to be conservative and slow to react to technological change compared with Western countries advocating free markets. However, as our analysis shows, China adopts a middle way that is neither liberalization nor complete prohibition. The Chinese regulators cut off the path of risk transfer by forbidding financial institutions from being involved with Bitcoin, while at the same time they allow other actors to enter the Bitcoin market under some elaborate conditions. The policy response of the Chinese government has been effective until now, as China hosts the largest Bitcoin market, which is relatively stable despite violent fluctuations in the global Bitcoin price.

Emergent technology alone might not permit developing countries to catch up with leading developed countries. Indeed, technology may be yet another point of polarization in the North–South divide. Developing countries tend to prohibit Bitcoin for fear of domestic wealth fleeing through its easily accessible global network. Yet while developed countries cannot control and manage all the impacts of emergent technologies, they tend to enjoy their potential benefits. The advent of Bitcoin and blockchain technology has been considered equivalent to the invention of the Internet in the 1970s (Benzinga, 2015). The Internet has provided profound benefits as well as problems over the past 50 years. It is still unclear what further opportunities, as well as challenges, that Bitcoin will bring. However, technology change is certain to continue provoking policy responses from governments, which would benefit from understanding the case of Bitcoin.

Acknowledgment

Thanks to Malcolm Campbell-Verduyn for his review and constructive comments on this chapter.

Notes

1 Many scholars consider how Bitcoin is underlined by anarchism, or syndicalism, both of which had a long history of revolutionary praxis. A comprehensive overview can be

found here: https://btctheory.com/ and https://btctheory.com/2015/03/19/revolutionary-syndicalism-bitcoin/. See also http://peerproduction.net/issues/issue-4-value-and-currency/

2 A genesis block is the first block of a blockchain. Modern versions of Bitcoin assign it block number 0, though older versions gave it number 1. The genesis block is almost always hardcoded into the software. It is a special case in that it does not reference a previous block, and for Bitcoin and almost all of its derivatives, it produces an unspendable subsidy.

3 U.S. Constitution, Article I, section 10.

4 Although critics argue that New York State license requirements imposed unfair burdens on the emergent technology, it should be noted that the regulatory requirements are still in the direction of liberalized governance of technology, especially compared with other countries from a global perspective. At least, the state did not prohibit any institution from conducting businesses in this field.

5 See: http://bitcoincharts.com/charts/volumepie/

6 There are many reasons that explain the sharp drop of Bitcoin price at that time. However, the precise time point of the intervention of the Chinese government in 2013 and 2017 shows a close relationship between China and the global Bitcoin market.

Bibliography

Abrami, R.E., Kirby, W.C., and McFarlan, F.W. (2014, March). Why China can't innovate. *Harvard Business Review.*

Baczynska, G. (2014). *Russia authorities say Bitcoin illegal.* Retrieved August 23, 2017, from www.reuters.com/article/2014/02/09/us-russia-bitcoin-idUSBREA1806620140209

Benzinga, L. (2015, March 25). *Coin.co CEO: Bitcoin's impact on society will rival the internet.* Retrieved August 23, 2017, from http://finance.yahoo.com/news/coin-co-ceo-bitcoins-impact-114107872.html

Bershidsky, L. (2013, October 4). Goodbye Silk Road, Hello Sheep Marketplace. *Bloomberg.* Retrieved August 23, 2017, from www.bloomberg.com/news/2013-10-04/goodbye-silk-road-hello-sheep-marketplace.html

Buntinx, J.P. (2016, March 22). *Using the blockchain for decentralized ride-sharing with La'Zooz.* Retrieved August 23, 2017, from www.newsbtc.com/2016/03/22/using-blockchain-decentralized-ride-sharing-lazooz/

Cannon, R. (2004). State regulatory approaches to VoIP: Policy, implementation, and outcome. *Federal Commations Law Journal, 57*: 479.

CCID. (2014). *Review of the development of the ASIC chip of Bitcoin mining machines.* Retrieved August 23, 2017, from http://cpu.qudong.com/2014/0504/168553.shtml

Chaum, D. (1983). Blind signatures for untraceable payments. In D. Chaum, R.L. Rivest, and A.T. Sherman (eds.) *Advances in cryptology* (pp. 199–203). New York: Springer US.

Christin, N. (2013, May). Traveling the Silk Road: A measurement analysis of a large anonymous online marketplace. In *Proceedings of the 22nd International Conference on World Wide Web* (pp. 213–24). New York: ACM.

Coldewey, D. (2012). $250,000 worth of Bitcoins stolen in net heist. *NBC.* Retrieved August 23, 2017, from www.nbcnews.com/technology/250-000-worth-bitcoins-stolen-net-heist-980871

Coleman, L. (2016). China's mining dominance: Good or bad for Bitcoin? *Cryptocoins News.* Retrieved August 23, 2017, from www.cryptocoinsnews.com/chinas-mining-dominance-good-or-bad-for-bitcoin/

De Filippi, P., and Loveluck, B. (2016, September 30). The invisible politics of Bitcoin: Governance crisis of a decentralized infrastructure. *Internet Policy Review.*

de Geus, M. (2014). Peter Kropotkin's anarchist vision of organization. *Ephemera, 14*(4): 859.

Extance, A. (2015). The future of cryptocurrencies: Bitcoin and beyond. *Nature,* 30 September.

Fan, Y. (2016). Zhong Guo Fa Ding Shu Zi Huo Bi de Li Lun Yi Ju he Jia Gou Xuan Ze (The theoretical basis and structure choice of Chinese fiat digital currency). *China Finance,* (17): 10–12.

Farrell, M. (2013). *Strategist predicts end of Bitcoin.* Retrieved August 23, 2017, from http://money.cnn.com/2013/05/14/investing/bremmer-bitcoin/index.html

FCC. (2011). *FCC's VoIP regulation dilemma.* Retrieved August 23, 2017, from www.telephonyyourway.com/2011/04/30/fccs-voip-regulation-dilemma/

Feenberg, A. (2012). *Questioning technology.* London: Routledge.

FinCen. (2013). US Department of Treasury, Financial Crimes Enforcement Network, "Application of FinCEN's Regulations to Persons Administering, Exchanging, or Using Virtual Currencies" (Guidance FIN-2013-G001, March 18, 2013). Retrieved August 17, 2016, from www.fincen.gov/statutes_regs/guidance/html/FIN-2013-G001.html

Foster, J.B., and McChesney, R.W. (2014). Surveillance capitalism: Monopoly-finance capital, the military-industrial complex, and the digital age. *Monthly Review, 66*(3): 1.

Franco, P. (2014). *Understanding Bitcoin: Cryptography, engineering and economics.* Hoboken, NJ: John Wiley & Sons.

Gasser, U., Budish, R., and West, S.M. (2015, January 15). *Multistakeholder as governance groups: Observations from case studies.* Cambridge, MA: Berkman Klein Center, Harvard University.

Gilpin, R. (1975). Three models of the future. *International Organization, 29*(1): 37–60.

Hayek, F.A. (1945). The use of knowledge in society. *American Economic Review,* 519–30.

Hughes, E. (1993). *A cypherpunk's manifesto.* Retrieved August 23, 2017, from www.activism.net/cypherpunk/manifesto.html

Hutt, R. (2016, December 13). Beyond bitcoin: Four surprising uses for blockchain. *World Economic Forum.*

Jonathan, M. (2013). *Bitcoin market cap breaks $10 billion.* Retrieved August 23, 2017, from http://coinalert.eu/2015013630-Bitcoin+Market+Cap+Breaks+10+Billion.html

Kaminsky, D. (2013). *I tried hacking Bitcoin and I failed.* Retrieved August 23, 2017, from www.businessinsider.com/dan-kaminsky-highlights-flaws-bitcoin-2013-4

Kenney, M., and Zysman, J. (2016). The rise of the platform economy. *Issues in Science and Technology, 32*(3): 61.

Kostakis, V., and Giotitsas, C. (2017, January 8). Beyond Bitcoin: Is Bitcoin a misguided information technology tool here to create more problems than it solves? *Evonomics.*

Kropotkin, P.A., and Baldwin, R.N. (1970). *Kropotkin's revolutionary pamphlets: A collection of writings.* Mineola, NY: Dover Publications.

Kurzweil, R. (2005). *The singularity is near: When humans transcend biology.* London: Penguin.

Lahrichi, K. (2016). Growing number of Venezuelans trade bolivars for bitcoins to buy necessities. *Guardian.* Retrieved August 23, 2017, from www.theguardian.com/technology/2016/dec/16/venezuela-bitcoin-economy-digital-currency-bolivars

Lazanis, R. (2015). *How technology behind Bitcoin could transform accounting as we know it.* Retrieved August 23, 2017, from https://techvibes.com/2015/01/22/how-technology-behind-bitcoin-could-transform-accounting-as-we-know-it-2015-01-22

Li, D. (2013). The US/EU regulation enlightenment to China. *Journal of Beijing Institute of Economic Management, 28*(4): 30–3.

Liu. (2016). *PBC confirms to issue digital currency*. Retrieved August 23, 2017, from http://finance.sina.com.cn/roll/2016-01-22/doc-ifxnvhvu6975097.shtml

Lombardo, H. (2015). *Hong Kong gov says Bitcoin regulation unneeded, highly speculative and not currency*. Retrieved August 23, 2017, from http://allcoinsnews.com/2015/03/25/hong-kong-government-bitcoin-regulation-unnecessary-warns-highly-speculative-not-lawful-tender/

Mac, R. (2013). *False alarm: Silk Road competitor Black Market Reloaded staying online*. Retrieved August 23, 2017, from www.forbes.com/sites/ryanmac/2013/10/18/false-alarm-silk-road-competitor-black-market-reloaded-staying-online/

Matthewman, S. (2011). *Technology and social theory*. London: Palgrave Macmillan.

May, C. (2013). *The global political economy of intellectual property rights: The new enclosures?* London: Routledge.

Mayer, M., Carpes, M., and Knoblich, R. (eds.) (2014). *The global politics of science and technology – Vol. 1: Concepts from international relations and other disciplines*. New York: Springer.

Mayer, M., Carpes, M., and Knoblich, R. (eds.) (2014). *The global politics of science and technology – Vol. 2: Perspectives, cases and methods*. New York: Springer.

Nakamoto, S. (2008). *Bitcoin: A peer-to-peer electronic cash system*. Retrieved August 21, 2017 from https://bitcoin.org/bitcoin.pdf

PBC. (2016). *People's Bank of China holds seminar on digital currency in Beijing*. Retrieved August 23, 2017, from www.pbc.gov.cn/goutongjiaoliu/113456/113469/3008070/index.html

PBC. (2014). *2013 Nian Zhong Guo Ren Min Yin Hang Gui Zhang Ji Zhong Yao Gui Fan Xing Wen Jian Jie Du (Explanations of the rules and important normative documents of People's Bank of China in 2013)*. Beijing: China Financial Publishing House.

Pielke, R., Wigley, T., and Green, C. (2008). Dangerous assumptions. *Nature, 452*(7187): 531–32.

Raczynkski, J. (2016). How might blockchain technology revolutionize the legal industry? *Thomson Reuters*. Retrieved August 23, 2017, from https://blogs.thomsonreuters.com/answerson/might-blockchain-technology-revolutionize-legal-industry/

Rizzo, P. (2015). Russian lawmaker: Bitcoin is a CIA conspiracy. Retrieved August 23, 2017, from www.coindesk.com/russian-politician-us-bitcoin-finance-terrorism/

Rosenau, J.N., and Singh, J.P. (2002). *Information technologies and global politics: The changing scope of power and governance*. New York: SUNY Press.

Rosov, S. (2015). Beyond Bitcoin. *CFA Institute Magazine, 26*(1).

Ruggie, J.G. (1975). International responses to technology: concepts and trends. *International Organization, 29*(3): 557–83.

Salmon, F. (2013). *The Bitcoin bubble and the future of currency*. Retrieved August 23, 2017, from https://medium.com/money-banking/2b5ef79482cb

Schatsky, D., and Muraskin, C. (2015). *Beyond Bitcoin: Blockchain is coming to disrupt your industry*. New York: Deloitte University Press.

Singleton, R. (2008). Knowledge and technology: The basis of wealth and power. In D. Balaam and M. Vesath (eds.) *Introduction to international political economy*. 4th ed. (pp. 196–214). Upper Saddle River, NJ: Prentice Hall.

Tillet, A., and Lesser, B. (2014). *Science and technology in central and eastern Europe: The reform of higher education*. London: Routledge.

van Wirdum, A. (2016). New EU directive may impose anti-money laundering regulations on Bitcoin wallet providers. *Bitcoin Magazine*. Retrieved August 23, 2017, from https://bitcoinmagazine.com/articles/new-eu-directive-may-impose-anti-money-laundering-regulations-on-bitcoin-wallet-providers-1468424029/

Vodovnik, Ž. (2013). *A living spirit of revolt: The infrapolitics of anarchism*. Oakland, CA: PM Press.

Wachhaus, A. (2014). Governance beyond government. *Administration and Society, 46*(5): 573–93.

Wang, K., and Safavi, A. (2016). Blockchain is empowering the future of insurance. Retrieved August 23, 2017, from https://techcrunch.com/2016/10/29/blockchain-is-empowering-the-future-of-insurance/

Wharton. (2016). How blockchain technology will disrupt financial services firms. Retrieved August 23, 2017, from http://knowledge.wharton.upenn.edu/article/blockchain-technology-will-disrupt-financial-services-firms/

Whittaker, Z. (2015). *Bitstamp exchange hacked, $5m worth of Bitcoin stolen*. Retrieved August 23, 2017, from www.zdnet.com/article/bitstamp-bitcoin-exchange-suspended-amid-hack-concerns-heres-what-we-know/

Willcocks, L.P. (2006). Michel Foucault in the social study of ICTs: Critique and reappraisal. *Social Science Computer Review, 24*(3): 274–95.

Young, J. (2016). *Why Bitcoin continues to become increasingly popular*. Retrieved August 23, 2017, from www.newsbtc.com/2016/02/27/bitcoin-continues-become-increasingly-popular/

Zhang, L. (2013). The Google-China dispute: The Chinese national narrative and rhetorical legitimation of the Chinese Communist Party. *Rhetoric Review, 32*(4): 455–72.

Zhou, Y. (2017). *CBC criticized Bitcoin exchanges to loan money to users illegally*. Retrieved August 23, 2017, from www.thepaper.cn/newsDetail_forward_1603964

6 Cryptocurrencies and digital payment rails in networked global governance

Perspectives on inclusion and innovation

Daivi Rodima-Taylor and William W. Grimes

Over two billion people live outside the formal financial sector. Digital financial inclusion has emerged as a novel paradigm to enhance access to financial services through e-currency platforms in many emerging economies. These processes started with the "mobile money revolution" in Africa and Asia a few years ago, transforming the way people transferred money in domestic and regional settings. Cryptocurrencies present a promise to build on that digital inclusion revolution by disrupting global remittance systems – cross-border and transnational person-to-person money transfers.

These are important developments both practically and theoretically. Practically, digital financial inclusion will likely be the way in which hundreds of millions, or even billions, of "unbanked" people interact with formal financial and regulatory systems. Theoretically, the examination of digital financial inclusion provides a novel – and likely revealing – lens for investigating the effects of the novel peer-to-peer digital payment infrastructures on agency, participation, and authority. In this chapter, we contend that the growing employment of digital money transfer circuits for remittance transfers profoundly affects their regulatory and normative conceptualizations, and has important implications for the global governance as well as broader legitimation of digital currencies. Arguing that crypto-remittances and mobile money transfers can facilitate a paradigm change in financial inclusion, the discussion highlights the novel dynamics of the communicative networks and local innovation ecosystems where the money transfers circulate.

Digital financial services in developing countries provide the essential but often missing infrastructures of finance, enabling many people to access formal financial services for the first time in their lives. In many communities, the poor live in a cash economy and engage mostly in informal economic activities. Emerging markets currently represent 75 percent of the world's 4.8 billion mobile subscribers (Bayen and Ajadi, 2017). Novel mobile-phone-based digital financial services have been launched in more than 80 countries worldwide (GSMA, 2014), enabling the poor to transition to electronically mediated financial services and connect to formal financial institutions. The new digital rails in low-income communities are used predominantly for person-to-person payments or remittances, both domestic and international. Payments are the "connective tissue of an economic system" (Radcliffe and Voorhies, 2012) and remittances often serve as an important entry point to the formal financial system in cash-based economies.

While e-money transferred through mobile platforms has significantly reduced the costs of money transfers *within* countries, money transfer fees in the traditional *cross-border* remittance industry remain extremely high. Digital currencies such as Bitcoin appear particularly suitable for migrant workers' remittances that are relatively small in size. Remittance transfers to the poorest areas in the world often tend to be the costliest. As of 2014, the global cost of sending $200 averaged at around 8 percent of the sum sent, whereas the costs of sending remittances to Africa remained close to almost 12 percent and as high as 30 percent in some remittance corridors (World Bank, 2016). The United Nation's Sustainable Development Goals call for a reduction of the migrant remittances transaction costs to less than 3 percent by 2030, and eliminating remittances corridors where transfer costs are higher than 5 percent. While this seems unrealistic under current institutional and legal conditions, digital currency offers one possible solution.

Hundreds of millions of people now live outside their countries of birth, and the recent global refugee crisis has resulted in further mass displacement. The contexts of forced migration and violent conflict have been shown to often produce enhanced remittance flows, but remittance transfers to fragile countries are among the costliest and most difficult (Rodima-Taylor, 2013). Meanwhile, recent "de-risking" initiatives[1] by global banks have re-marginalized many money transfer operators and correspondent banks in poor and conflict-affected states, pushing remittance flows further underground.

Blockchain applications have made possible a conceptually novel approach to sending and receiving migrant remittances that includes new digital forms of money, novel payment infrastructures, and new types of remittance actors. The technology facilitates decentralized systems of trust and secure financial transactions: as an immutable and time-stamped public ledger, it provides a permanent record of money transmissions. Bitcoin as a global decentralized currency holds a promise to facilitate direct and transparent cross-border remittance transfers, theoretically eliminating intermediaries such as correspondent banks of traditional remittance systems. The technology is also suitable for micropayments – the sums regularly transacted can be small in many developing economies (Realini and Mehta, 2015). Cryptocurrencies can therefore contribute towards more efficient remittance systems and enhance financial inclusion, particularly in economies with inefficient payment systems and underdeveloped infrastructures of traditional finance.

We build our analysis using both emerging theoretical approaches to infrastructures and ethnographic research. In this respect, we seek to lay the groundwork for future work by researchers in both political economy and economic anthropology. The chapter begins by examining the emergence of the digital financial inclusion paradigm, including the role of new communicative technologies in facilitating inclusive innovation practices. Next, it examines the "mobile money revolution" in East Africa, exploring in particular the central role of local practices of money management and user innovations in the success of that digital finance initiative. Building on the analysis of the impact of mobile money, it considers emerging practices of person-to-person payments based on blockchain technologies in developing economies. The chapter next examines the conceptually novel approaches to sending and receiving migrant remittances made possible by the blockchain technology, which include new digital forms of money, novel payment infrastructures, and new types of remittance actors such as fintech start-ups and other non-bank financial service providers. It demonstrates that the social meaning attached to actual financial practice helps to illuminate the broader impact of the digital financial technologies as they move through the material and human infrastructures.

Digital financial inclusion: towards "platformization" of financial innovation

Financial inclusion is increasingly emerging as both a development policy concern as well as a market opportunity for industry players in global finance. Traditionally defined by access to the formal banking system, the meaning of financial inclusion has been transformed by new technologies that offer financial functions at extremely low cost. There is an increasing recognition of the relevance of diverse institutions as players in financial inclusion, including various non-bank and non-financial institutions, as well as the informal sector. We now understand financial inclusion as occurring within a broader, interconnected financial ecosystem "of market actors and infrastructure needed for safe and efficient product delivery for the poor" (Ledgerwood, 2013). The concept of financial inclusion has been increasingly intertwined with the notions of innovation, interconnectedness, and institutional diversity in the recent development discourse. The Group of Twenty (G20) recently highlighted the role of financial inclusion in moving "towards an Innovative, Interconnected and Inclusive World Economy" (Global Partnership for Financial Inclusion, 2016), while affirming its commitment to assist the low-income developing countries in leveraging digital financial inclusion towards advancing the UN 2030 Sustainable Development Agenda.

This chapter contributes to conceptualizing the novel dynamic of financial inclusion that occurs with the growing role of technology in the circulation of credit in global finance. By involving masses of the global "unbanked" in novel financial access structures, digital financial inclusion has a potential to introduce new forms of disempowerment and marginality. Modern technology and the emerging "fintech–philanthrophy–development complex" that guides digital financial inclusion initiatives can facilitate novel opportunities for accumulation and exploitation through the use of digital financial access and data (Gabor and Brooks, 2017: 2). Gabor and Brooks contend that this new form of "financialized inclusion" of the global unbanked that is based on digital footprints can be used by states to render populations "legible" as well as generate financial assets for the emerging "digital elite" with little involvement from official development actors and actual consumers. Bernards (2016: 2) suggests attention to the "organization and forms of financial practice" and relevant political and institutional dimensions that emerge in local political struggles of the post-colony. Global regulatory projects such as financial inclusion are enacted in local spaces through articulation of a "complex network of local organizations, non-governmental organizations, international organizations and state institutions" (ibid.: 9) and defined by ambiguities between private and public interests, profit and social protection agendas. This also implies attention to the interaction of financial inclusion frameworks with the emerging economic informality.

We argue that the analysis of the impact and new connections emerging with spreading digital financial inclusion should consider a broad set of practices and actors involved in their actualization and governance. The social field of digital financial inclusion has been conceptualized as a "global assemblage of subjects, technics and rationalities that aim to develop poor-appropriate financial products and services" (Schwittay, 2011: 381), with attention at how diverse material, normative, and institutional elements "constitute a technical field fit to be governed and improved" (Li, 2007: 286). The assemblage approach to development interventions highlights the issue of agency – as exploring the work of situated subjects who "pull together" disparate elements "from an existing repertoire, a matter of habit, accretion, and bricolage" (ibid.: 265). Schwittay suggests more attention to "culturally grounded monetary practices and logics" (ibid.: 381) to overcome the quantitative focus on measuring impact and producing accountability, and to illuminate the growing tensions between the social mission of financial inclusion enterprise and the private accumulation logic of industry players (ibid.: 393).

These dilemmas are characteristic of the current era of global governance that is shaped by an increasing disaggregation of global political and regulatory processes, but also new opportunities for forging connections that redefine and expand the autonomy and sovereignty of individual actors. Slaughter (2004) suggests that the emerging global networks of regulators and legislators are leading towards a novel type of "networked world order" where sovereignty is "relational rather than insular" (ibid.: 188). This "disaggregated sovereignty" in the international system of government networks reaches beyond traditional autonomy and interdependence of various national and supranational entities, involving new types of connections defined by participation and agency – "the political ability to be an actor" within the networked order (ibid.: 187).

The rise of these novel nodes of connection highlights the intersection between new technologies and agency. Discussing the dimensions of technological emergence that are relevant for informed policy-making and governance, Rotolo, Hicks and Martin (2015) point out the need to incorporate qualitative research on human agency and "niche-regime dynamics" (see Chapter 1 of this volume for more discussion on emerging technologies).[2] As these technologies are characterized by uncertainty and ambiguity – regarding their future impact as well as meanings and importance attributed to them by different social groups – scientometric approaches produce only limited effectiveness (ibid.). This calls for a study of local practices and systems of inclusive innovation that occur in the contexts of spreading digital finance. The notion of "local innovation ecosystems" (Toivanen et al., 2012) entails viewing new technology infrastructures and the material aspects of technology diffusion in a dynamic interplay with local human and social resources. Driven by interactive learning and experimentation – "co-creation" and cooperation between different types of actors (ibid.: 12) – these ecosystems incorporate important social and cultural elements.

Digital financial initiatives are increasingly shaped by the financial technology (fintech) sector, which has effected profound changes in the financial industry landscape, particularly in emerging markets. The industry is disrupted and transformed by novel business models and partnerships. The emergence of fintech is accompanied by a disaggregation of various financial services and products from the traditional banking sector, but also new ways of consolidating and channeling these along new digital pathways. Particularly in developing countries, mobile platforms are increasingly consolidating payments, lending, investment, and micro-insurance services. This chapter argues that digital currencies are instrumental in the novel modes of platformization of global payment rails that increasingly shape financial services in low-income communities.

Digital financial platforms carry a powerful potential to integrate other actors and institutions in the predominantly cash economies of developing countries (see Kendall et al., 2012). Kendall et al. argue that mobile money platforms function as a network infrastructure that facilitates new forms of moving goods and services and new ways of integrating actors. Similarly to other ICT-based platforms, such as the Internet, they provide existing financial actors with new opportunities to "stimulate innovation and change existing business models," as well as "radically reconfigure how retail finance is done in developing countries" (ibid.: 49). By facilitating the exchange of cash and electronic value between diverse sets of actors, mobile money platforms become a novel type of communicative network with potential to affect and transform the financial system as well as a country's economy.

A novel ecosystem emerged around the mobile money platform in Kenya that includes both established financial institutions as well as innovative startups, ranging from "traditional banks, savings and credit cooperatives (SACCOs), and insurance providers to newer mobile-based credit, insurance and mobile savings offerings" (Kendall et al., 2012: 52). Mobile money has also given rise to new initiatives that provide connections between the established players and the digital currency platform. Kendall et al. pinpoint three types of engagement: "integrators" who add the electronic money channel to existing products; "innovators" who launch new products or ventures around mobile-money-based models; and "bridge builders" who create connections of mobile money platforms to financial and payment services.[3] This "platformization" of the financial environment highlights the catalytic powers of digital currencies and e-money to facilitate institutional integration in the Global South. It is particularly important to investigate the impact of the emerging connective nodes to the changing configurations of power and agency on local as well as global scales.

The emergence of digital technologies that reshape financial services and access infrastructures poses novel challenges to consumers as well as regulators. A new model of global governance of financial inclusion was outlined in the G20 Financial Inclusion Action Plan (FIAP), which emphasizes the need to integrate financial inclusion in the activities of global standard-setting bodies[4] and "increase understanding of the interdependence of financial inclusion, stability, integrity, and consumer protection" (GPFI, 2016: 6). As digital modes of financial inclusion involve a radical change in customer and financial data use and handling, data protection is critical. The complex digital technology platforms combine with a pervasive unfamiliarity of the low-income customers with the formal financial sector and customer rights (Lauer and Lyman, 2015). Customer concerns around digital finance platforms include the lack of transparency regarding fees and terms, poor customer recourse, and inadequate data protection (Zimmerman and Baur, 2015). Addressing these risks remains crucial, as the livelihoods of many low-income consumers involve chronic instability. The recent White Paper of the Global Partnership for Financial Inclusion (GPFI, 2016) calls for a coordinated collaboration between the global standard-setting bodies (SSBs) and country-based regulators in exploring challenges to financial data security, and the development of guidelines for financial technology companies. It also highlights some opportunities of blockchain applications for enhancing financial data protection and customer privacy.

Disrupting financial inclusion in East Africa: amplifying networks through mobile money platforms

In East Africa, traditional bank-based notions of financial inclusion have been largely superseded by the development of client-driven mobile money networks. While enabled by technology and services provided by large-scale telecom and IT hardware companies, it has been the actual practices of households and individuals – in many cases using mobile technologies to build on existing social practices and cultural norms – that have led to widespread access to core financial services (payments, credit, and savings). While these practices began largely outside the banking system, banks are now also using mobile money to provide lower-cost financial services, thus improving the opportunities for households that previously found the costs and practical challenges associated with brick-and-mortar banks to be daunting. In this section, we focus on the successful adoption of mobile-money-based financial inclusion in Kenya; similar stories can be told elsewhere, with other well-documented cases including Uganda and Tanzania. We contend that reflection on the successes and challenges of the adoption of mobile money – a form of digital finance that has rapidly become ubiquitous in many unbanked areas of the Global South – illuminates the potential role of cryptocurrencies in facilitating cross-border remittances and broadening financial inclusion in the developing world.

M-Pesa is one of the first and most successful mobile money initiatives in East Africa, and its inception and continued evolution provide instructive insights into the dynamics of digital financial networks and inclusive innovation in the Global South. M-Pesa is a system for small-scale electronic payment and store of value (up to $500) that is accessible through a simple feature phone. Customers can transfer money to other users, pay bills, and purchase mobile airtime credit by using text messages (SMS). There is a flat fee for most transactions. It is significant that Kenya's mobile money system was inspired by a local payment innovation – with the rise of mobile phones, people started forwarding pre-paid airtime to each other as currency.[5] The recipient could use it for calling, utilize it as credit at the local store, or turn it into cash by informal means (Maurer, 2015). M-Pesa is mostly used for person-to-person money transfers – Kenyan mobile-phone-based domestic remittances are triple of those in sub-Saharan Africa (Rosengard, 2016: 11). Other functions include retail payments for goods and agricultural services, receiving salaries and government funds, payment of utilities, as well as emerging savings and credit products that utilize the mobile money platform (e.g., M-Shwari). In 2015, M-Pesa had over 19 million subscribers in Kenya, with daily transactions of $150 million (Ochieng, 2016). M-Pesa has significantly impacted financial inclusion in the country – in ten years, from 2006–15, the number of adults using formal financial services almost tripled, rising from 27 percent to 75 percent (FinAccess, 2016).

The market success of M-Pesa has been attributed to certain economic, social, demographic, and regulatory conditions, but also to effective design and strategy that helped the platform scale up rapidly (Mas and Radcliffe, 2010). M-Pesa has managed to effectively balance regulation, financial inclusion, and innovation, without threatening the country's financial stability (Ndungu, 2017). It capitalizes on a flexible collaboration between the main actors of the mobile money ecosystem that included banks, telecommunications and fintech companies, regulators, as well as retail agents and consumers. At the time of the inception of the M-Pesa platform in 2007, its executor, Safaricom, held a dominant position in the country's telecommunications sector (with a 73 percent market share) and did not have to coordinate with other providers for interoperability (Rosengard, 2016). The Bank of Kenya was open to the experimentation by Safaricom with mobile financial access models, exempting the new mobile money platform from stringent KYC/AML rules and branch banking requirements with higher operation costs (Rosengard, 2016). Money transfers between individuals as well as institutional payments benefited from the 2006 Kenyan government legislative amendment to the communication law to "recognize electronic units of money" (Ndungu, 2017: 49). In the absence of the national payments and settlement law, the mobile money platform developed through the practicality of transactions and broader public acceptance of the service. The regulators also encouraged banking intermediation around M-Pesa virtual savings accounts, and cross-border remittances and payments were facilitated by appropriate provisions in the National Payments Act (ibid.). At the same time, the Bank of Kenya provided adequate measures of protection to consumers and the national payments system – by addressing cybersecurity concerns, establishing appropriate KYC measures in the form of national identity cards, and stipulating depositing of customer funds in prudentially regulated institutions (Rosengard, 2016).

Despite the unprecedented success in Kenya of M-Pesa's mobile money system, its telecom-led mobile banking model ("new products via existing delivery channels") is facing new competition from Airtel Money, a bank-led service ("existing products via new delivery channels") offered by Kenya's Equity Bank (Rosengard, 2016: 16).[6] Dynamic partnerships between banks and non-banks in Kenya are continuing at the present moment, as the Kenyan Bankers Association announced in February 2017 the planned launch of PesaLink, a banking-industry-based mobile money transfer platform that links customers' bank accounts via M-Pesa infrastructures.[7]

There is an increasing recognition that the rapid progress of mobile money transfer services in Africa has been facilitated by the central importance of informal credit networks in developing economies. Through its person-to-person money transfers, M-Pesa tapped into informal networks of mutuality and financial security – a market that was previously handled "through personal trips, friends, and public transport networks" (Mas and Radcliffe, 2010: 5). A large part of these transactions represented various reciprocal transfers within networks of relatives, friends, and business associates that functioned as mutual insurance. Mobile money services link into existing cycles and networks of reciprocity, rather than one-way money transfers or remittances (Jack et al., 2013: 357). Mobile money systems allow their users fuller integration with existing financial systems – which do not include just the formal sector – and expand their circle of debt and credit partners and networks of mutual obligations. In sum, mobile money has been empowering for East African households, by decreasing the cost of payments and remittances within existing networks and improving their efficiency, as well as opening up new opportunities to expand these networks. As Mas and Radcliffe suggest, the mobile money experience in Kenya could therefore highlight an alternative approach to financial inclusion as compared with the traditional credit- or savings-led model – the initial focus in low-income communities could be on establishing the "payment rails" for a broader set of financial services.

Digital finance in Africa building on local financial practices

The East African mobile money initiatives owe much of their success to their close correspondence to people's financial practices and money management needs. Studies of Kenyan low-income households highlight the unstable nature of household income and pivotal importance of remittances from social networks. The 2014 Kenyan Financial Diaries study[8] indicates that such external resources comprised 25 percent of the household total income and were particularly important for women (Zollmann, 2014: iv). Mobile money transfers from male migrant workers in Kenyan urban areas had a positive impact on the income of rural households as well as on women's empowerment (Morawczynski and Pickens, 2009).[9] Customers appreciated that the M-Pesa service enabled them to store small amounts of money[10] for daily consumption as well as emergencies (ibid.: 3). Negotiating credit at retail shops, market stalls, schools, hospitals, and diverse local savings groups was widespread (Zollmann, 2014: 11). Strategies to increase liquidity and gain credit centered around people's social networks and informal savings–credit groups. Not surprisingly, the main function of mobile money became mediating remittance transfers from other regions, but also moving money within local social networks. Morawczynski and Pickens indicate that M-Pesa money transfers in their relatively early stages already substantially increased money flows in Kenya, particularly in rural areas. Mobile money spread through the network effect of users and remitters once its effects to increased income inflows were understood.

These studies show that the adoption of digital finance is dependent on local practices and concepts of savings and debt. Mobile money taps into the relationships of mutuality that are central in the fiduciary culture among low-income Kenyans. While people relate to the oligopolistic formal banking sector on a more hierarchical basis, informal financial groups operate on the basis of equality (Johnson, 2014: 17). Mobile money transfers capitalize on long-term relationships of reciprocity that often function based on delayed returns. It provides more opportunities for risk-sharing among social networks, facilitating increasingly open-ended and diverse connections (ibid.: 18).

An important feature of these informal debt networks is their flexibility and negotiability (Johnson, 2014). Social networks have historically constituted an important avenue of resource access in African communities, where production and resource access have been plagued by chronic uncertainties (Berry, 1995). New opportunities that the money economy has brought have expanded that institutional diversity: "monetization has often been accompanied by the preservation or even multiplication of local institutions for obtaining credit or managing savings" (Berry, 1995: 309, in Rodima-Taylor, 2014). Mobile money serves to facilitate a further expansion of existing networks of mutuality that are central to local economies.[11]

Rodima-Taylor (2014) argues that there has been a recent rise in informal financial groups in African communities, and these institutions entail an apparent paradox of cooperation and sharing that occurs inside the expansion of money economy. The groups are seen as "hybrid organizational forms" that combine traditional as well as modern values, organizational templates, and resources, and where fragmented elements of formalization co-mingle with customary and kin-based norms and idioms (Rodima-Taylor, 2014). Although outwardly focusing on the egalitarian and peer-oriented dimensions of the collective activities, the groups also encouraged individual accumulation and advancement. As such local financial institutions and practices therefore entail a hybridity between the formal and informal, they challenge the conceptualization of financial inclusion as inevitable movement towards greater formalization and regulation. Instead, more attention is called to the interplay between local financial forms and practices, and the new institutions and technologies of spreading digital finance.

The mutual learning and experimentation characteristic to these new networks involves an increasingly diverse set of local and global actors – "mobile money professionals" that include people and organizations from diverse industries – development experts, researchers and programmers, investors, businesspeople and startup founders, NGO staff, regulators and policy-makers (Maurer, Nelms, and Rea, 2013: 53).[12] The role and functioning of local mobile money retail agents can be particularly illustrative of the dynamic of power and innovation occurring in these communicative networks. The agents – who serve as "cash-in/cash-out points" and mediate the "last mile" access as local shop-keepers or kiosk operators – represent the "human face" of the network (ibid.: 55). They use their social knowledge to manage and recruit clients, while simultaneously also representing banks, mobile network operators and regulators – thereby combining both mediating (transformative) and intermediary (acting on behalf of someone else) functions (ibid.; see also Latour, 2005). The agents exemplify the non-hierarchical dynamics of the network, but also the ambiguities it creates for agency and representation. Increasingly based on relationships between multiple actors, power and agency in the network are diffuse but more situational and politically motivated.

The emerging communicative infrastructures also facilitate changes in the meanings of money and payments by establishing new connections and relationships. Instead of consuming the product of mobile money, its users actively modify and remake this technology – for example, when using airtime minutes as money (Maurer, 2012). These increasing ambiguities about the nature of agency as well as money could end the "state monopolization of the means of exchange" and lead to the "democratization of the form and process of money as an open-ended, ongoing, socio-technical experiment" (ibid.: 592), as well as alter the form and process of financial inclusion. The new payments space is thereby characterized by "user-driven innovations" of a specific character, ensuing from the capacity of communication technologies to involve "an active state of readiness to forge new relations" (ibid.: 590). The study of the operation of money in these novel digital structures also calls more attention to the functioning of money as a means of payment – not merely as a neutral and depersonalized medium of exchange separate from its social context (Maurer, 2015). New payment technologies such as mobile money and cryptocurrencies can reveal new perspectives about money and its different roles and forms.

Blockchain technology: implications for trust, governance, and monetary pragmatics

The rapid diffusion of mobile money in East Africa suggests that developing economies are ripe targets for digital currencies as well. Just as mobile protocols were able to circumvent the existing challenges to financial inclusion by lowering transaction costs and speeding access, digital currencies appear to be well configured to solve additional challenges or to further drive down cost curves. In particular, digital currencies such as Bitcoin may be able to reduce concerns about abuse of market power by fintech monopolies or lower-level fraud, while also eliminating barriers and inefficiencies in cross-border transactions.

This chapter argues that the monetary innovation of Bitcoin involves novel technologies and infrastructures and new conceptualizations of money and value that elicit new forms of cooperation and collective action. Blockchain technologies promise solutions to the growing problems of public distrust with traditional financial institutions and transactions. In the blockchain-empowered system, where the traditional coupling of fiat with digital forms of bank credits and debits has been replaced by cryptocurrency, the database of transactions is shared by a network of autonomous computers and enables a novel and transparent approach to recording transactions and verifying information – a "trustless" and decentralized transaction system. Historical changes in trust-bearing and ledger-keeping institutions – from barter to digital finance – have shown us how systems of trust redefine tokens of money as mediums of exchange as well as stores of value (Casey and Dahan, 2016).[13] The novel decentralized trust protocols bring about changes not only in ledgers and record-keeping, but also in contract – the two "central legal devices of the modernity" (DuPont and Maurer, 2015: 4). The authors assert a connection between the systems of record keeping and modes of governance.[14] The new digital contracts as "self-executing law-like services" are managed and enforced without human intervention, altering the nature of social contracts as negotiable and grounded in uncertainty: in crypto-contracts, code replaces law (ibid.).

A blockchain-based system of self-executing contracts would therefore have potential to facilitate novel decentralized and participatory organizations and systems of governance. Wright and De Filippi (2015: 3) contend that blockchain applications would allow eliminating the regulatory and administrative "middlemen" and lead to novel participatory governance systems that can replicate "the benefits of the formal corporate structures, while at the same time maintaining the flexibility and scale of informal online groups." The new digital currency promises its followers both material and social values; the strengthening of the autonomy of the individual as well as a new peer-based community.

The practical effects of blockhain-based networks can be illustrated by analyzing how value is produced and distributed in the new peer-to-peer transfers (Mallard et al., 2014; Maurer, Nelms, and Swartz, 2013). Bitcoin occupies an ambiguous position between "commodity money" – currency as a material device that has an intrinsic value – and "credit money," where currency is a series of mutually accepted debts. It aims to break with the centralized lending authorities and their chains of guarantors, which are credit money features (Mallard et al., 2014: 6–7). At the same time, the monetary value of Bitcoin is also subject to the trust of its adherents in the decentralized community peers, affording it with credit aspects. Maurer et al. (2013: 263) indicate that this trust is embedded in the crypto-protocol, allowing for a peculiar combination of a "practical materialism" of Bitcoin with a "politics of community and trust." The authors contend that a dynamic dialectic between commodity money and credit money defines the essence of Bitcoin. The new evolving monetary pragmatics is grounded in trust embedded in technical code, but also shared among individuals using the system, and dependent on multiple infrastructures and institutions involved in its functioning.

Mallard et al. (2014: 2) point out that the emergence of trust in such systems occurs "through interactions between actors and technologies, transactions, discourses and debates, in several arenas ranging from governance to social interaction and technology implementation." While conventional networks are based on chains of belonging and cooperation, heterogenous networks also incorporate material and ideational elements that allow attention to the points in the web of actors where important connections are revealed and value conversions occur (Rodima-Taylor, 2016).

Bitcoin, remittances, and growing global mobility

This spatial and temporal heterogeneity of the novel digital ledger applications that affects the emerging monetary pragmatics of Bitcoin, particularly in low-income, non-Western societies, calls for a closer examination of diverse connections forged along the increasingly global digital pathways. The ambiguous alliance of new technologies and customary social money uses creates a hybrid combination of tradition and modernity, of expanding individual networks, and traditional kin and community values. We contend that this novel connective hybridity can be most clearly observed in the functioning of transnational remittance transfers and networks – an expression of family values and community loyalties in the novel context of rapidly growing global mobility; traditional payments moving along new payment rails.

Despite its potential to revolutionize global remittance transfers, the use of Bitcoin for cross-border remittances faces several regulatory, institutional, and logistical challenges. This section explores these in the example country cases from Asia and Africa. It argues that the emerging digital currency space is increasingly recognized and regulated on national and international levels by the means of the transmission of that currency through person-to-person payment rails – one could say that Bitcoin is increasingly legally defined as remittance.

The regulation of the remittance transfer industry is still largely defined by the consequences of the recent "de-risking" movement that began as a 2013 initiative of the US Department of Justice to investigate the banking activities of companies deemed as posing high risk. This resulted in many commercial banks closing the accounts of the correspondent banks and remittance companies in developing countries. While the initiative formally ended in 2015, many banks remain cautious of doing business with money transfer companies. US-based digital currency companies also face burdensome federal and local regulation. The law of digital currency in the United States is governed by two regimes: money transmitter regulation of the Department of the Treasury's Financial Crimes Enforcement Network (FinCEN), and securities regulation of the Securities and Exchange Commission (Santori, 2013). Businesses transacting Bitcoin are designated as money services businesses and have to follow FinCEN's Anti-Money-Laundering and Know-Your-Customer policies (AML/KYC). As they have to collect identifying customer information and report suspicions of criminal activity, the regulation potentially conflicts with the inherent nature of privacy and anonymity of Bitcoin transactions (Santori, 2013). Fintech companies do have the option of applying to be regulated as "special purpose banks," which offers some additional flexibility.[15] Still at present, only three US Bitcoin exchanges have been issued the license (Circle, Ripple, and Coinbase).

Although US regulations appear burdensome to potential digital money transfer companies, the United States remains one of the few countries in the world that has made systematic efforts to regulate digital currencies.[16] In many emerging economies, digital currencies continue to be regarded with distrust. The Central Bank of Kenya recently cautioned citizens about Bitcoin's status as "unregulated currency" – a caution typical to many central banks. Meanwhile, recent regulatory developments in the Philippines (an economy highly dependent on remittances) demonstrate some of the developing country ambivalence about digital currency. In February 2017, the Central Bank of the Philippines (BSP) published guidelines for Bitcoin exchanges, de facto designating these as a form of a remittance company. The new money transfer businesses are required to apply for a Certificate of Registration and also register with the country's Anti-Money Laundering Council Secretariat. BSP positioned these new regulations of cryptocurrency exchanges "from the perspective of anti-money laundering and financial stability."[17] It emphasized that its intention was not to endorse Bitcoin as a currency as it "is neither issued or guaranteed by a central bank nor backed by any commodity."

Bitcoin remittances are subject to various constraints relating to financial market ecosystems, liquidity, as well as price volatility. There are several components to a cross-border Bitcoin remittance corridor: in most cases, the "first mile" remittance outlets or online services where migrant remittance senders deposit their remittances; and the "last mile" partner who receives the money and client details, and forwards the payment to the payout channels. The payout channels can include banks, post offices, and various local cash pickup outlets (jewelry stores, pawnbrokers, etc.) (Buenaventura, 2017). Thus, corridors utilize Bitcoin only as a "middle" currency to facilitate instant settlement and avoid going through the international wire transfer system. The problems in that chain frequently lie with the last mile partner, which may not have enough Bitcoin liquidity to convert the incoming remittances to local currency (ibid.).

The institutional partnership issues in these digital ecosystems are most clearly revealed in interfacing with existing money delivery businesses and pathways. Particularly in countries with large migrant populations, there exist multiple ways for local delivery of transnational remittances – including retail stores, mobile money wallets, courier delivery, and collection in physical bank branches. While this redundancy may make markets less vulnerable to disruption, the lack of a clear "market leader" can challenge local-level integration for remittance transfer operators (Allison, 2016; Buenaventura, 2014). Existing service charges may still apply – for example, in the Philippines, Bitcoin-based remittance services continue to operate along the "last mile" rails of traditional remittance outlets that have no incentive to lower their fees for cryptocurrency transfers.[18]

Partnering with mobile money networks for local delivery can be essential for the success of cryptocurrency-based remittance systems, but this raises new challenges since Bitcoin remittance startups must acquire enough customers to take advantage of network effects. Paradoxically, integrating with such platforms for local distribution may only be feasible in areas of already existing viable mobile money ecosystems, but this may also reduce the scalability of the business model and its adaptiveness in different contexts (Breloff and Bond, 2015). On the other hand, well-functioning international remittance services can add to the viability of domestic mobile money platforms and could incentivize mobile money companies to seek such partnerships.

There has been extensive experimentation with Bitcoin-based remittance transfers in South-East Asian remittance markets in recent years. Cryptocurrency remittance markets are particularly developed in the Philippines and in Vietnam (where the Bitcoin company Bitcoin Vietnam operates a remittance platform, cash2vn).[19] The Philippines is the third-largest remittance recipient in the world, receiving an estimated US\$27.5 billion in 2014 (Buenaventura, 2017). Multiple cryptocurrency companies have entered the Philippines remittance market, offering easy and convenient ways for transacting Bitcoin by utilizing both bank and non-bank institutions to access the services. Among the country's best known Bitcoin-based remittance initiatives are the mobile wallet-based coins.ph, which runs on blockchain technology, and a remittance platform Rebit.ph (Satoshi Citadel Industries). Coins.ph has a network of 17,000 locations in the Philippines (which is more than the number of bank offices and branches in the country), collaborating in remittance delivery with banks and a variety of licensed local retail agents. The mobile payments company provides remittance transfer services and institutional and retail payments by means of Bitcoin and Philippine pesos. Facilitating international remittance transfers via Bitcoin medium, it bypasses high exchange rate margins and fees of traditional remittance operators.[20] (The transaction fees of coins.ph range from 1–3 percent, instead of the 7–8 percent traditional remittance fees.[21])

The growing popularity of Bitcoin in the Philippines could be explained by the inefficiencies of the formal financial sector in expanding financial access as well as high remittance transfer fees of traditional channels. Despite the recent rapid economic growth, financial inclusion in the country remains limited, and migrant remittances are central to local livelihoods. Only about a third of the adult population keeps their savings in a bank account (Bangko Sentral ng Pilipinas – BSP, 2015). Migrant senders and remittance receivers have been increasingly relying on local remittance transfer outlets over formal banking services. It has been estimated that there are over 11,000 remittance outlets in the country. Digital finance is increasingly seen as a tool to enhance financial inclusion as well as encourage e-commerce and empower small businesses in the Philippines. The central bank has facilitated experimentation with digital financial services and encouraged the entry of non-bank companies to the financial services arena.

The crypto-remittance company Bitpesa in Africa is an illustrative case of both the challenges and potentials of digital global payment rails within changing financial inclusion ecosystems. Bitpesa sought to revolutionize African cross-border remittance space by providing fast, transparent, and low-cost cryptocurrency remittance services. It facilitates a Bitcoin-based digital currency platform alongside a network of global foreign currency brokers. Its customers include small businesses and enterprises as well as individuals who send money from developed and emerging economies (including the UK, US, and China) to Sub-Saharan Africa. The company is currently operating in Nigeria, Kenya, Uganda, Tanzania, Senegal, and the Democratic Republic of Congo. Its coverage spans over 85 countries, and the company has integrated with six mobile platforms and 60 banks. The traditional banking sector in Kenya has limited outreach, particularly among low-income and rural populations. Other remittance actors in Kenya include large international money transfer operators, such as Western Union and MoneyGram, which have a globally well-established customer base, as well as local and regional mobile network operators such as M-Pesa and Airtel (MIT, 2016). Western Union and MoneyGram deduct $10–17 to wire $200 to Kenya from the US, including charges to exchange funds, in a process that can take anything from an hour to five days.[22] Bitpesa employs a flat transaction fee of only 2 percent, compared with an average 12 percent cost of traditional remittance transfers in the continent. These fees are possible as the Bitcoin-based remittance services bypass traditional intermediaries such as correspondent banks and their high fees in many less competitive corridors.[23] Engaging in Africa–Asia remittance corridors, Bitpesa has created cost-effective ways for individuals and businesses to transfer payments in local currency from African bank accounts to Chinese bank accounts, without relying on the US dollar as an intermediary currency. Despite the inherent appeal of low-cost digital remittances, however, Bitpesa has yet to make a significant impact. In 2015, Bitpesa transmitted $2.7 million of an estimated $32 billion African remittance market, generating revenue of $67,000 (MIT 2016).

Because the regulatory framework around cryptocurrencies is still emerging in many African states, compliance continues to pose challenges, as demonstrated by a recent regulatory controversy in Kenya's $1.5 billion remittance market. A number of legal disputes have occurred between digital currency operators and Kenyan authorities over the implications of Bitcoin to AML/KYC regulations. In 2015, the Central Bank of Kenya issued a statement that the operations of the Bitcoin platform Bitpesa did not fall under the purview of the money transfer and remittance regulations of the Central Bank of Kenya, finding instead that Bitcoin was an unregulated currency.[24] In response, Safaricom suspended its collaboration with an M-Pesa affiliated payments platform that was utilized by Bitpesa,[25] arguing that its activities were not in compliance with Kenyan AML laws.[26]

Bitpesa and other Bitcoin competitors have faced regulatory challenges and the lack of a viable local cryptocurrency ecosystem as existing players in the remittance market have been reluctant to expand into Bitcoin-based platforms. For example, Kipochi, a cryptocurrency remittance platform, integrated with Safaricom's M-Pesa network in 2014, but ceased its activities within a year.[27] Bitpesa does remain active in several African countries, including Kenya, and has successfully expanded to West Africa. However, its primary focus is no longer on private remittances, but digital business-to-business payments, including serving as a platform for wholesale remittance companies. Perhaps the most developed jurisdiction for digital currency is South Africa, which has several Bitcoin exchanges and platforms for services such as utility payments.[28]

The market position of crypto-companies such as Bitpesa is also affected by fintech players that provide support services, the most important of which are payment aggregators. Payment aggregators are companies that facilitate the "collection, disbursement, and circulation of digital payments across multiple payment providers." Aggregators enable payment instrument providers – such as mobile money services, credit card companies, or banks offering mobile banking – cost-efficient integration with entities that send money to or receive money from end customers (McKay and Pillai, 2016). Most of the aggregators in the East African mobile money landscape are ICT companies that provide value-added services to banks and mobile network operators, such as running switches, providing forex and settlement services, and coordinating the services of merchants and agents (Realini and Mehta, 2015: 61–2). Other important but little-known actors in the global cryptocurrency chains include smaller wholesale remittance companies in diaspora communities, shaping the evolving transnational payment rails through social and cultural knowledge. Diaspora communities and businesses are the main customers of these startups.[29]

In the country cases discussed above, the rapid rise of Bitcoin as a competitive player in the diverse cross-border remittance market in the Philippines could be largely attributed to the effective (albeit constantly challenged) partnerships of the crypto-remittance companies with the existing local distribution channels, which were diverse and widespread, taking care of the "last mile" issue. Mobile money platforms frequently invest heavily in the last mile infrastructure, then establish exclusive control and use rights.[30] In the case of Bitpesa in Kenya, the failure of partnering with the effective but monopolistic M-Pesa delivery infrastructure could be seen as a central reason for the Bitcoin company to shift its activities geographically as well as refocus from individual remitters to businesses as their main customer group.

Thus, the success of crypto-remittances depends on the existence of robust money delivery infrastructures in the area, as well as effective partnering with them. This also suggests that crypto-remittance companies could be more competitive in environments with a diversity of established delivery channels and outlets, as monopolistic delivery markets may currently not have enough incentives to include crypto-startups in their activities. The widely existing exclusivity arrangements of many banks and telecommunications companies involved in cross-border remittance delivery are among the main impediments to crypto-remittances in many parts of the developing world (Overseas Development Institute, 2014; Financial Sector Deepening Africa, 2017). Much of this is driven by regulation, including AML/KYC rules in developed economies and competition policies in developing economies. To make digital financial transfers (including both e-money as well as cryptocurrencies) work in developing economies, a "tiered" approach to KYC rules has been advocated when working with the unbanked – a regulatory innovation that still remains to be implemented in many areas of the developing world.[31]

Development experts and donor organizations advocate a risk-based approach to customer identification strategies that facilitates financial inclusion of culturally and socially diverse financial norms and institutions (including Islamic finance) (FSD Africa, 2017; Gelbard et al., 2014). The impact of regulation to innovation is particularly pronounced in underdeveloped financial markets, where it coordinates the input of the fragmented and fragile private sector (FSD Africa, 2017). However, regulation must also be understood as political in nature; in order to understand the choices made in a given country, it is essential to delve more deeply into legal systems, macroeconomic management, and patterns of ownership, among other factors. While this task is beyond the scope of this chapter, it offers a fertile research agenda for scholars of comparative public policy.

Digital payment rails in the networked world order: concluding remarks

Bitcoin has a theoretical potential to profoundly transform the ways people transfer and use money, and associate with each other and broader social institutions. The legal definition as well as social conceptualization of digital currencies occur mainly as based on their movement through payment infrastructures – cryptocurrencies are often defined through their role as remittances or person-to-person payments. Because of the profound inefficiencies of traditional remittance systems in many developing economies, the remittance industry has been ripe for disruption through the blockchain technology. Remittances also often serve as an important entry-point to the formal financial system in cash-based economies.

The emerging concept of digital financial inclusion captures the increasing relevance of mobile-money-based domestic transfers as well as cryptocurrency-based cross-border remittances in the livelihoods of many developing economies. It also highlights a possible paradigm change in the financial inclusion concept, which instead of savings- or credit-led models is now increasingly focused on the establishment of digital payment rails for broader financial access. This new model builds on an increasing recognition of the ubiquitous informal networks of mutual obligation and debt in developing economies, as well as their role in integrating and transforming financial inclusion initiatives.

The discussions of the chapter demonstrated the capacities of e-money and digital currencies to amplify and transform existing reciprocal networks of person-to-person transfers and exchange. Evidence from East Africa showed that mobile money services link into existing cycles and networks of reciprocity, as well as alter social relationships by bringing about more impersonal bases of exchange. Digital financial services enabled their users a fuller integration into the financial system that encompassed both the formal and informal sectors. They also facilitated a transformation and democratization of the financial inclusion phenomenon through enhanced local participation and innovation.

The innovation ecosystems that emerged around mobile and digital currencies built on local knowledge and patterns of resource management, cultural monetary practices, and customary kin and community values. The discussions revealed how actors in these ecosystems assembled diverse material and normative elements belonging to different repertoires and regimes of value, and how new economic and financial elements and functions emerged from that creative *bricolage*. Local retail agents and outlets constituted an important part of the digital finance innovation ecosystem, and their dual functions of mediation and representation illustrated the ambiguities that digital finance networks pose for agency and participation. As indicated, many of the hybrid organizational forms prevalent in local developing economies combine peer-oriented and egalitarian dimensions with new forms of individual advancement. Similar duality characterizes the promise of the digital currencies of decentralized resource management and governance systems that advance novel forms of individual autonomy based on crypto-code and smart contract, while heralding a new peer-based community. That necessitates more attention to the interplay of the contingent knowledges of local monetary pragmatics, and new institutions and technologies in emerging digital finance assemblages.

The communicative network of digital payment rails could be seen as illustrative of a broader dynamic of an emergent "networked world order" (Slaughter, 2004), where global governance is shaped by a growing disaggregation of actors and processes, but also by a new type of relational sovereignty stemming from connections forged through participation and agency. As seen, the digital payments space includes a multiplicity of global and national standard-setting bodies, development agencies and experts, funders and philanthropists, financial institutions, fintech companies, retail agents, and consumers. The emerging financial technology landscape brings along a novel type of disaggregation of financial services, but also new forms of consolidation of these along digital financial platforms. These platforms function as a network infrastructure with a potential to integrate other actors and institutions, as the analysis of mobile money systems in East Africa revealed. The digital networks are amplified but also instilled with new qualities through that process of "platformization," where new services, actors, and modes of business are added on to existing templates, stimulating innovation and user-based initiatives. The chapter contends that digital and e-currencies are instrumental in the new modes of platformization of global payment rails that increasingly shape financial inclusion in low-income communities.

The challenges and potentials inherent in the digital concept of financial inclusion highlight the centrality of novel institutional partnerships and new connections between the local and the global. They also call for a systematic study of local practices and systems of inclusive innovation that occur in the contexts of spreading digital finance. Both mobile money and digital currencies multiply existing networks of credit and reciprocity and facilitate novel connections and transfer chains. They disrupt financial inclusion and the traditional financial sector by involving novel types of actors and forms of partnership, with a potential to change the power balance among traditional financial institutions. As the still novel digital-currency-based remittance transfers are introduced and embedded in a growing number of global remittance corridors, regulators, policy-makers, and development experts need to pay attention to fostering competitive markets and sustainable institutional partnerships.

This chapter describes a situation where informal financial practices and financial inclusion initiatives in the Global South are increasingly intermingling with new communication infrastructures. As noted, the adoption of digital finance in East African communities may have been motivated by the opportunity to expand networks of mutual obligation, rather than the advantages of the more efficient money transfer and savings options provided by the digital money platform. In these new currency ecosystems, researchers should focus on how inclusive innovation practices arise within the emerging network dynamics of digital transactions. By more fully understanding the emerging meanings of the circulating digital currency, we can better analyze their broader social and political governance effects.

Acknowledgments

The authors of this chapter would like to thank the volume editor Malcolm Campbell-Verduyn for his valuable advice and insights, and the participants of the "Bitcoin and Beyond" workshop (Balsillie School of International Affairs, February 27, 2017) for providing a stimulating venue for discussions that inspired the revisions of this chapter. We also thank participants of the panel discussion on Digital Remittances in Crisis-Affected Contexts at the International Monetary Fund in October 2015, where earlier versions of the chapter material were presented.

Notes

1 The "de-risking" movement that started in 2013 with a purpose to investigate the banking activities of companies deemed as posing high risk resulted in many commercial banks closing the accounts of the correspondent banks and remittance companies in developing countries.

2 Rotolo et al. (2015: 1840) define emerging technologies as

> a relatively fast growing and radically novel technology characterized by a certain degree of coherence persisting over time and with the potential to exert a considerable impact on the socio-economic domain(s) which is observed in terms of the composition of actors, institutions and the patterns of interactions among those, along with the associated knowledge production processes.

3 An example of innovators includes the Equity Bank's M-Kesho product that is a deposits and savings bank product linked with M-Pesa. Innovators include many new savings, credit, and insurance products that utilize the existing mobile money platform (e.g., a new person product of Jua Kali, the association of informal workers). Bridge builders include software developers and other specialists who facilitate mobile money connections with established financial institutions, or build interoperability with other digital payments providers (ibid.).

4 The GPFI 2016 White Paper outlines standards and guidance to the following global bodies:

> the Financial Stability Board (FSB), which exists as a coordinating body of SSBs with respect to financial stability, and six SSBs: the Basel Committee for Banking Supervision (BCBS), the primary SSB for supervisors of banks and other deposit-taking institutions; the Committee on Payments and Market Infrastructures (CPMI), the primary SSB with respect to payment systems, including retail payment systems; the Financial Action Task Force (FATF), the SSB responsible for protecting the integrity of financial systems by preventing financial crime, particularly through standards and guidance on anti-money laundering and combating financing of terrorism (AML/CFT); the International Association of Deposit Insurers (IADI), the SSB for deposit insurance systems; the International Association of Insurance Supervisors (IAIS), the primary SSB for insurance supervision; and the International Organization of Securities Commissions (IOSCO), the primary SSB for the securities sector.
>
> (GPFI, 2016: xii)

5 At first, M-Pesa started as a platform for microfinance loans, utilizing airtime vendors as entry points to the payment system. It gradually grew into a complex platform for person-to-person as well as retail payments by means of forwarding value via text messages (Maurer, 2015).

6 Due to regulatory, socio-economic, and institutional conditions, country contexts can significantly differ. The M-Pesa platform that was launched in Tanzania in 2008 by Vodacom has recently overcome the challenges caused by prevalent interoperability and multi-agent networks. In South Africa, however, M-Pesa services were recently discontinued – possibly because of the existence of an advanced and inclusive banking sector, and regulatory reasons (Rosengard, 2016: 21).

7 https://citizentv.co.ke/business/banks-cut-out-middleman-with-pesalink-launch-158005/

8 The Kenyan Financial Diaries research project (FSD Kenya) aimed at a comprehensive overview of people's money use patterns and financial inclusion needs, recording the transactions of 300 low-income households in five locations of the country over the period of a year.

9 The 2009 study highlighted the cost-effectiveness and convenience of mobile domestic remittances over other available transfer options: "sending 1,000 Ksh (US$13.06) through M-PESA cost US$0.39, which is 27 percent cheaper than the post office's PostaPay (US$0.52), and 68 percent cheaper than sending it via a bus company (US$1.16)" (2).

10 "Small money" refers to "deposits ranging from 100 Ksh (US$1.30) to 1,000 Ksh (US$13.00), or approximately one week's wages" (3).

11 Among Tanzanian micro-entrepreneurs, mobile telephony led to the emergence of "socio-technical capital" – "productive resources which inhere in patterns of social relations that are maintained with the support of information and communication technologies" (Molony, 2009: 78). Molony argues that this novel form of social capital that is facilitated by the means of ICT applications helped African micro-entrepreneurs to expand their customer base and move from personal towards impersonal exchange.

12 The global centers of expertise on mobile money include the Consultative Group to Assist the Poor (CGAP), the GSMA or global trade association of telecommunication

providers, the Bill and Melinda Gates Foundation, the International Finance Corporation (IFC), USAID and some other bilateral development agencies, various IT and design firms, and payments industry firms – including major card networks as well as small startups or third-party payment providers (54).

13 The contemporary traditional banking model includes a hybrid of commercial banks as "dispersed and fragmented" nodes of ledger keeping, and the central bank operating as a "trust backstop" (ibid.).

14 With the historical evolvement of double-entry ledger systems and public accounting manuals, the systems of data management became a "vehicle for promoting emerging mercantile power against the King's traditional rule" (11) – by making ledger systems public, they were turned into powerful tools of governance and political restructuring.

15 www.orrick.com/Insights/2016/12/National-Bank-Charters-for-Fintech-Companies

16 Please see the chapter by Campbell-Verduyn and Goguen in this volume for more details about the impact of the global anti-money-laundering regime on blockchain applications.

17 www.coindesk.com/philippines-just-released-new-rules-bitcoin-exchanges/

18 https://medium.com/cryptonight/bitcoin-doesn-t-make-remittances-cheaper-eb5f437 849fe#.shqxjn4d3

19 www.cash2vn.com/

20 http://asia.nikkei.com/Politics-Economy/Economy/Asia-has-all-the-ingredients-for-a-fintech-revolution

21 http://fintechnews.sg/5978/philippines/top-24-fintech-startups-forbes-philippines/

22 The World Bank Send Money Africa database.

23 www.forbes.com/sites/laurashin/2016/06/15/elizabeth-rossiello-describes-how-bitpesa-slashes-international-payment-fees/#105259c6475d

24 www.cryptocoinsnews.com/telecombitpesa-legal-tangle-aml-threatens-mobile-payments-kenya/

25 The partnership between the companies allowed customers to convert Bitcoin into Kenyan shillings for remittances and retail payments.

26 www.cryptocoinsnews.com/central-bank-kenya-threatened-bitcoin/

27 https://motherboard.vice.com/en_us/article/the-western-myth-of-bitcoin-in-kenya

28 https://bitcoinmagazine.com/articles/cash-still-trumps-mobile-payments-and-bitcoin-in-africa-1481148103/

29 E. Rossiello, CEO of Bitpesa, January 2017, interview with the author.

30 E. Rossiello, CEO of Bitpesa, January 2017, interview with the author.

31 While presenting new challenges in the areas of customer verification, digital finance technologies also carry a promise of enhanced transparency and monitoring not only of the identities of money senders and receivers, but also transactions. A new "Know Your Transaction" paradigm enabled by the immutable blockchain technology could enable an "unprecedented level of forensic analysis to be carried out on the transactions themselves" (Buenaventura, 2017: 26).

Bibliography

Allison, I. (2016). *Cross-border payments experts debate Bitcoin remittances*. Retrieved August 24, 2017, from www.ibtimes.co.uk/cross-border-payments-experts-debate-bitcoin-remittances-1561983

Bangko Sentral ng Pilipinas (BSP). (2015). *National Baseline Survey on Financial Inclusion*.

Bayen M., and Ajadi, S. (2017, January 13). *Building synergies: How mobile operators and start-ups can partner for impact in emerging markets*. Retrieved August 24, 2017, from www.gsma.com/mobilefordevelopment/programme/ecosystem-accelerator/building-synergies-how-mobile-operators-and-start-ups-can-partner-for-impact-in-emerging-markets

Bernards, N. (2016). The International Labour Organization and the ambivalent politics of financial inclusion in West Africa. *New Political Economy, 21*(6): 606–20.

Berry, S. (1995). Stable prices, unstable values: Some thoughts on monetization and the meaning of transactions in West African economies. In J.I. Guyer (ed.), *Money matters*. Chicago: University of Chicago Press.

Breloff, P., and Bond, J. (2015). *Picking winners in the great remittance disruption.* Washington, DC: CGAP.

Buenaventura, L. (2017). *Reinventing remittances with Bitcoin.* Singapore: Bloom Solutions.

Buenaventura, L. (2014). *The short-term view on Bitcoin remittances.* Retrieved August 24, 2017, from www.coindesk.com/short-term-view-bitcoin-remittances/

Casey, M., and Dahan, M. (2016). *Blockchain technology: Redefining trust for a global, digital economy.* Retrieved August 24, 2017, from https://medium.com/mit-media-lab-digital-currency-initiative/blockchain-technology-redefining-trust-for-a-global-digital-economy-1dc869593308

DuPont, Q., and Maurer, B. (2015, June 23). Ledgers and law in the blockchain. *King's Review.* http://kingsreview.co.uk/articles/ledgers-and-law-in-the-blockchain/.

FinAccess. (2016). *2016 FinAccess household survey.* Nairobi: FSD Kenya.

Financial Sector Deepening Africa. (2017). *Financing the frontier: Inclusive financial sector development in fragility-affected states in Africa.* Report. Nairobi: FSD Africa.

Gabor, D., and Brooks, S. (2017). The digital revolution in financial inclusion: International development in the fintech era. *New Political Economy, 22*(4): 423–36.

Gelbard, E., Hussain, M., Maino, R., Mu, Y., and Yehoue, E. (2014). *Islamic finance in Sub-Saharan Africa: Status and prospects.* Washington, DC: International Monetary Fund.

Global Partnership for Financial Inclusion. (2016). *Global standard setting bodies and financial inclusion: The evolving landscape.* Washington, DC: GPFI.

Global Partnership for Financial Inclusion. (2014). *Digital financial inclusion and the implications for customers, regulators, supervisors and standard-setting bodies.* Issues Paper. Washington, DC: GPFI.

GSMA. (2014). *2013 state of the industry report on mobile financial services for the unbanked.* London: GSMA.

Jack, W., Ray, A., and Suri, T. (2013). Transaction networks: Evidence from mobile money in Kenya. *American Economic Review, 103*(3): 356–61.

Johnson, S. (2014). *Informal financial practices and social networks: Transaction genealogies.* Nairobi: FSD Kenya.

Kendall, J., Machoka, P., Veniard, C., and Maurer, B. (2012). An emerging platform: From money transfer system to mobile money ecosystem. *Innovations, 6*(4): 49–64.

Latour, B. (2005). *Reassembling the social: Introduction to actor-network theory.* Oxford: Oxford University Press.

Lauer, K., and Lyman, T. (2015). *Digital financial inclusion: Implications for customers, regulators, supervisors, and standard setting bodies.* Washington, DC: CGAP.

Ledgerwood, J. (2013). *The new microfinance handbook: A financial market system perspective.* Washington, DC: World Bank.

Li, T. (2007). Practices of assemblage and community forest management. *Economy and Society, 36*(2): 263–93.

Mallard, A., Méadel, C., and Musiani, F. (2014). The paradoxes of distributed trust: Peer-to-peer architecture and user confidence in Bitcoin. *Journal of Peer Production, 4.*

Mas, I., and Radcliffe, D. (2010). *Mobile payments go viral: M-PESA in Kenya.* Seattle: Bill and Melinda Gates Foundation.

Maurer, B. (2015). *How would you like to pay? How technology is changing the future of money.* Durham, NC: Duke University Press.

Maurer, B. (2012). Mobile money: Communication, consumption and change in the payments space. *Journal of Development Studies, 48*(5): 589–604.

Maurer, B., Nelms, T., and Rea, S. (2013). "Bridges to cash": Channeling agency in mobile money. *Journal of the Royal Anthropological Institute, 19*(1): 52–74.

Maurer, B., Nelms, T., and Swartz, L. (2013). "When perhaps the real problem is money itself!": The practical materiality of Bitcoin. *Social Semiotics, 23*(2): 261–77.

McKay, C., and Pillai, R. (2016). *Aggregators: The secret sauce to digital financial expansion.* Washington DC: CGAP. Retrieved August 24, 2017, from www.cgap.org/blog/aggregators-secret-sauce-digital-financial-expansion

MIT. (2016). *Exploring the competitive landscape.* Example Project Group 11, Module 4. Boston: MIT.

Molony, T. (2009). Carving a niche: ICT, social capital, and trust in the shift from personal to impersonal trading in Tanzania. *Information Technology for Development, 15*(4): 283–302.

Morawczynski, O., and Pickens, M. (2009). *Poor people using mobile financial services: Observations on customer usage and impact from M-PESA.* Washington, DC: CGAP.

Ndungu, N. (2017). Regulatory environment and technological innovation in Africa. In Brookings Institution (ed.) *Boosting transformational technology.* Report. Washington, DC: Brookings Institution.

Ochieng, L. (2016, April 27). M-Pesa reports 27 pc jump in global users to 25 million. *Daily Nation.*

Overseas Development Institute. (2014). *Lost in intermediation: How excessive charges undermine the benefits of remittances for Africa.* London: ODI.

Radcliffe, D., and Voorhies, R. (2012). *A digital pathway to financial inclusion.* Seattle: Bill and Melinda Gates Foundation.

Realini, C., and Mehta, K. (2015). *Financial inclusion at the bottom of the pyramid.* Altona, Canada: FriesenPress.

Rodima-Taylor, D. (2016). Gathering up mutual help: Work, personhood, and relational freedoms in Tanzania and Melanesia. In K. Myhre (ed.) *Cutting and connecting: 'Afrinesian' perspectives on networks, relationality, and exchange.* New York, Oxford: Berghahn.

Rodima-Taylor, D. (2014). Passageways of cooperation: Mutuality in post-socialist Tanzania. *Africa: The Journal of the International African Institute, 84*(4): 553–75.

Rodima-Taylor, D. (ed.) (2013). *Remittance flows to post-conflict states: Perspectives on human security and development.* Boston: Boston University.

Rosengard, J. (2016). *A quantum leap over high hurdles to financial inclusion: The mobile banking revolution in Kenya.* Working Paper. Cambridge, MA: Harvard Kennedy School.

Rotolo, D., Hicks, D., and Martin, B. (2015). What is an emerging technology? *Research Policy, 44*(10): 1827–43.

Santori, M. (2013). *Bitcoin law: What U.S. businesses need to know.* Retrieved August 24, 2017, from www.coindesk.com/bitcoin-law-what-us-businesses-need-to-know/

Schwittay, A. (2011). The financial inclusion assemblage: Subjects, technics, rationalities. *Critique of Anthropology, 31*(4): 381–401.

Slaughter, A. (2004). Disaggregated Sovereignty: Towards the Public Accountability of Global Government Networks. *Government and Opposition 39*(2): 159–190.

Toivanen, H., Mutafungwa, E., Hyvönen, J., and Ngogo, E. (2012). *Pro-poor social and economic opportunities in the African ICT innovation ecosystem.* Finland: VTT Technical Research Center of Finland.

World Bank. (2016). Migration and Development Brief 26.

Wright, A., and De Filippi, P. (2015). Decentralized blockchain technology and the rise of lex cryptographia. Available at SSRN: https://ssrn.com/abstract=2580664

Zimmerman, J., and Baur, S. (2015). *Understanding how consumer risks in digital social payments can erode their financial inclusion potential.* Washington, DC: CGAP.

Zollman, J. (2014). *Kenya financial diaries – Shilingi kwa shilingi, the financial lives of the poor.* Nairobi: FSD Kenya.

7 Governing what wasn't meant to be governed

A controversy-based approach to the study of Bitcoin governance

Francesca Musiani, Alexandre Mallard, and Cécile Méadel

Introduction

Is it possible to implement trustworthy governance mechanisms for Bitcoin – the technology that, by design and by manifesto, "was not meant to be governed" to begin with?[1] This question has been raised several times since the creation of Bitcoin, which has been presented as an "alternative" currency circumventing state-backed financial and economic institutions. It is no coincidence that Bitcoin's birth and swift rise took place at the very moment in recent history, 2008, when the worldwide financial crisis exposed the shortcomings and unsavory inner workings of the global financial system. Not meant to be controlled by any central authority, Bitcoin's monetary supply is shaped and defined by its name-sake protocol – its cornerstone being that from the inception of the system, the total amount of Bitcoins that could ever be created was known and established in advance (21 million), and so was their generation rate over time. The generation of Bitcoins is based on an activity called mining, based on the principle that Bitcoins are assigned as a reward to those users – the miners – that lend their computing and hard-disk resources to the system for operational and security purposes. The establishment of the system's functioning as "purely" technical, as mentioned, was strictly related to the alleged aim of wiping corruption and "human-made" dangerous and speculative practices from finance and markets. Banks and states could not be trusted anymore, opening the way to a trustless, cryptography-reliant, architecture-based solution. However – and as we have explored in previous work (Mallard et al., 2014) – when Bitcoin started becoming a global network and raised interest and business opportunities for a variety of actors worldwide, including a number of new market intermediaries, the issue of trust came back in full color, raising questions related to the global redistribution of authority and power – and governance.

This chapter tackles the question of Bitcoin governance from a perspective grounded in science and technology studies, in particular the sociology of socio-technical controversies. Following the foundational work of authors in the actor–network theory (ANT) tradition (Callon, 1986; Latour, 1987), we use the term "socio-technical controversy" to refer to every debate questioning the distinction between the technical and social elements involved in an issue, exploring the boundary between the known and the uncertain, and transforming the components of the issue as well as the networks of entities involved. We also draw from the argument, frequent in ANT-derived perspectives, that the size and magnitude of a controversy is not predictable at the beginning, and that in any case, it does not explain its resolution in the end. As a whole, one can find in the short yet charged history of Bitcoin manifold such debates, where what seemed to be a technical issue ends up as a political problem, where the explanations of a crash mix technical limits and financial crisis, where doubt is raised on the frontier between what belongs to the blockchain and what belongs to intermediaries, and so on. Furthermore, these debates have variable magnitudes: they may be restricted to a temporary dispute in an online forum, or extend to a large array of actors intervening on the cryptocurrency. We postulate that such controversial events in Bitcoin's recent history, that brought to light tensions, conflicts, or divergences among relevant Bitcoin actors on specific aspects – be they the modification of a technical feature, the organization and hierarchy among core developers, or the introduction or disappearance of an intermediary – are useful loci to observe the "making of" Bitcoin governance. Thus, by observing such events, the chapter seeks to answer the following research questions: how are structuring dynamics of governance, such as collective action and debate, consensus, and intervention of public actors, "unveiled" by controversy? Who are the actors taking, or being entrusted with, responsibility and authority, in particular when it comes to decentralizing or re-centralizing specific components of the system?

To seek an answer to these questions, we examine three core events of Bitcoin's short yet tumultuous history that were the subject of widespread public debate and controversy in instances when "revealing" events took place – and thus relevant to investigate the issue of governance. A first controversy concerns the reliability of the networks and protocols subtending the blockchain and its integrity, which has been challenged, for example, by a number of security failures and hijacks between 2010 and 2014, as well as, more recently, by the implementation of a "hard fork," Bitcoin XT, in late 2015. A second controversy is the currency's ambiguous links with the dark economy epitomized by the Silk Road affair, started in 2011. A third controversy is the development of an articulate ecosystem of Bitcoin intermediaries that gradually introduced the digital currency into international networks of commerce and finance and exposed it to a number of "non-purely-technical" points of vulnerability and exploitation. The landmark episode in this regard was the dramatic shutdown of the MtGox platform in 2014.

This chapter offers a reading of Bitcoin's governance history alongside these three dimensions. We adopt a science and technology studies (STS) informed controversy-analysis perspective to examine in which ways, as the manifold facets of this digital currency developed, the issue of governance has been at the center of different problematizations, at the articulation of technology, economy, and politics. The controversies examined in this chapter vary greatly in size and magnitude, as well as types of actors involved and dynamics set in motion. Following the STS tradition, we do not postulate here that there needs to be a set of minimal or maximal requirements for a controversy to be considered as such. From a pragmatic standpoint, the three events we examine have sparked debates, conflicts, tensions, and re-alignments on aspects of the Bitcoin system that we consider important to investigate its governance.

As the following section will address in more detail, our analysis builds on two primary strands of STS literature: on one hand, work that explores the role of information intermediaries and technical infrastructures and architectures as instruments of Internet governance and "control points" (DeNardis, 2014), around which issues of technical and economic performance, as well as battles over values and civil liberties, play out; on the other hand, we also build on research that addresses the structuring and performative effects of socio-technical controversies on governance, and analyzes the very processes by which norms are created, negotiated and put to the test as no less important than the "stabilized" norms themselves.

This study relies on a qualitative exploration of a corpus of press articles and expert contributions, having Bitcoin as their core subject from its birth to the present day. For each of the cases, we "unwrap" and decode several ($n=6-8$) written pieces – mainly specialized press and web articles, but also technical documents and forum excerpts – concerning the controversial episodes. Through the chapter, we attempt to highlight how these different data and the particular ways in which controversies are narrated and understood contribute to defining the world they address and, thereby, propose specific forms of governance. In conclusion, the chapter will propose a general reflection on the issue of blockchain technology governance, thanks to the "already-historical" experience of Bitcoin.

Approaching (Bitcoin) governance through an STS lens

The rise and development of Bitcoin, and the interdisciplinary attention it has enjoyed, is one of the most telling examples in recent Internet history of why a predominantly institutional view of Internet governance, which was dominant in the field's early days, is being increasingly criticized for partially missing what actually constitutes governance in a networked and global system. In contrast, the latter has come to be understood as more about "environments with low formalization, heterogeneous organizational forms, large number of actors and massively distributed authority and decision-making power" (van Eeten and Mueller, 2013: 730). In response to such criticism, approaches informed by the field of STS are increasingly part of the "toolbox" used to study Internet governance, broadly understood as social ordering occurring less exclusively in formal political institutions, but also enacted through mundane practices of people engaged in maintaining or challenging social order, supported and mediated by technical artefacts (Woolgar and Neyland, 2013). Two STS traditions, concepts, and methodological tools at once appear especially useful to study Bitcoin governance: the sociology of controversies and infrastructure studies.

Studying Internet governance (IG) through the prism of controversies (Pinch and Leuenberger, 2006) is one STS-informed way to unpack the complex realities subtending the "Internet" and its "governance." As we have examined (Epstein et al., 2016), terrains such as interconnection agreements between Internet service providers, the debate around net neutrality, the use of deep-packet-inspection and content filtering technologies, ubiquitous surveillance measures, the use of domain name systems for intellectual property-related regulatory aims – and, as we will see, the deployment of decentralized technologies such as Bitcoin – are indeed key sites of contestation and tension over the Internet and how formal and informal systems of normativity interact in it. STS-informed approaches to IG analyze the structuring and performative effects of controversies shaping these various formal and informal arrangements of governance. Such approaches are particularly useful to analyze controversies around claims made by different actors or groups about "doing Internet governance," contributing to the creation of different worlds in which specific notions of governance make sense (Brousseau et al., 2012). Thus, controversies unpack "governance" as a theoretical and operational concept, by exposing the plurality of notions it refers to, and the consequences of their being in conflict (Cheniti, 2009; Ziewitz and Pentzold, 2014). This point is explored in international relations and political science literature on how crises expose the implicit character of governance (to give but one example, Hay, 1999). The very processes by which norms are created, renegotiated, put to the test, re-aligned, raise conflicts, are as crucial – and perhaps more crucial – in STS perspectives as the "stabilized" norms themselves.

The particular subfield of STS that has been labeled as "infrastructure studies," stemming from Bowker and Star's pioneering work, addresses the agency of non-human actors and technical infrastructures as loci of mediation, and explores their "political role" in interplay with a plurality of normative systems: law, markets, discourses, and practices (Brousseau et al., 2012). In the case of the Internet, information intermediaries, critical Internet resources, Internet exchange points, surveillance, and security devices play crucial governance roles alongside political, national, and supra-national institutions and civil society organizations (Musiani et al., 2016). The governance of the Internet thus takes shape through a myriad of infrastructures, devices, data fluxes, and technical architectures that are often discreet and invisible, yet nevertheless crucial in subtending building the increasingly public and articulate network of networks. Laura DeNardis (2014: 11) defines these entities as infrastructural "control points," around which are entangled matters of technical and economic efficiency, as well as negotiations over human and societal values such as intellectual property rights, privacy, security, transparency.

A few recent contributions apply STS perspectives more specifically to the study of Bitcoin and the interplay of technology and politics at stake within it. Bill Maurer et al. (2013) coin the notion of "digital metallism," drawing from both STS and the anthropology of money, to account for the combination of materiality and virtuality that characterizes Bitcoin. The concept underlines

Bitcoin's dematerialization, in which the value is embedded, such as commodity money is in gold. Digital metallism also emphasizes how, as with every technology supported by digital networks, the dematerialization of money itself is accompanied by the implementation of heavy material infrastructure. In a blend of STS and economic sociology, Henrik Karlstrøm (2014) sees the "material embeddedness" of market interactions as the primary analytical key to understand the ways in which virtual currencies are just as intimately linked to the institutional setup of the material world as non-virtual currencies. This analysis thereby helps to bridge Bitcoin's specificities with the history of money to draw useful lessons from it. Karlstrøm also notes the challenging task that a qualitative, social science study of Bitcoin represents, due to the novelty of the phenomenon, widespread anonymity among core actors, and the nature of the sources, many of which "are to a certain degree non-verifiable in the traditional academic sense – many are from transient web pages rather than published research." In a methods-oriented contribution, also using Bitcoin as a particularly emblematic case of challenge to digital humanities approaches, Pablo Velasco (2016: 100–1) notes the distributed currency's status as a "metamorphous" research object, observing that "[b]ecause Bitcoin is at the same time a protocol, a currency, a software, a network and a cultural phenomenon, it can play the discontinuous role of instrument, method, and object of research." Velasco also notes that data on cryptocurrencies is "democratically scarce" as opposed to what is available to researchers of social networks, for example.

In today's context of frequent hype surrounding blockchain technology, praising in particular its capacity to entirely self-regulate via the algorithms it subtends, Primavera De Filippi and Benjamin Loveluck's (2016) contribution uses the late 2015/early 2016 controversy over the Bitcoin XT fork to illustrate the limitations of an over-reliance on purely technical tools to address complex issues of governance, including elements of social coordination and economic exchange. A previous contribution from the authors of this chapter (Mallard et al., 2014) has showed how, introducing and discussing specific devices, dynamics or operations as being in some way related to the building of trust, early expert knowledge on Bitcoin has contributed to the very definition and shaping of this trust within the Bitcoin system – ultimately contributing to perform the shared definition of its value as a currency.

Taken together, these contributions draw upon STS approaches' suitability to analyze in a detailed and situated manner the design, construction, establishment, and appropriation of technology in a complex system such as Bitcoin. They helpfully explore the connections between the politics of Internet infrastructure and infrastructure as Internet politics.

Three controversies unveiling Bitcoin governance

This central section of the chapter presents three core, controversial events of Bitcoin history that we identify as particularly relevant to investigating its governance. In these instances, "revealing" events took place and led to widespread public debate on different governance dimensions. A first dimension concerns the reliability of the networks and protocols underpinning the blockchain and its integrity, which has been challenged, for example, by a number of security failures and hijacks between 2010 and 2014, or more recently, by the implementation of a "hard fork," Bitcoin XT, in late 2015. A second dimension concerns the development of an articulate ecosystem of Bitcoin intermediaries that gradually introduced the digital currency into the international networks of commerce and finance and exposed it to a number of "non-purely-technical" points of vulnerability and exploitation – a landmark episode in this regard being the dramatic shutdown of the MtGox platform in 2014. A third dimension addresses the ambiguous links with the dark economy epitomized by the Silk Road affair, which started in 2011. This case sheds light on the role of police investigations on the functioning of Bitcoin architecture.

March 2013's "involuntary fork": protocol reliability, trust, and decentralized governance

To address the issue of the relationship between the reliability of the technical protocol and users' trust – and its consequences for Bitcoin governance – we first examine the events surrounding the "involuntary fork" of March 2013. These events are of particular interest as they reveal how the Bitcoin community, from core developers to miners to at-large users, responded to a moment of crisis deeply embedded in the technical architecture, for which both a technical response and a "political" consensus on the solution needed to be developed. The events proceeded as follows: on March 11–12, 2013, a miner running version 0.8 of the Bitcoin software created a large invalid block (i.e., incompatible with earlier versions of the software). This created an unintended split or "fork" in the Bitcoin blockchain, since computers with the most recent version of the software at the time (0.8) accepted the invalid block and continued to build on the diverging chain, whereas older versions of the software rejected it and continued extending the older/original blockchain without the offending block. This split resulted in two separate transaction logs being formed without clear consensus or even knowledge of the other event happening, which allowed for the same funds to be spent twice on each chain – the very act of double spending whose avoidance was meant to be the chief improvement of Bitcoin over earlier digital currencies.

Beyond relating the incident in a straightforward manner, interestingly, Wikipedia's account of the event adds that:

> Miners resolved the split by downgrading to version 0.7, putting them back on track with the canonical blockchain. User funds largely remained unaffected and were available when network consensus was restored. The network reached consensus and continued to operate as normal a few hours after the split.[2]

This account raises a number of interesting questions inasmuch as this unprecedented technical "glitch" required the negotiation of a new norm to reorganize Bitcoin operations into only one blockchain – and the implementation of a successful "mix" of technical, political, and social elements required to do so. What actually happened behind the "resolution of the split," and who was responsible for it? How did the network "reach consensus"? Did the network "operate as normal" after this episode? Who were the actors and the actants of this sequence of events?

The first documents addressing these questions were the alert report on the Bitcoin website[3] and its related "post-mortem" improvement proposal,[4] which was authored by Bitcoin core developer Gavin Andresen. Albeit succinct and impersonal, the former clarifies that the cause of the problem was the creation, mining, and broadcasting of a "large block [...] that is incompatible with earlier versions of Bitcoin." Meanwhile the latter argues that the issue with the block being was that it displayed a "larger number of total transaction inputs than previously seen." In a subsequent analysis of the incident, Vitalik Buterin[5] further clarifies that the problem was linked to the release of the most recent version of "bitcoind," the most popular implementation tool/interface for running Bitcoin used by miners. Developers of this release, labeled 0.8, switched the database that bitcoind used to store blocks and transactions from one called BerkeleyDB to another called LevelDB, considered as more efficient and more suitable to reduce blockchain synchronization time. However, Buterin explains:

> what the developers did not realize at the time was that by doing so they also accidentally introduced a change to the rules of the Bitcoin protocol. In order to make an update to the database, the database process must make a 'lock' on the part of the database which stores that particular item of information, a mechanism implemented to prevent two changes from occurring simultaneously.

LevelDB had no restrictions on the possible number of locks, but BerkeleyDB had, and failed when a single block required more locks than this limit.

Nodes running the most recent version of the Bitcoin software, 0.8, were able to manage this large block, but some nodes running previous versions of the software rejected it. The unintended fork of the blockchain, we learn, was due to the fact that at the time of the incident, the nodes running pre-0.8 software versions had more sheer computing power than those running the newest version, thus automatically gaining pre-eminence:

> The pre-0.8-incompatible chain (from here on, the 0.8 chain) at that point had around 60% of the mining hash power ensuring the split did not automatically resolve (as would have occurred if the pre-0.8 chain outpaced the 0.8 chain in total work, forcing 0.8 nodes to reorganise to the pre-0.8 chain).[6]

At this time, the incident's account begins mentioning some specific actors of the Bitcoin broader ecosystem. Two mining pools, BTCGuild and Slush, downgraded their Bitcoin 0.8 nodes to 0.7 "so their pools would also reject the larger block." Because of their central position in the Bitcoin mining process, the move by these two mining pools shifted the majority of hashpower (the processing power of the Bitcoin network) on the chain without the larger block, eventually causing the 0.8 nodes to reorganize to the pre-0.8 chain. Later on, the report mentions this aspect – one of the early defining moves to return to one and only stabilized norm – as a positive aspect and one in which the two mining pools were seen as having behaved altruistically, as the downgrading of their nodes was beneficial to the system but "caused them to sacrifice significant amounts of money." Since they had previously mined with the 0.8 version and come back to 0.7, BTCGuild and Slush lost what they had mined.

The report records one important instance of double-spending – the act of successfully spending some money more than once, which the distributed-yet-unique blockchain ledger subtending Bitcoin generally protects against – and the involuntary fork made temporarily possible. However, and interestingly, the report notes that the act was "done by someone experimenting to see if it was possible and was not intended to be malicious." This person subsequently identified himself[7] as a "lead user" (see von Hippel, 1986) trying to establish evidence that this type of operation was possible, and revealed the details of his actions with a deposit of a substantial sum, equivalent to US$10,000, over the online payment system OKPay. The post-mortem report includes this event in the "What went right" list – thereby emphasizing that the user's actions ultimately made the system stronger, by providing a test of a weakness without malicious intent. However, subsequent analyses tend to contest this interpretation, arguing that "[a] longer-running fork would likely have exacerbated the problem and allowed malicious attackers to figure out a systematic way to create double-spend transactions," and pointing out that other exchanges or payment services might have taken even longer to upgrade their clients (or disable transactions) in far more adversarial contexts (Naranayan, 2015).

The principal arena of negotiation of a possible solution was the bitcoin-dev Internet relay chat (IRC) channel, where most core developers quickly gathered. The central controversial issue was which one of the two blockchains should be supported – knowing that a choice needed to be made, and as soon as possible. The 0.8-supporting blockchain had to its advantage more computing power-per-node than the 0.7 one: nodes were fewer, but more powerful. However, as Buterin (2013) explains, legitimizing the chain based on 0.8 would have imposed a heavier burden on a lot more users: "thousands of users on 0.7 would be forced to upgrade in order to use Bitcoin at all, something which would not happen if the 0.7 fork took over since both versions of bitcoind can read it." Time was also of the essence, and a resolution would have been reached faster with a few powerful actors putting their weight behind the return to 0.7, instead of a more time-consuming distributed response involving the entire community. As developer Pieter Wuille pointed out in the chat discussions: "we _cannot_ get every bitcoin user in the world to now instantly switch to 0.8 so no, we need to roll-back to the 0.7 chain" (Naranayan, 2015). For these reasons, consensus was eventually reached on downgrading to 0.7.

What was needed at this point for the decision to be enforced was that most major actors in the community decided to support 0.7 – those with dedicated computing resources, and widespread user trust. The bitcoin-dev IRC channel became the place where developers deployed, to put it in Callon's (1986) terms, mechanisms of *intéressement* and enrollment vis-à-vis core miners, mining pool operators, and merchants. A defining factor in both Buterin and Naranayan's accounts appears to be the decision of mining pool operator BTCGuild, in particular, to proceed with the downgrade. At some point, the operator points out how it has the computing capacity to end the incident: "I can single handedly put 0.7 back to the majority hash power. I just need confirmation that thats [*sic*] what should be done." This was confirmed shortly thereafter by several developers. Most exchange and deposit platforms proceeded to shut down their deposits, updated their servers to the 0.7-led blockchain, and returned to operation. Interestingly, in the IRC message that basically summarizes instructions from developers to Bitcoin actors and effectively ends the emergency, the central role of BTCGuild is cited by developer Wuille as the reason that the 0.7 downgrade is indeed the good choice and network activities will indeed be back in order soon because of sheer computational power, because BTCGuild has rallied behind it: "If you're a miner, please do not mine on 0.8 code. Stop, or switch back to 0.7. BTCGuild is switching to 0.7, so the old chain will get a majority hash rate soon" (Naranayan, 2015). The switch in hash power shortly followed, as Buterin (2013) reports:

> At about 03:30 the tipping point came. The 0.7 chain quickly caught up to being only 10 blocks behind, then 8 blocks, and at 06:19 both chains converged to the same length at block 225454, leading to nearly all remaining miners abandoning the other.

The incident was over, and the involuntary fork repaired – but not before providing some enlightening indications on how power is co-constructed in Bitcoin. The incident revealed the nodes of authority, power, and hierarchy in the highly distributed system, the degree to which the system is characterized by the intersection of the technical and political.

More precisely, Bitcoin's involuntary fork unveils a number of dynamics illustrating at least three aspects of governance in Bitcoin, and more broadly in blockchain-based distributed environments. First, we observe how individual leadership/initiative and community consensus-building were both central to solving a moment of tension and controversy that could have led to Bitcoin's demise. "Classical" decision-making processes, made of the dialogue between the individual and the collective, are appearing for the blockchain. However, we can also observe the inherent power asymmetries between actors that underlie the blockchain's functioning: most notably, the asymmetry between a multitude of users and a small oligarchy of mining pools.

Second, this case illustrates that what made the fork "just" an incident, rather than an enduring hard fork or a permanent damage to the system, was the combination of a human "semi-centralization" or centralization *tout court* in the response to the risk, and a decentralization of the blockchain itself that remained compatible with this human action. The existence of a decentralized blockchain presupposes an infrastructure whose maintenance, and whose "care," needs to be recentralized somehow, and draws inspiration from mechanisms of governance that are able to engage a variety of actors (users, miners, developers) but coordinate according to well-known dynamics typical of open-source communities such as the "benevolent dictator."

Third and last, this event underlines the materiality of Bitcoin's infrastructure as a governance tool. With its complex ecosystem of intermediaries, mediations, and control points, this "governance by infrastructure" is evident in both the cause of the incident (a change in the type of database used to store results has unintended consequences for the organization of the community and the value of the currency) and its solution (an actor that is "powerful" in terms of computing power is capable of single-handedly bringing the controversy to a stabilized point, if not to an end).

The shutdown of MtGox

The shutdown of the MtGox platform provides an opportunity to investigate the governance mechanisms underlying Bitcoin exchange from another point of view. Contrary to the case of the "fork," governance uncertainties here do not concern the core of the system, the blockchain, but rather one of the intermediaries with the rest of the economy. MtGox was a major actor of the Bitcoin ecosystem during its rise, and the troubles it encountered offer fruitful insights into issues of governance associated with the specific position of key intermediaries.

Online press articles make it possible to reconstruct a short history of MtGox from its emergence to its downfall.[8] MtGox was created in 2007 by an Internet innovator named Jed McCaleb. Only in July 2010 did it become a full-fledged platform for the exchange of Bitcoins into money. In 2011, the platform was purchased by another Internet entrepreneur, Mark Karpelès. Karpelès developed MtGox during the period where Bitcoin experienced its tremendous success, starting in 2011 with an exchange rate of $1 and reaching $1,000 at the end of 2013. MtGox then played a central role in the Bitcoin market, capturing at its peak 80 percent of the global exchange. The platform is also partly associated with the collapse following this euphoria phase, in which a series of jolts led the Bitcoin exchange rate to around $250 at the beginning of 2015. MtGox's bankruptcy in February 2014 was a milestone in a long descent punctuated by crises, crashes, and bounces. Yet the platform had encountered a number of troubles much earlier: between 2011 and 2014, a series of problems mixing up the technical, legal, and economic dimensions occurred. Here, we will examine four episodes emphasizing issues of governance posed to intermediaries in an ecosystem organized around the Bitcoin blockchain.

The first episode is known as the "Dwolla" case. In May 2013, the US financial authorities urged Dwolla, an e-business for payment and money transfer, to stop transacting with "Mutum Sigillum LLC." This company was a subsidiary of MtGox, serving as an intermediary to operate transactions between Dwolla and MtGox. Customers would use their Dwolla account to circulate money to the Mutum Sigillum LLC account, where they were in turn circulated to the platform to convert dollars into Bitcoins. The bridging of Dwolla (headquartered in the US) and MtGox (domiciliated in Japan) through Mutum Sigillum LLC was problematic for US federal authorities as it enacted the systematic and massive circulation of currencies at the international level that had never been declared as such to the authorities. In other words, it breached American law on "unlicensed money transmitting business." This is a classical case of conflict with economic actors operating through electronic media at the borders of national territories in a borderless Internet, rather than within national borders and subject to domestic regulations that are often plagued by loopholes. The scenario described in the press involves all the characteristics of a typical situation of conflict (Siluk, 2013): a regulation attempt,[9] a contestable financial arrangement with shell companies, a judge, a warrant, and, in the end, a heavy financial penalty. Indeed, in August 2013, the case ended with a seizure of $2,900,000 from the Mutum Sigillum LLC account by the US government, a penalty that contributed to the deterioration of the financial position of MtGox (Spaven, 2013). In this context, governance – in a "classical" way – is reduced to compliance with regulation.

A second instance reflecting important dynamics of governance is when MtGox encounters technical problems hindering the normal flow of transactions. This is what happened in November 2013, when exchanges on MtGox were temporarily slowed down or even paralyzed by a technical failure that was later described as a denial-of-service (DoS) attack. These interruptions of market functioning usually trigger two reactions: on the one hand, users gather information or express their discontent in Internet forums; on the other hand, the online press echoes the problem and indulges in diagnosis attempts.[10] Both processes enable the activation of public spaces associated with the market as locations where technical and economic conflicts can be expressed – and, sometimes, fixed.

Furthermore, such processes enact mechanisms of governance that are at the same time generic and very telling about Bitcoin's peculiarities. They are generic to the extent that appealing to this kind of arena constitutes a usual means to foster public debate on the modalities of organization of global markets. The notion of "hybrid forum" can be mobilized to apprehend the modalities of governance that are at stake (Callon et al., 2002). Yet these processes of communication are also symptomatic of Bitcoin, not only because online forums and online press have played a major role in spreading practices and uses associated with the electronic money (Mallard et al., 2014), but also because this modality of intervention in the market builds on the effects of transparency of the transactions that are specific of its functioning. Notably, in these online debates, actors evoke the discrepancy between information on transactions given on the platform and in the blockchain. For instance, on November 18, 2013, a user posted the following question on one of the main Bitcoin forums: "I just withdrew some BTC from Mt Gox to address 1Mvk4YAtKZAP43wEhZ6ZQrTzLZwZ-zPxtTJ, transaction id 3dfa979af56ff061efbceed0dd7c9dc9fd8c774249544018f-6bbf646323ff03b, but didn't receive the coins and the transaction isn't in the chain. Should I be worried?"[11] The modalities of traceability enabled by the block-chain – that is, the very fact that anyone can examine the public ledger of trans-actions and verify whether an order is recorded or not – provide peculiar resources for governance processes based on communication in the market.

A third emblematic episode occurred in the turmoil of the collapse of MtGox. At the beginning of February 2014, the platform encountered significant new troubles characterized initially by a delay in the execution of money withdrawal and, ultimately, by the complete interruption of this service. In a first step, the market as a whole is disturbed and exchange prices go up and down erratically, raising the fear of a domino effect (Kate, 2014). The signs of a technical failure of the platform accumulate, and MtGox issues a series of press releases received by market actors as less and less comforting and credible. In these declarations, Mark Karpelès indicates that a problem of "malleability" of the Bitcoin money might be at the origin of the failure, a problem that the platform staff and Bitcoin developers would be jointly trying to fix (Martinez, 2014). This argument is interesting because it shows an attempt to shift the problem and to allocate the responsibility of the MtGox failure to a weakness that would be inherent to Bitcoin. Many in the Bitcoin community regarded this attempt as an insult to the electronic money. Above all, this attempt to allocate responsibility to the techni-cal underpinnings of Bitcoin proved unconvincing, particularly as it became evident that the troubles encountered by MtGox would not propagate to other actors in the Bitcoin ecosystem. The fact that instability would not spread became obvious in the last transaction recorded on the platform around February 20, at a moment when it displayed a rate of $110 for 1 Bitcoin, while other plat-forms maintained a rate around $500 (Kinsley, 2014a). In the end, MtGox col-lapsed without dragging down the rest of the market. The exact reason of this collapse remained an object of speculation during the following months. One of the scenarios that emerged during the crash and was confirmed much later (Mott, 2015), involves a technical failure in the platform rather than the Bitcoin protocol. A "leak" in the exchange had slowly caused 750,000 Bitcoins being stolen, and was discovered only at the beginning of 2014. What is important for our analysis is that the capacity to enact boundary work between what belongs to the blockchain and what belongs to an intermediary actor is a component of the dynamics of governance that are at stake here.

Let us finally move to the end of the story of MtGox, and examine a last inter-esting modality of governance for Bitcoin intermediaries. The episode occurs on February 24, 2014, when trading on the platform is almost stopped. Mark Kar-pelès takes account of the defeat of the battle by resigning from the board of the Bitcoin Foundation (Southhurst, 2014).[12] Thus, he publicly admits to the dis-connect between the trajectory followed by the platform and the new ventures of Bitcoin innovators. This action echoes a public statement made in the same period by six leaders of the Bitcoin industry (Blockchain.info, Coinbase, Kraken, Bitstamp, BTC China, and Circle) to break ranks with MtGox (Titcomb, 2014). The text of the declaration clearly shows the wish to prevent any interlinkage between the fate of MtGox and the future of Bitcoin:

> This tragic violation of the trust of users of MtGox was the result of one's company actions and does not reflect the resilience or value of bitcoin and the digital currency industry. (…) As with any new industry, there are certain bad actors that need to be weeded out, and this is what we are seeing today.

The public display of the exit of one of the members of the coalition supporting the market, and the claim of a disconnect between what happened to MtGox and what other Bitcoin intermediaries do, comes under a modality of governance that, as is the case for the first episode, is quite generic: simply restoring confidence in the Bitcoin market.

Silk Road

Our third case study links Bitcoin history to a digital market on the "dark web," the Silk Road, and addresses the issue of responsibility allocation within this platform. This case illustrates the large number of intermediaries involved in a market that exclusively accepted Bitcoins for exchange. More specifically, this case addresses the role of public authorities facing an outlaw website market.

The original Silk Road was a peer-to-peer commerce website, like eBay or Amazon, connecting providers and customers through a transaction infrastructure platform and financed by commission on sales. Unlike other digital marketplaces, Silk Road was novel in that its only accepted currency was Bitcoin and the transaction is operated through TOR, the peer-to-peer network enabling anonymous communication. Together, these traits were supposed to provide anonymity of actors and transactions, two major advantages given the specificity of proposed goods: drugs, in their great majority, with a choice of 13.000 drugs including LSD, but also computer-hacking services, malicious software, fake passports, credit card statements, and perhaps even, according to the FBI complaint,[13] murder for hire.

Silk Road (SR) ran between January 2011 and October 2013, before its shutdown when Ross William Ulbricht, the alleged owner and inventor of the site, was arrested by the US Federal Bureau of Investigation. Despite pleading not guilty, Ulbricht was sentenced to perpetuity in May 2015. As our previous case study, this one relies on three data resources: a study of press material, with particular attention to the magazine *Wired*, which followed this story closely,[14] debates on the Bitcoin forum, and case documents online.[15]

From its inception, Silk Road presented itself as an activist system, advocating the libertarian philosophy of the Austrian school of free market economics; it claimed its continuity with the Bitcoin paradigm, distrustful against public market policy. Silk Road explicitly promoted a libertarian model of market connecting directly supply and demand for products wrongly prohibited by governments. Its founder considered that people are free to use drugs to the extent that their consuming does not disturb anyone. The website argued, in its terms of service (Chen, 2011), that it banished anything that may cause harm (although the status of particular weapons' trade remained ambiguous).

This libertarian discourse was favorably received within the Bitcoin community. As explained in one of the first articles devoted to Silk Road[16] in June 2011:

> Since it launched this February, Silk Road has represented the most complete implementation of the Bitcoin vision. Many of its users come from Bitcoin's Utopian geek community and see Silk Road as more than just a place to buy drugs.
>
> (Chen, 2011)

Ulbricht, interviewed right before his arrest, asserted that he had "an important message for the world": "The people now can control the flow and distribution of information and the flow of money. Sector by sector the State is being cut out of the equation and power is being returned to the individual" (Greenberg, 2013a). On the Bitcoin forum, this discourse seems successful: some commentators present Ulbricht as a "hero," "our own Che Guevara," "a name [that] will live [on] among the greatest men and women in history as a soldier of justice and freedom," and so on.[17]

However, as was highlighted by police investigations, this "perfect" market model, driving out intermediaries and chasing out state interventions, acting in the sole hands of direct players, was mostly a thought experiment and unable to operate on its own. Indeed, such a web market actually needed a strong governance model and involved a multiplicity of actors. Not only did the three-year-long police work shed light on Silk Road's functioning, but it contributed to shape it as the investigation procedures unfolded.

The first and central question asked by the agencies, such as the US FBI, investigating Silk Road since the summer of 2011: who was responsible for the illicit trafficking on the website? Buyers and sellers, in line with Silk Road philosophy? The first were easy to find for investigators, who only needed to offer products at a good price to entice them – and all over the world, lawsuits were filed against them. Sellers, however, were more difficult – albeit not impossible – to identify: according to the press, national police was able to locate and pursue vendors in more than ten different countries, including the United States, Australia, Europe, and Israel. American police wanted more and looked for the "inner circle" of the Silk Road. Investigators explored in all its dimensions the functioning of Silk Road and highlighted the chain of intermediaries required for conducting, under appropriate conditions, a "direct transaction." In the police's steps, we identify the issue of responsibility allocation in three points. The first dimension concerns the banking system able to facilitate Bitcoin use and regulate currency exchanges. The second dimension leads us to the technical infrastructures of Silk Road, de facto controlled by a central authority. The third dimension focuses on the specific Silk Road market rules and their application, concerning dispute resolution, regulation of forbidden goods, competition management, and so on.

Concerning the banking aspects, police investigations show that Silk Road needed a specific system and could not rely entirely on the Bitcoin protocol; a new service layer was implemented with different functions. First, Silk Road acted as a bank or, more exactly, as an escrow. As was explained in June 2011 on the main Bitcoin forum,[18] Silk Road deposits protected buyers and sellers against scammers as the money deposited into a Silk Road account was sent to the seller only when the transaction was satisfactorily completed. As a trusted third party, Silk Road acted as an "obligatory passage point," which implies a centralized system of control. The police investigations concluded that the escrow account was controlled directly and exclusively by Ulbricht. The FBI held him liable for a first level of responsibility and he was personally charged for money laundering (Count 3 of the sealed complaint[19]).

The second point concerns the money "trapped" in the deposit account, and requiring an intermediary to be laundered. How could the money be re-injected into the legitimate economy, eliminating the direct link with Silk Road? An important drug salesman, Steven Lloyd Sadler, who cooperated with the police, explained that the most optimal solution was to go through LocalBitcoins.com, a website that connected Bitcoin traders and buyers for a low fee. This site organized a physical encounter between a seller who wanted to get rid of his electronic money, even with a low exchange rate, and buyers with disposable hard currency. Sadler concluded: "Any Silk Road vendor not on LocalBitcoins is losing a lot of money" (O'Neill, 2014).

The third point on banking concerns the difficult use of Bitcoin. The vast majority of the 150,000 unique Silk Road buyers (according to the indictment) were not sufficiently skilled to accomplish transactions with the electronic currency. The FBI enquiry identified at least two intermediaries, among many others, able to support illicit transactions and prosecute them. Robert Faiella resold Bitcoins on the Silk Road website (probably on the forum) and bought them through the intermediary of Charlie Shrem, Chief Executive Officer of The Company, a firm that was designed to enable customers to exchange cash for Bitcoins. Ironically, the criminal complaint reveals that Shrem was, furthermore, "in charge of ensuring the Company's compliance with federal and other anti-money laundering," which means he was fully aware of the illicit nature of transactions on Silk Road. The definition of responsibility is then expanded to the service concerning all the financial aspects of transactions, which indirectly links Silk Road with the Bitcoin Foundation, as Shrem is one of its administrators (Hill, 2014).

In sum, the Silk Road's decentralized payment instrument could not assume on its own the proper treatment of the financial transaction. To function properly, Silk Road needed the dynamic involvement (thus, the responsibility) of a series of actors who add rules of conduct and perform the market.

The second dimension we analyze addresses the Silk Road's technical infrastructure. This became more and more complicated so as to ensure the confidentiality of exchanges both from the police and increasingly frequent and fine-tuned cyberattacks (O'Neill, 2014). To that extent, encryption tools, cyber attackers, and police inspectors participated in the reconfiguration of the transaction apparatus and thereby in the governance of the Silk Road.

However, Bitcoin itself, initially perceived by the police as the weak link of confidentiality, resisted more than expected, as shown by the unfortunate adventure of two computer science scholars (Ron and Shamir, 2013; Greenberg, 2013b). Their analysis of Bitcoin circulation was quickly debunked by a Bitcoin user on a Reddit forum. However, as later demonstrated in police investigations, Silk Road considered that TOR and Bitcoin gave no sufficient anonymity guarantees. Silk Road used a reinforced layer of encryption in order to conceal individual transactions. As the above-cited FBI complaint explains, "According to the Silk Road wiki, Silk Road's tumbler 'sends all payments through a complex, semi-random series of dummy transactions (…) making it nearly impossible to link your payment with any coins leaving the site'." Those encryption tools were not only meant as means to avoid prosecution, but also to resist the many cyberattacks by hackers or by competitors. Commentators on the Bitcointalk forum suggested that the most serious attack in April 2013, by denial-of-service, which took advantage of unknown vulnerabilities in TOR, was engineered by a newcomer in the market, Atlantis.

In addition to encryption tools, SR, with its growing popularity, needed a wide infrastructure reliant on a powerful park of computer servers spread across multiple countries as the FBI later discovered. These physical infrastructures weakened the security of the platform, as indicated by commentators in the forum or the press. Police exploited a first weakness in seizing a Silk Road server farm in Finland. Yet this was not enough to locate the core of the system, the specific actor or group of actors in control of the wider Silk Road infrastructure.

The traces left by the uses of all those infrastructures did not permit the identification of the specific governance actors. The FBI needed to seize physical materials, such as Ulbricht's hard disk, to shut down the website. Ulbricht was eventually identified through one misleading use of an email address. According to *Wired*, he had become too self-confident in the ability of his hard drive's encryption system to hide his illicit activities. Had he employed stronger anonymization tools, his traces might have been more difficult to identify. Yet those digital traces were useful to demonstrate the functioning of the site – and his eventual guilt – once his identity was spotted and his computer seized.

Silk Road encapsulated various technical devices, from Bitcoin blockchain to server, encrypted mail, monetary tumbler, and so on, in fulfilling illicit transactions. Just as with the fork case, the governance of the Bitcoin market is encapsulated in particular, highly interdependent infrastructures.

The third and last governance dimension of Silk Road are its market devices. As in every digital market, trust was central to Silk Road. Yet the particular goods and services it exchanged made this issue more problematic. Buyers had to trust (Luhman, 2000) the quality of products, the confidentiality of exchanges, and the good execution of transactions. The website provided trust mechanisms, like seller ratings or, as we have seen, a trusted third party. Thus, a journalist could assume that Silk Road's core service was not the commerce of illicit products, but the selling of "insurance and financial products (…). The business model is to commoditize security" (Greenberg, 2013a). This point leads us to another mode of governance: the rules and operating instructions, part explicit and part implicit. As shown by Burnett and Bonnici (2003), these rules specified the authorized merchandises and services but also instructions for use and terms of service. According to Sadler (see above and O'Neill, 2014), reselling vendors' closed accounts was, for example, not allowed, and site administrators shut them down if they were made aware of this practice. The Silk Road site proclaimed its will to satisfy its customers, in particular through a forum and a dispute settlement arrangement (about which, unfortunately, nothing is known).

Such organization required a lot of work and a de facto staff. As such, Ulbricht had to hire several people for substantial salaries. For example, ChronicPain (Bearman, 2015), a former volunteer who moderated the forum and gave free advice on drugs' uses, was hired to deal with customer service, resetting passwords, consumers' dispute resolution, and so on. The staff interacted through a special anonymized forum. Yet while Ulbricht knew everything about his staff members, it was in no way reciprocal. This system was also meant to protect Ulbricht in case staff members were arrested, and complicated the organization of work and the execution of rules, especially since the development of competitors led Silk Road to make itself more visible on the market. The press (in particular Chen (2011), who was extensively requoted) played an important role in popularizing the site, so much so that most media commentators established a link between Silk Road-related articles and Bitcoin's first strong growth in June 2011.

The management of his successful commerce led Ulbricht to gain visibility. He spoke to journalists, played a more active role in forums, and replaced his "Admin" pseudonym with a more strongly identifying one, DPR (acronym of Dread Pirate Robert): "As time went on, the administrator became an important voice, the site's theorist and advocate for individual liberty" (Bearman, 2015). According to the FBI complaint and to press articles, the Silk Road model of governance seems classical: pyramidal, not to say autocratic. DPR hired, fixed the rules, earned commissions, animated the staff forum, spoke in the press and in the forums. However, as repeatedly stressed on the forum, Ulbricht's technical competencies were limited and it is likely that he was unable to set up all aspects of the device alone.[20] The assumed community of users, led by Silk Road, was hardly visible and did not manifest itself, except through the wave of protest on forums when the site was first closed.

All those governance devices were actually under the control of one exclusive, hardly benevolent, despot. Yet, their failings resulted in the intervention of various other governance actors. Formal action by both the police and through international justice systems contributed to define the organization of the Silk Road system, by "forcing" it to formalize and transform its rules (so as to functioning better) and to modify its organization. The FBI, for example, exerted a strong influence on the downfall of the site. To better protect buyers or sellers, or to insure the quality and security of transaction, Silk Road had to strengthen its security and multiply firewalls through particular governance actors. Furthermore, Silk Road influenced the collective ethos of the participants, as can be seen in the press interventions of its managers or in the Bitcoin forum: Ulbricht had to publicly assume his libertarian position and to deal with it in depth (it seems that he sought to maintain his authority at every price, even by suggesting a murder for hire) (Greenberg, 2015b).

Thus, the Silk Road case shows that, even in such a hierarchical and autocratic organization, the governance of a Bitcoin-based market resulted in a complex eco-system of actors and technical devices, who were responsible for configuring the execution of transactions, modifying the functioning of the website and its terms of use, and other governance functions. In addition to formal public authorities, various intermediaries, involved in banking or security aspects, but also in consumption or uses, contributed governance functions as well. As we have seen, together these actors shaped the exchanges and the transactions. The central role granted to Ulbricht thereby hides a more complicated governance organization. That the site was able to temporarily return back online in the form of two successive avatars[21] illustrates that its existence could survive the despotic rule of a central leader.

Conclusion

Adopting an STS perspective informed, in particular, by the sociology of controversies and infrastructure studies, this chapter analyzed three events in Bitcoin's recent history in order to observe the "making of" Bitcoin governance. We have particularly sought to examine how structuring dynamics of governance, such as collective action and consensus, are co-shaped and brought to light by controversies such as the modification of a technical feature or the introduction or removal of an intermediary. We also observed how responsibility and authority are created and redistributed among different actors in the system. Thanks to the "already-historical" experience of Bitcoin, this general conclusion provides some reflections on the broader issue of blockchain technology governance.

First, the three cases reveal the need for further nuance in the "technical governance vs. community governance" point made in some prior studies. We see intermediaries that are an integral part of infrastructure and their agency supersedes the blockchain as "core" technical arrangement of the system. Furthermore, behind the "purely technical" protocol of the blockchain, developers appear, in all their variety of roles and activities, to maintain and further develop the code. These developers' actions vis-à-vis their object can be likened to other well-known forms of governance, those of open-source communities, as De Filippi and Loveluck (2016) have shown in the more recent case of the Bitcoin XT controversy. However, in this situation, we see the developers involved in the very process of the "care of the blockchain." Paraphrasing the expression of Denis and Pontille (2015), one could say that events such as the involuntary fork offer the opportunity to investigate the link between the digital order and the care of distributed infrastructures, and to identify governance mechanisms in the maintenance of a "thing" – the blockchain – that accordingly shows very particular forms of vulnerability. As this case has shown, technical updates involved in the care of a distributed infrastructure become "heavy with governance," as dynamic processes that restore uniformity, continuity, connectivity among different components of a system. Yet such updates also prioritize decisions, manage conflicts, align themselves with norms, allow the elimination of offenders and weak links, and so on. Updates become regulators of technical incoherences. An update's conditions of success depend upon the asymmetry of power inscribed in a complex network of actors.

Controversial episodes also reveal a number of "micro-hierarchies" among developers, and between developers and intermediaries. On one hand, we observe dynamics when intermediaries are called upon by developers to help resolve issues; on the other hand, some developers – even among the "core" team – are clearly "more core" than others. This leads us to novel questions concerning the distribution of authority in the system, and questions the "points of control" (DeNardis, 2014) in a blockchain-based system. This also questions Nakamoto's early "decentralization manifesto," confronted to multiple realities of bottlenecks and tensions. These features bring back in full force the materiality of the blockchain: where the ideological/technical discourse contributes to the invisibility of the infrastructure that brings together the blockchain. Yet points of control and tensions also unveil this infrastructure by showing the multitude of entities and sub-entities that compose it and need to attain some sort of alignment so that the blockchain can keep on existing as a coherent entity.

The three cases also permit to nuance the notion of "users" at large, that one would be tempted, by default, to categorize as "all those who don't mine." We see how, at times, all users are not directly central stage. Rather, the representation of an entity mobilized by developers trying to anticipate their demands or needs, according to what is mirrored in the press, or on forums, and other supports of conversation and debate. However, an important "range" of roles for users is unveiled by these controversies. Certainly, "ordinary users" are there, those that are "passive" exclusively relying on intermediaries. As are miners, who in some instances can no longer be considered as "users" in any traditional sense, but become a power to be reckoned with, because they form an obligatory "passage point" in the network. Most interesting from a governance standpoint are all the figures in between, from "users/teachers" intervening on forums on specific aspects to users "testing" the system in moments of crisis, not for their personal advantage but for the sake of improving it.

This notion of "tester" itself can, indeed, be extended beyond the technical nature of their activities and towards governance functions: for example, specialized journalists "test" in order to better understand and explain the technical. Police explore technical architectures in an extremely careful manner, probing their frontiers and limits. As in other open-source projects, extremely varied and specific formats of governance contributions appear. There are the actors dealing with an involuntary fork, the actors challenging embedded "security" devices, and the actor-evangelists. Along this continuum two ideal-type extremes can be identified. At one end, the "passive" user profile relying on an intermediary to acquire some specific competencies, yet participating in the work of creation and spreading of information. At the other end, quasi-mythical figures of the "first user," such as Satoshi Nakamoto, whose very existence as a single person is doubtful but fuels all kinds of Bitcoin's "founding histories," from decentralization to the less savory ones such as the existence of a Ponzi pyramid. All these figures and their ways of tinkering with Bitcoin infrastructure add to the complexity of its governance, to certain nodes and bottlenecks that are prone to vulnerabilities and controversies.

Finally, our study provides examples of structuring dynamics of governance at play in the functioning and maintenance of Bitcoin exchange. In the three cases, discussion on online forums can play a primary role in the resolution of a controversy, such as in the identification of mechanisms for securing exchange on the Silk Road platform, in the detection of service failure on MtGox, or in the communication with all stakeholders implied in the management of the fork incident. The intervention of public authorities may also play a structuring role in delineating the controversy. In the Silk Road affair as well as in the MtGox history, formal governance contributed to drawing the chain of custody, to allocating responsibility, and eventually to eliminating specific players so as to circumscribe an arena that would be more legitimate for Bitcoin exchange/ activities. Collective action and consensus are also necessary mechanisms for the ordering and maintenance of the blockchain. In the episode of the involuntary fork, for example, these mechanisms were mobilized to secure an agreement with actors such as the mining pools, who had a dominant position in the sociotechnical configuration at play – notwithstanding the supposed capacity of the cryptocurrency to defy hierarchical schemes of power.

Doubtlessly, among the different directions that future Bitcoin-related research can take, there is a place for STS approaches to examine its governance, and more broadly to investigate the governance of blockchain-based activities. Most importantly, there is a need to better understand how different actors situate themselves around the blockchain – which may lead us to challenge the very fact that, in a system such as Bitcoin, the blockchain is *the* core element of the system.

Acknowledgments

From 2010 to 2014, all three authors were supported by the French National Agency for Research (*Agence Nationale de la Recherche, ANR*), CONTINT programme, ANR-10-CORD-004 – ADAM – *Architectures distribuées et applications multimédias*. Francesca Musiani is currently supported by the European Union's Horizon 2020 Framework Programme for Research and Innovation (H2020-ICT-2015, ICT-10–2015) under grant agreement number 688722 – NEXTLEAP.

Notes

1 As already hinted in Satoshi Nakamoto's (2008) seminal paper.
2 https://en.wikipedia.org/wiki/History_of_bitcoin#The_fork_of_March_2013
3 https://bitcoin.org/en/alert/2013–03–11-chain-fork
4 https://github.com/bitcoin/bips/blob/master/bip-0050.mediawiki
5 Buterin (2013).
6 Ibid.
7 On the bitcointalk.org forum, see thread https://bitcointalk.org/index.php?topic= 152348.0
8 The post (Southhurst, 2014) on coinreport.net, from which we borrow some episodes, gives an overview of this history.
9 www.law.cornell.edu/uscode/text/18/1960
10 The role of the press is not limited to echoing problems experienced by customers. It can also carry out specific operations in order to qualify and measure these problems. For instance in February 2014, following repeated dysfunctions of MtGox expressed on the online forums, Coindesk commissioned a poll intended to measure the extent of what the platform's communication service described as "troubles encountered by a handful of users" (Wong, 2014a). This operation showed that the problem in reality concerned 68 percent of platform users (Wong, 2014b).
11 http://bitcoin.stackexchange.com/questions/16870/mtgox-withdrawal-transaction-not-in-blockchain
12 The Bitcoin Foundation is a non-profit corporation founded in 2012 with the mission to promote the development and use of the cryptocurrency. It is funded mainly through grants made by companies operating in the Bitcoin ecosystem. Interestingly, three of the main characters of the stories we tell in this chapter have been members of the board of the Bitcoin Foundation: Charlie Shrem, who resigned after arrest (Hill, 2014), Mark Karpelès, and Gavin Andresen.
13 https://assets.documentcloud.org/documents/801028/silkroad.pdf
14 See in particular Bearman (2015).
15 The case is commented by Trautman (2014).
16 Two senators addressed an urgent appeal to federal authorities, giving more visibility to the articles.
17 https://freeross.org/
18 https://bitcointalk.org/index.php?topic=28824.msg365665#msg365665
19 https://assets.documentcloud.org/documents/801028/silkroad.pdf
20 As for "Satoshi Nakamoto" himself, there is an ongoing debate on the actual identity of the Silk Road creator (Greenberg, 2015a).
21 https://silkroaddrugs.org/guide-on-how-to-access-the-silk-road-3–0/

Bibliography

Bearman, J. (2015, June). The untold story of Silk Road. Parts 1 & 2. *Wired*. Retrieved August 24, 2017, from www.wired.com/2015/04/silk-road-1/ and www.wired.com/2015/05/silk-road-2/

Brousseau, E., Marzouki, M., and Méadel, C. (eds.) (2012). *Governance, regulation and powers on the Internet*. Cambridge: Cambridge University Press.

Burnett, G., and Bonnici, L. (2003). Beyond the FAQ: Explicit and implicit norms in Usenet newsgroups, *Library and Information Science Research, 25*(3): 333–51.

Buterin, V. (2013). Bitcoin network shaken by blockchain fork. *Bitcoin Magazine*. Retrieved August 25, 2017, from https://bitcoinmagazine.com/articles/bitcoin-network-shaken-by-blockchain-fork-1363144448

Callon, M. (1986). The sociology of an actor-network: The case of the electric vehicle. In M. Callon, J. Law, and A. Rip (eds.) *Mapping the dynamics of science and technology: Sociology of science in the real world* (pp. 19–34). London: Macmillan Press.

Callon, M., Méadel, C., and Rabeharisoa, V. (2002). The economy of qualities. *Economy and Society, 31*(2): 194–217.

Chen, A. (2011, January 6). The underground website where you can buy any drug imaginable. *Gawker.* Retrieved August 25, 2017, from http://gawker.com/the-underground-website-where-you-can-buy-any-drug-imag-30818160

Cheniti, T. (2009). *Global Internet governance in practice: Mundane encounters and multiple enactments.* Unpublished DPhil thesis, Oxford University.

De Filippi, P., and Loveluck, B. (2016). The invisible politics of Bitcoin: governance crisis of a decentralised infrastructure. *Internet Policy Review, 5*(3). DOI: 10.14763/2016.3.427.

DeNardis, L. (2014). *The global war for Internet governance.* New Haven, CT and London: Yale University Press.

Denis, J., and Pontille, D. (2015). Material ordering and the care of things. *Science, Technology, and Human Values, 40*(3): 338–67.

Epstein, D., Katzenbach, C., and Musiani, F. (2016). Doing internet governance: Practices, controversies, infrastructures, and institutions. *Internet Policy Review, 5*(3). DOI: 10.14763/2016.3.435.

Greenberg, A. (2013a, August 3). Meet the Dread Pirate Roberts, the man behind booming black market drug website Silk Road. *Forbes.* Retrieved August 25, 2017, from www.forbes.com/sites/andygreenberg/2013/08/14/meet-the-dread-pirate-roberts-the-man-behind-booming-black-market-drug-website-silk-road/#346f8d58190c

Greenberg, A. (2013b, November 25). Israeli researchers' theory debunked: No clear ties between Bitcoin's creator and Silk Road. *Forbes.* Retrieved August 25, 2017, from www.forbes.com/sites/andygreenberg/2013/11/25/israeli-researchers-theory-debunked-no-clear-ties-between-bitcoins-creator-and-silk-road/

Greenberg, A. (2015a, September 9). Ross Ulbricht didn't create Silk Road's Dread Pirate Roberts. This guy did. *Wired.* Retrieved August 25, 2017, from www.wired.com/2015/02/ross-ulbricht-didnt-create-silk-roads-dread-pirate-roberts-guy/

Greenberg, A. (2015b, January 4). Silk Road boss' first murder-for-hire was his mentor's idea. *Wired.* Retrieved August 25, 2017, from www.wired.com/2015/04/silk-road-boss-first-murder-attempt-mentors-idea/

Hay, C. (1999). Crisis and the structural transformation of the state: Interrogating the process of change. *British Journal of Politics and International Relations, 1*(3): 317–44.

Hill, K. (2014, January 27). Winklevosses, Bitcoin community shocked by arrest of BitInstant CEO Charlie Shrem. *Forbes.* Retrieved August 25, 2017, from www.forbes.com/sites/kashmirhill/2014/01/27/winklevosses-bitcoin-community-shocked-by-arrest-of-bitinstant-ceo-charlie-shrem/#242d7623242d

Karlstrøm, H. (2014). Do libertarians dream of electric coins? The material embeddedness of Bitcoin. *Distinktion: Scandinavian Journal of Social Theory, 15*(1): 23–36.

Kate, L. (2014, March 25). The rise and fall of MtGox: Everything you need to know. *Coinreport.* Retrieved August 25, 2017, from https://coinreport.net/editorial-rise-fall-mtgox/

Kinsley, J. (2014a, February 20). Mt.Gox falls: Drags Bitcoin along for a ride. *Coinreport.* Retrieved August 25, 2017, from https://coinreport.net/mt-gox-falls-bitcoin-price-new-low/

Kinsley, J. (2014b, February 12). Mt.Gox meltdown initiates domino effect in Bitcoin world. *Coinreport.* Retrieved August 25, 2017, from https://coinreport.net/mt-gox-meltdown-bitcoin/

Latour, B. (1987). *Science in action: How to follow scientists and engineers through society.* Cambridge, MA: Harvard University Press.

Luhman, N. (2000). Familiarity, confidence, trust: Problems and alternatives. In D. Gambetta (ed.) *Trust: Making and breaking cooperative relations* (pp. 94–107). Oxford: Oxford University Press.

Mallard, A., Méadel, C., and Musiani, F. (2014). The paradoxes of distributed trust: Peer-to-peer architecture and user confidence in Bitcoin. *Journal of Peer Production* (4). Retrieved August 25, 2017, from http://peerproduction.net/issues/issue-4-value-and-currency/peer-reviewed-articles/the-paradoxes-of-distributed-trust/

Martinez, F. (2014, February 25). The MtGox Bitcoin scandal explained. *Fusion.* Retrieved August 25, 2017, from http://fusion.net/story/4947/the-mtgox-bitcoin-scandal-explained/

Maurer, B., Nelms, T.C., and Swartz, L. (2013). "When perhaps the real problem is money itself": The practical materiality of Bitcoin. *Social Semiotics, 23*(2): 261–77.

Mott, N. (2015, April 12). Mt.Gox lost most of its Bitcoin years before it shut down in 2014. *Pando.* Retrieved August 25, 2017, from https://pando.com/2015/04/20/mt-gox-lost-most-of-its-bitcoins-years-before-it-shut-down-in-2014/

Musiani, F., Cogburn, D.L., DeNardis, L., and Levinson, N.S. (eds.) (2016). *The turn to infrastructure in Internet governance.* New York: Palgrave/Macmillan.

Nakamoto, S. (2008). *Bitcoin: A peer-to-peer electronic cash system.* Retrieved August 21, 2017, from https://bitcoin.org/bitcoin.pdf

Naranayan, A. (2015, July 28). Analyzing the 2013 Bitcoin fork: Centralized decision-making saved the day. *Freedom to Tinker Blog.* Retrieved August 25, 2017, from https://freedom-to-tinker.com/2015/07/28/analyzing-the-2013-bitcoin-fork-centralized-decision-making-saved-the-day/

O'Neill, P.H. (2014, January 22). The final confessions of a Silk Road kingpin. *DailyDot.* Retrieved August 25, 2017, from www.dailydot.com/crime/silk-road-confession-steven-sadler-nod/

Pinch, T., and Leuenberger, C. (2006). *Studying scientific controversy from the STS perspective.* Paper presented at the Science Controversy and Democracy Conference, Taipei, Taiwan.

Ron, D., and Shamir, A. (2013). *Quantitative analysis of the full Bitcoin transaction graph.* BT – Financial Cryptography and Data Security: 17th International Conference, Okinawa, Japan, April 1–5.

Siluk, S. (2013, May 15). Why are the feds seizing Mt. Gox and Dwolla funds? *Coindesk.* Retrieved August 25, 2017, from www.coindesk.com/why-are-the-feds-seizing-mt-gox-and-dwolla-funds/

Southhurst, J. (2014, February 24). Mt. Gox CEO Mark Karpeles resigns from Bitcoin Foundation Board. *Coindesk.* Retrieved August 25, 2017, from www.coindesk.com/mt-gox-ceo-mark-karpeles-resigns-bitcoin-foundation-board/

Spaven, E. (2013, August 20). Government seized $2.9 million from Bitcoin exchange Mt. Gox. *Coindesk.* Retrieved August 25, 2017, from www.coindesk.com/government-seized-2-9m-from-bitcoin-exchange-mt-gox/

Titcomb, J. (2014, February 25). Bitcoin under threat as MtGox goes offline. *Telegraph.* Retrieved August 25, 2017, from www.telegraph.co.uk/finance/currency/10659768/mtgox-down.html

Trautman, L. (2014). Virtual currencies Bitcoin and what now after Liberty Reserve, Silk Road, and Mt. Gox? *Richmond Journal of Law and Technology, 20*(4).

Van Eeten, M.J., and Mueller, M. (2013). Where is the governance in Internet governance? *New Media and Society, 15*(5): 720–36.

Velasco, P.R. (2016). Sketching Bitcoin: Empirical research of digital affordances. In S. Kubitschko, and A. Kaun (eds.) *Innovative methods in media and communication research* (pp. 99–122). New York: Springer International Publishing.

Von Hippel, E. (1986). Lead users: A source of novel product concepts. *Management Science, 32*(7): 791–806.

Wong, J.I. (2014a, February 4). Poll: Are you having Mt.Gox withdrawal issues? *Coindesk*. Retrieved August 25, 2017, from www.coindesk.com/poll-mt-gox-withdrawal-issues/

Wong, J.I. (2014b, February 15). 68% of Mt. Gox users still awaiting their funds, survey reveals. *Coindesk*. Retrieved August 25, 2017, from www.coindesk.com/mt-gox-users-awaiting-funds-survey-reveals/

Woolgar, S., and Neyland, D. (2013). *Mundane governance: Ontology and accountability*. Oxford: Oxford University Press.

Ziewitz, M., and Pentzold, C. (2014). In search of Internet governance: Performing order in digitally networked environments. *New Media and Society, 16*(2): 306–22.

8 Experiments in algorithmic governance

A history and ethnography of "The DAO," a failed decentralized autonomous organization

Quinn DuPont

This chapter describes a short-lived experiment in organizational governance that attempted to utilize algorithmic authority through cryptocurrency and block-chain technologies to create a social and political world quite unlike anything we have seen before. According to the visionaries behind the project, by encoding the rules of governance for organizations and governments in a set of "smart contracts" running on an immutable, decentralized, and potentially unstoppable and public blockchain, new forms of social interactions and order would emerge. This experiment was an example of a new form of organization, called a "decentralized autonomous organization," or DAO. The forms of sociality that would emerge – they promised – would be transparent, efficient, fair, and democratic.

While the idea of decentralized autonomous organizations had been mooted since the early days of cryptocurrencies, the launch of sophisticated blockchain platforms with built-in programming interfaces gave enthusiasts a practical, technical apparatus to realize their vision. Foremost among these emerging blockchain platforms was Ethereum, a so-called distributed "Turing-complete" computer. The Ethereum platform is a new and expanded version of the Bitcoin system in that it adds a layer of software on top of a blockchain. Like Bitcoin, Ethereum also comprises decentralized "mining" computers, but whereas the Bitcoin miners primarily authenticate transactions, the Ethereum miners authenticate and run executable code.

It seemed like decentralized autonomous organizations would finally get their day in 2016, when a design built on the Ethereum platform emerged from a small blockchain company called Slock.it. Earlier, in June 2015, Slock.it began development of a decentralized autonomous organization framework, accepting contributions from the open-source software community. By March 2016, a large community had begun to form around the open-source framework, and Christoph Jentzsch of Slock.it published the corresponding white paper on March 15, 2016 (Jentzsch, 2016). The community formed through the Slack messaging service initially, and then launched an online forum independent of Slock.it, calling themselves DAOhub, which was co-founded by Felix Albert and Auryn Macmillan, and joined by a core team of six other members. Slock.it was sympathetic and encouraging of the DAOhub, and wanted their design to become a "standard" for future decentralized autonomous organizations to build on. In April 2016, the DAOhub community appointed 12 "curators," backing the project with the imprimatur of industry heavyweights, including Vitalik Buterin himself, the wunderkind and inventor behind Ethereum.

The very model of simplicity, a mere 900 or so lines of software source code, this design was given the placeholder name of "The DAO." The DAO was intended to allow cryptocurrency "investors" to directly fund and manage new enterprises – all to be run on the Ethereum blockchain. Because The DAO was backed by Ethereum, complex business logic could be programmed, and once set in action, the organization would be virtually unstoppable. The blockchain would ensure that all business transactions and organizational changes would be immutably recorded on a public ledger authenticated and controlled by a large, decentralized network of computers. Moreover, because the organizations spawned by The DAO were directly funded through digital token-holding "investors," each organization would be, in effect, directly managed by its investors, as per the investment stake of the individual (i.e., those investors who contributed more tokens would get a correspondingly larger number of votes on organizational decisions). No need for messy and inefficient human negotiation – so it seemed!

The DAO was launched on April 30, 2016, at 10:00am GMT/UTC (by several "anonymous" submissions associated with DAOhub, who executed the open-source bytecode on the Ethereum blockchain), with a set funding or "creation" period of 28 days (A2be, 2016). As the funding period came to a close (concluding May 28, 2016), The DAO went live with the equivalent of about US$250 million in funding, breaking all existing crowdfunding records. Some 10,000 to 20,000 (estimated) people invested in The DAO, contributing 11,994,260.98 Ethereum tokens (known as ether, or ETH), which amounted to about 14 percent of the total ETH supply.[1] However, shortly after the minimum two-week "debating" period, on June 17, 2016, The DAO's code was "exploited" by an unknown individual. This exploit used unintended behavior of the code's logic to rapidly drain the fund of millions of dollars' worth of ETH tokens. Immediately, Slock.it, the leaders of the Ethereum platform, numerous cryptocurrency exchanges, and other informal technical leaders stepped in to stem the bleeding – shutting down "exits" through the exchanges, and launching counterattacks. It is at precisely this point that we see the vision of future governance structures break down, and devolve into traditional models of sociality – using existing strong ties to negotiate and influence, argue and disagree – all with nary a line of code in sight. In the end, the whole project was disbanded, with an inglorious "hard fork" rolling back the ostensibly "immutable" ledger.

This chapter details the governance structures that were promised by the developers and community members involved in the making of The DAO, and in contrast, those that were observed in its discourses before, during, and after the "exploit." With the term "governance," I intend a broad scope: governance is the "conduct of conduct" through the plurality of (human and non-human) actors that are interdependent but lack the power or authority to decide and enact solutions unilaterally and directly (Introna, 2016: 19), which enables a broad set of "governance options" as risks and solutions (Saurwein et al., 2015). In analyzing "discourses," I mean the "cohesive ensemble of ideas, concepts, and categorizations about a specific object that frame that object in a certain way and, therefore, delimit the possibilities for action in relation to it" (Epstein, 2005: 2). The discourses surrounding The DAO reflect governance through its technical makeup, as a deeply embedded socio-technical apparatus that permits, prohibits, enables, disables, promotes, and limits courses of action.

My goal in this chapter is not to discredit the idea of decentralized autonomous organizations, but rather to highlight some of the ways that such discourses and their operationalization do and do not (currently) work. Thus, "true believers" in the technology will see that the world is simply not yet ready for decentralized autonomous organizations, or that Slock.it and the DAOhub's version was flawed (such criticisms were widespread well before its launch). Critics of The DAO's utopia, on the other hand, will realize that human sociality crops up whenever humans are involved, and that existing governance structures are in fact well refined through thousands of years of social commerce, government, and exchange – not the idealistic, pre-social vision that arguably never existed. Either way, The DAO introduced and explored an interesting technology for experimenting with governance issues and new models of society.

Visions of Decentralized Autonomous Organizations

The DAO was a decentralized, crowdfunded, direct-management (or direct-democracy) organization and investment platform. The DAO was the first high-profile realization of a decentralized autonomous organization (DAO) running on the Ethereum platform (other DAOs exist, and existed).[2] Whereas The DAO had visions of being the DAO to end all DAOs, most DAOs differentiate from one another by offering slightly different functionality, market verticals, and governance structures.

In the original vision of decentralized autonomous organizations, as proposed by Vitalik Buterin, founder and member of the Ethereum Foundation, a DAO is a pseudo-legal organization run by an assemblage of human and "robot" participants. The robotic participants are algorithmic rules that run on the distributed Ethereum blockchain, and automatically respond to inputs according to programmed rules. Inputs can be varied in type, including fully autonomous sensors (e.g., a digital thermometer), online inputs (e.g., a change in stock price), or "real-world," external decisions by human agents.[3] Based on these inputs and the pre-programmed logic stored on a distributed blockchain, the idea is that a DAO would automatically initiate action in an irreversible way (all changes would be written into an immutable distributed ledger). Potential actions a DAO might take include distributing cryptocurrency (such as ETH, for "fuel" or payment), or making a computation and issuing an output, such as triggering software or electromechanical (or IoT) devices.

From the inception of Ethereum and its much lauded decentralized autonomous organization concept there had been very little concrete development of DAOs until The DAO was launched. The DAO was an attempt to build a funding platform, similar to Kickstarter, but one that specifically used decentralized autonomous organization (blockchain) technologies for its operation. Whereas Kickstarter raises funds from many individuals through their centralized administration, typically for the development of commercial products (often "rewarding" the funders through a pre-sale mechanism), The DAO sought to raise funds direct from peers (decentralized, peer-to-peer crowdfunding). This "funding" mechanism remains a contentious, poorly understood, and increasingly prevalent practice. Later, in conversation with Christoph Jentzsch, he described his vision of The DAO's economics as a very large joint bank account, not a "sale," or "security." Following The DAO, through 2016–17, numerous "initial coin offerings" would be launched that continued to skate on legal thin ice with respect to securities and finance law, raising impressive amounts of investment from unvetted and typically amateur investors.

To raise funds for a pool of investment (controlled by The DAO token-holders), the first stage of The DAO was a funding period or "creation phase" of 28 days (beginning April 30 and concluding May 28, 2016), during which time anyone could exchange ETH cryptocurrency for DAO tokens in return. During the initial funding period, the price of DAO tokens rose programmatically (from an initial value of $1:100$) – encouraging early buy-in (a masterful sales tactic, encouraging people to "act soon, limited supplies!"); formally, the price increase was to reward the riskier (information-deficient) behavior of early investors. After the initial funding period, no more tokens would be created; however, it would be possible to trade existing tokens on public cryptocurrency exchanges.

Tokens would be used to directly fund and control "proposals" on The DAO platform. Anyone with a (refundable) minimum token deposit could create a proposal to be voted on by token-holders. Investors voted by allocating DAO tokens for specific proposals.[4] Since tokens would be valuable (comprising exchange-convertible ETH cryptocurrency), "voting" for a proposal was conceptually the same as funding it, in much the same way that projects are funded on Kickstarter. Unlike Kickstarter, however, DAO voting members would have significant control over projects. Since proposals were expected to be as transparent as possible (ideally, with their operational logic programmed into the blockchain), DAO voting members would directly control an organization by voting for (i.e., funding) specific decisions. For example, voting members could decide – directly – if a new employee was hired or not by using their votes to approve or deny the decision (or even, in fact, use their tokens to directly pay the employee). The level of management granularity would be set by the decentralized autonomous organization contract that runs on the blockchain, and projects could choose to have the minutia of decisions voted on by members, or decide to have only major decisions go to vote. Those members holding the most tokens – majority stakeholders – would have greater influence over decisions.[5]

The DAO proposals

On May 28, The DAO officially went "live" after an initial 28-day funding period. During this "creation phase" the community of investors discussed "proposals" for how The DAO funds might be used. The proposal with clearly the most community support was Slock.it's own: use The DAO funds to hire Slock.it to design and manufacture a "smart" lock system that would enable "sharing economy" members (such as AirBnB homeowners) to programmatically grant access to their homes to approved renters. Since The DAO was intended to fund the development of this smart lock system, to be built by Slock.it, The DAO token-holders would earn rent on each transaction that used the system. The proposal was enticing to many investors because it used many aspects of blockchain technology to accomplish its primary function, such as payment and granular management of access that would function through smart contracts on the blockchain, in an open, immutable, and verifiable manner. That rent was being extracted on each use did not seem to bother many people interested in the idea of a "sharing" economy. That Slock.it developed a funding platform for the primary purpose of enticing investors to fund their own enterprise *was*, however, a concern for many in the community. Early on, foreseeing future problems, commentators on The DAO worried about potential conflicts of interest between Slock.it's development and control of The DAO and Slock.it's status as potential hired contractor.

Although vastly less popular than Slock.it's proposal, a few other ideas for The DAO emerged, including one by a French company hoping to create a ride-sharing vehicle (Mobotiq), and a proposal for an online gaming system (Firstblood). Given my own interest in understanding the dynamics of distributed funding and governance platforms, I also began the process of setting up an organization that would use The DAO. My hope was that in creating an environmental charity using The DAO, along with fellow researchers (at University College Dublin and the University of California, Irvine), we would be able to study real-world activities through participant observation. By participating in and observing The DAO community and its technology, we hoped to see how these new forms of economics and management were being used. Unfortunately, none of these ideas made it to the formal proposal stage prior to the exploit.

The DAO of Whales

The research groups that had loosely formed to study The DAO had been collectively studying cryptocurrencies and blockchain technologies since the early days of Bitcoin. We had observed many early cryptocurrency challenges, such as when the then-leading Mt.Gox cryptocurrency exchange was hacked, Bitcoin went through violent price swings, and Silk Road facilitated the sale of drugs and guns online. We also observed how cryptocurrencies were transitioning away from cypherpunk ideologies, and away from use as an online replacement for cash. Principally, I wondered if the emerging venture-capital-backed blockchain companies would lead to a new era of respectability or legitimacy for cryptocurrencies. At the time, it seemed like The DAO was clearly a part of this trend of cryptocurrencies moving towards dominant capital (cf., Bichler and Nitzan, 2004), and I hoped that by studying the formation and operation of The DAO, from the inside, we would see how such systems might facilitate new forms of democratic control and enable massively crowdfunded financing.

The environmental charity I proposed was called "The DAO of Whales." Running on The DAO platform, the charity sought to directly and *autonomously* care for a pod of orca whales in the Pacific Northwest. The entire charity would run in a transparent fashion on the blockchain, and through a series of smart contracts, its primary function would be to disburse funds to a scientific research group studying our "adopted" pod of orcas (the choice of research group to receive the funds would also be decided through the voting mechanisms supplied by The DAO). Using techniques made possible by blockchain technologies, the payments from the charity would be automated, verifiable, and censorship-resistant (or "unstoppable," in the sense that the system would need to be changed or eliminated). I believed that charity organizations, in particular, would benefit from these kinds of capabilities, since charities are sometimes accused of financial mismanagement and opaque governance.

Additionally, to see how far I could push the idealistic vision of decentralized autonomous organizations, I proposed reviving the concept of a deodand to create a human–whale–robot hybrid organization. A deodand is a medieval idea that imbued all created things with legal status, which therefore would give rights and duties to all things, just like human law (the concept of the deodand has in the past led to legal cases where farm animals have had to stand trial for their crimes – which, humorously, included being dressed in appropriate clothing and sitting in the witness stand). For my human–whale–robot hybrid, The DAO would legitimize the identity of the hybrid by realizing its programmatic operation and economic performance – in effect creating a new kind of legal entity.[6]

Why whales? I was inspired by a science fiction idea mooted in the Ethereum community (Schroeder, 2014), which imagined that a DAO might work as a kind of legal counsel on behalf of a pod of whales. So, for example, to ensure their own safety, The DAO could automatically (and irrevocably) disburse funds if certain programmed criteria were met, such as if an oil spill occurred in the region. In this way, The DAO (on behalf of the whales) would automatically hold humans financially responsible for their actions, and redress any negative events by funding appropriate countermeasures (such as paying for oil cleanup). As the original author of the idea stated, "This is not 'save the whales,' it's 'give the whales the tools to save themselves'" (Schroeder, 2014).

The exploit

In the months leading up to the post-funding, launch date of The DAO, numerous community members expressed worry about the security and governance of The DAO. One community member called it an "experiment in responsibility," and, in general, it was becoming clear that Slock.it might not be the safe shepherd the community had hoped for (Ryan, 2016). The most pressing and vocal critique came from cryptocurrency researchers Dino Mark, Vlad Zamfir, and Emin Gün Sirer, who released a white paper on May 26, 2016 (when The DAO was launched but in the static "funding" period), outlining eight possible security risks (Mark et al., 2016). Although these security risks were based on game theory issues, rather than actual code bugs, given the status of these researchers in the field, and the unexpected success of The DAO's funding stage, their call for a temporary "moratorium" was well supported in the community. Nonetheless, Stephen Tual, founder and COO of Slock.it (who had taken on a de facto corporate messaging role), assured the community that such concerns would be addressed, and that there was no need for panic. Later, in conversations with both Tual and Jentzsch, they expressed concern to me that between the unexpected success of the launch, the DAOhub's quasi-control, and their de facto lack of control, The DAO was becoming a fearsome worry.

Between June 5 and June 9, 2016, another issue was discovered – a technical bug this time, called a "race to empty" attack – just days before the first activities of The DAO were to begin (2016).[7] To address the rising tide of security issues, and to reassure an increasingly worried public, on June 13, Tual issued a statement about a 1.1 software update to The DAO framework, which had been in the works for "over a month" (Tual, 2016a). This updated version purported to address the game theory issues identified by Mark, Zamfir, and Sirer (2016), as well as technical fixes for other issues, including the "race to empty" attack. However, during this time, Tual was also increasingly vocal that Slock.it did not "own" or "run" The DAO – a fact they had begun emphasizing as The DAO grew relatively large and wealthy – motivated to keep their role as hired contractor distinct from the ostensibly leaderless DAO framework. Because of the algorithmic governance structure, Tual reported to the community, the needed technical fixes (supplied for the most part by Slock.it) could not be implemented until (a) The DAO token-holders affirmatively voted for an upgrade (after a proposed two-week community review), and (b) Ethereum miners approved and implemented the change.

Meanwhile, as the Slock.it team was preparing the version 1.1 update and trying to move it through the community governance process for upgrading, the "race to empty" attack was out in the open. This exploit would enable an attacker to utilize the "split" function to exit the DAO while repeatedly calling a function to withdraw funds before the balance could be updated. The attack had been tested by a similar (but much smaller) DAO project called "MakerDAO," which confirmed that it was executable, and had alerted The DAO developers about the security risk. On June 12, just prior to his prepared statement about the launch of the version 1.1 update, Tual issued a statement about this security risk, insisting that "no funds were at risk" (a statement that, while technically true, he later regretted), and that the forthcoming 1.1 software update would address this exploit (2016c).

With ostensibly no funds at risk, and little true control over the platform at this point, the Slock.it and DAOhub teams pressed forward, insisting that The

DAO would stick to its original schedule, but that they *might reconsider* moving forward with new features and improvements until after "the deployment of a DAO Framework 1.1," which was supposed to fix existing security issues (2016c). Slock.it and community members thoroughly vetted the by-now immutable code, looking for the "re-entry" bugs that had been previously identified, and found none. Besides, in theory, all The DAO funds were safe, at least for the time being, due to built-in debating periods for proposals and creating new child DAOs, and a seven-day delay window for the withdrawal-like "split" action (Christoph, 2016). Therefore, Slock.it argued, token-holders – malicious or otherwise – could not immediately exit The DAO. Accounting for all of the various built-in delays, the earliest date token-holders could exit with their funds was July 15, 2016. In the end, no dates would be pushed back; The DAO launched with the 1.0 framework and an upgrade path to 1.1 software (requiring community approval and review).

On June 17, 2016, an unknown "attacker" launched a "race to empty" exploit that was similar to the one that had been previously identified, and began draining The DAO of funds (in the end, 3,689,577 ETH, or about 30 percent of the total). The first warning came from a Reddit community member, "ledgerwatch," who wrote, "I think TheDAO is getting drained right now" (ledgerwatch, 2016b). Within hours, Ethereum Foundation member George Hallam roused key Ethereum developers and other pertinent members of the community to an internal Slack communication channel (some of whom were already well into a Friday night). The members confirmed the attack and started to strategize. Knowing that the attacker would want to convert the "stolen" funds into "traditional" currency, the assembled group contacted several individuals in charge at the major exchanges responsible for trading ETH, and strongly requested that these exchanges halt trading. Worried that shutting down trading would cause panic and reputational damage, and potentially suggest fiduciary malfeasance, some exchanges resisted such a drastic action, but with US$250 million and an existential crisis for the entire Ethereum platform on the line, the major exchanges eventually relented. With nowhere to go, and counterattacks in place, the attack relented and the funds were effectively "frozen" for the time being (due to the built-in security delay required for child DAOs and "splits" from The DAO). At this point, long-term strategies were discussed, blame was placed (the community excoriated Slock.it, and especially Tual), and a countdown clock for a solution was started.

After the exploit

Over the next month, Buterin publicly debated solutions (which ranged from immediate counterattacks, to complicated "soft forks," to clean and *severe* "hard forks"), the founder and CTO of Slock.it Christoph Jentzsch publicly apologized, and The DAO funds continued to be attacked (and blocked through technical countermeasures). The value of ETH plummeted, and the community speculated that an unknown individual had shorted the price of ETH prior to the exploit and made millions in the aftermath, fueling the belief that the true purpose of the attack was to devalue ETH and make money by short selling (some of the evidence for this short sale, however, is circumspect, as it may have been a mere coincidence). Moreover, debates over solutions raged online, driven by ideologies that saw any kind of "hard fork" as tantamount to an existential deceit (a hard fork would conceptually, if not technically, erase the event from the collective and supposedly *immutable* ledger). Even more curiously, a letter purportedly written by the attacker circulated, arguing that since The DAO was defined by its code, the "exploit" was nothing more than a clever (and legal) loophole ("The Attacker," 2016).[8] The letter writer and a vocal minority in the community argued that "code is law," echoing Lawrence Lessig's (1999) influential slogan. Therefore, they argued, any effort to block the "attacker" would be morally wrong and against the very spirit of decentralized autonomous organizations.

Within the next few weeks, with the political clout of Buterin and the Ethereum Foundation behind the decision, a "hard fork" version of the Ethereum software was developed and released to miners. This hard fork created a special "withdrawal-only" contract on the Ethereum blockchain and moved all tokens to it. A majority of miners implemented this software, and the blockchain ledger was updated to effectively erase The DAO. The DAO, and its political vision, was dead.

"Moderates" saw the hard fork as evidence of the flexibility and practicality of Ethereum and its leaders, while the more ideological saw the hard fork as censorship by a powerful cabal, or proof that blockchain technology was unable to live up to its idealistic promises. For the minority of miners who refused to update their Ethereum software – refusing the hard fork – they split from the mainline blockchain. This new blockchain – still susceptible to The DAO-style attacks – was dubbed "Ethereum Classic" and gained a somewhat significant following, even being actively traded on exchanges. Over time, the Ethereum community put The DAO experiment behind them, and talk of decentralized autonomous organizations – previously a guiding light for blockchain platforms – was thereafter tainted.

An ethnographic study of the DAO governance

Seeing that my attempt to engage in participant observation research by proposing "The DAO of Whales" charity was cut short when The DAO was ignominiously canceled and erased by the hard fork, I then began retrospectively studying the ideals and imaginations of the community through their online discourse. Over the following year (2016–17), this course of study brought me into contact with the discourses of hobbyist participants and investors, amounting to an ethnography of digital culture focusing primarily on the Reddit community (which I had previously identified as a primary site of discourse). My study covered online discourses in the period immediately before, during, and after The DAO.

Numerous challenges occurred in my efforts to ethnographically study The DAO. Very little empirical research on cryptocurrencies and blockchains exists today. The research that does exist is predominantly quantitative in nature, and from a socio-economic perspective. The only existing *qualitative* study of actors and communities that I am aware of is Lustig and Nardi's (2015) analysis of the Bitcoin community. Consequently, there are very few research models to follow (qualitative research of online communities, in general, remains a challenge), and there is scant contextual data about these communities to help guide and ground my own research.

Nonetheless, Lustig and Nardi (2015) do provide a compelling snapshot of the composition, beliefs, and values of the Bitcoin community (and by extension, the larger cryptocurrency and blockchain community).[9] In their study, they used grounded theory methodology with an initial 36-question online survey and a follow-up series of interviews (with participants identified from the initial survey). Twenty-two participants were interviewed, and Lustig and Nardi found (perhaps unsurprisingly) that most members of the cryptocurrency and blockchain community believed algorithms were more trustworthy and authoritative than existing socio-political institutions. Yet, the views and values of the Bitcoin community were divided and complex – Lustig and Nardi reported that the community "recognized that it is not enough to just trust in the code" (2015: 751). This complex and sometimes contradictory view of trust and authority meant that other Bitcoin users needed to be trusted and consulted while using the cryptocurrency (especially when it came to matters of trading strategy), but that the technical structure of Bitcoin (using a "proof of work" network of "miners" cryptographically authenticating transactions) obviated worries about counterfeited coins or counterparty risk. Moreover, the development of the Bitcoin software itself, Lustig and Nardi pointed out (2015: 751), required complex socio-technical negotiations.

Research method

My research used a variant of grounded theory methodology; specifically, I followed Merriam and Tisdell's (2016) "Basic" qualitative method. Merriam and Tisdell characterize this method as richly descriptive, emergent, and flexible. Key to this "Basic" method is recognizing that existing bias – the expertise of the researcher – is a strength to the development of theory, by which the researcher works from observed behaviors and discourses to thick theories of human and social interaction.

Data were collected from online sources, in a retrospective fashion. Since The DAO had already ended, I used written traces of discourse from several online sources. In my initial research, I identified the Reddit community as being the richest source of non-technical discourse, especially since this community appeared to comprise both insiders and outsiders to The DAO. Within the larger Reddit community (organized around thematic "sub-Reddits") I found that the Ethereum sub-Reddit (/r/Ethereum) was the most vibrant and interesting place for online discussion of The DAO (unexpectedly, the /r/TheDAO sub-Reddit was less active). Therefore, I focused my data collection on the Ethereum Reddit community, but also researched broadly across blogs, technical websites, and news media as well.

Data were retrieved using opportunistic search queries across the entirety of the Reddit platform (global searches), and by following links and leads in an investigative manner with no predefined scope limitations. Additionally, data were collected from the Ethereum sub-Reddit *systematically* through June/July 2016 (the two months surrounding the exploit), using an online search tool to display sub-Reddit posts in chronological order. Discussions of interest (determined by a quick initial skim-read) were captured as PDF files, and ingested to Atlas.ti software for later processing (73 PDF documents, each ranging from a few pages to 50-plus pages, were ingested).

Once the Reddit discussions were ingested into Atlas.ti, I performed a form of "open coding" for qualitative content analysis. This method is similar to the constant comparative method developed by Glaser and Strauss (1967). I reflexively, iteratively, and interactively grouped, renamed, and abstracted data while building towards categories (a form of "axial coding"). My method of analysis was purposely loose and pragmatic, not high-minded analysis driven by formalities. Merriam and Tisdell espouse this deflationary view of qualitative data analysis for their "Basic" method: "Coding is nothing more than assigning some sort of shorthand designation to various aspects of your data so that you can easily retrieve pieces of the data" (2016). As I developed categories, I constantly returned to the data and re-evaluated my codes and categories, using my existing insights about cryptocurrency discourses to guide my decisions. I developed 23 codes over the 73 ingested documents (in addition to identifying 534 illustrative quotations). I soon learned that chronology became the most critical axis of analysis (files were renamed in Atlas.ti using their origin date to facilitate ordering), since discourse about The DAO shifted significantly before, during, and after the exploit.

Given the highly decentralized nature of the underlying blockchain technology and cryptocurrency's origins in cypherpunk and Internet culture, I felt justified in focusing solely on online discourses for data collection, since my previous experience told me that blockchain communities are especially well represented online. Nonetheless, the Reddit community constitutes a very particular snapshot of larger cryptocurrency discourse, and has its own form of rhetoric and shared lore. As such, my study cannot be understood as fully representative of all participants in The DAO (and certainly, Tual and Jentzsch, whom I spoke with later, disagree with many of the opinions expressed by the Reddit community). Moreover, Reddit discourse is "semi-public" and pseudonymous in nature, and often has a "performative" quality.[10] Additionally, given the extensive, decentralized, and often secret nature of cryptocurrency participants (and especially their trading strategies), there is almost certainly a shadow element not at all represented in the public discourses that I investigated. In fact, my past experiences within the community suggest that a significant number of cryptocurrency users are primarily "investors" interested in little more than high-risk profit, and therefore are motivated by economic incentives, which may also be underrepresented in the vibrant online discourses (with an inverse overrepresentation of idealist and polemic discourses existing online). Nonetheless, my analysis revealed hints at these and other complex motivations in the online communities.

Results

The DAO provides a compelling and rich snapshot of unrealized dreams, visions of new worlds, and quotidian struggle. Because The DAO ended in disaster, the results also speak to literatures on crisis and the governance thereof. Specifically, I am drawn to Samman's analysis (2015) of crisis and historical imagination, which conceives of crisis as both overdetermined and indeterminate. In the case of The DAO, there were numerous internal contradictions that overdetermined a single narrative history, and The DAO remained indeterminate because it was shuttered before long-term dynamics of governance could be further explored. Moreover, as a moment of crisis, the experimental goals that The DAO originally set out to achieve have yet to be brought to fruition. Therefore, assessing the governance of The DAO, and seeking sensible solutions and options for addressing risk (see Saurwein et al., 2015), remains a significant challenge.

Of the many potential themes that emerged in the complex discourses on The DAO, I identified three related to issues of governance: legal authority, practical governance, and the experimental nature of using algorithmic systems for distributed action.

Legal authority

Legal authority is now a well-known "issue" in the cryptocurrency and blockchain world. For years, strong (idealistic) proponents of blockchain technology have advocated that "code is law."[11] In the academic literature, this articulation of "code is law" has been described as a form of "algorithmic authority" – first identified by Clay Shirky (2009) and then later Frank Pasquale (2011) (as "automated authority"), among others. In much of this literature, in direct opposition to the idealistic proponents of blockchain technology, the concept of algorithmic authority is characterized critically, as tantamount to the biopolitical technologies that go about unknown by, and against the interests of, its subjects (Introna, 2016).

Lustig and Nardi (2015) characterize the Bitcoin community's beliefs about legal authority through the lens of algorithmic authority. In their analysis, they identified a complex array of views on algorithmic authority, and they found that according those in the Bitcoin community, the presence of algorithmic authority is not uniformly negative. Similar views about the role of algorithmic authority were also found in the discourses on The DAO. As I mentioned above, the person who purportedly exploited The DAO also wrote a letter to the community, arguing from this very position of algorithmic authority – that he or she "rightfully claimed 3,641,694 [*sic*] ether" by exploiting a "feature" of The DAO that was designed to "promote decentralization" ("The Attacker," 2016). Others in the community were also sympathetic to this view (despite sometimes being in a position to potentially lose a significant number of valuable tokens because of this very model of legal authority).

Therefore, rather than simply adopt a critical, normative position when assessing the community discourses on algorithmic authority, I reference a model of algorithmic authority in terms of its governance relations (Campbell-Verduyn et al., 2017). Using this model, I argue that the forms of algorithmic authority present in the discourses on The DAO properly exist in a continuum – as governance through algorithms, governance with algorithms, and governance by algorithms.

Those attuned to formal understandings of law will likely find the notion of algorithmic authority – as exemplified by the argument put forth in the attacker's letter – galling and borderline humorous. As though intent could not or does not play an important role in law, or that a terms of service agreement (which the attacker also cites) could trump common sense and legal process. Nonetheless, the concept of algorithmic authority crystalizes a point that many in The DAO community held – The DAO was supposed to represent a turning point in legal authority, where code really does form a new legal regime. For example, "IAMnotA_Cylon" (2016) argued that "Ethereum worked exactly as intended," and "Polycephal_Lee" (2016) argued that the exploit was "the protocol working as it was written." On the other hand, "UntamedOne" (2016) argued that "we don't live in this idealistic cryptoanarchy world *yet*" (emphasis added). For those in The DAO community, many (but certainly not all) saw The DAO as a realization of a new form of legal authority. Nonetheless, the subsequent exploit also helped expose the tensions necessarily present in the space between algorithmic and existing, juridical legal authority.

Some members of The DAO community expressed concerns about this tension. Early on, these voices also included Slock.it's, which attempted to balance this legal tension by rhetorically distancing itself from fiduciary involvement of The DAO, seemingly for fear of legal reprisal (and many community members picked up on this maneuvering). A clear example of the latent tensions between utopia and reality was expressed by Tual in an early blog post (March 1, 2016), entitled "DAOs, or how to Replace Obsolete Governance Models" (2016b). This blog post announced the coming realization of a practical technology for "anyone, anywhere in the world to set up a Decentralized Autonomous Organization" (later known as The DAO), which included the proviso that "if you create a DAO … [using our software] you will be responsible for its operation" (Tual, 2016b). Somewhat more skeptically, others noted that The DAO nonetheless involved "real people" (ledgerwatch, 2016a), which may or may not be able to "legally own assets" given the unique structure of ownership under existing law (Dunning_Krugerrands, 2016). Showing concern for the ways that existing legal authority might impinge on their collective experiment, taxes, regulation, and liability were also frequent points of conversation in the community.

Many members of The DAO community saw their experiment as embarking on a new legal world, and devised strategies to make this world a reality. Reddit community member "ledgerwatch" (and later, the individual to first discover The DAO exploit), thought that "the necessary legal framework" for The DAO could be "grown bottom up … [from] within the current legal system" (ledgerwatch, 2016a). This individual then invoked *Lex mercatoria*, or medieval merchant law, as a model for how The DAO might find its legal footing within the existing legal system (ledgerwatch, 2016a). Presumably, medieval merchant law was a suitable model on account of its rough-and-ready and pragmatic way of dealing with legal issues (medieval merchant law sat outside of more formal legal processes). For The DAO, this kind of pragmatism became a form of real governance, as seen in the views of those community members who believed the post-exploit hard fork was an example of pragmatic, good governance.

Practical governance

On the continuum of governance made possible by algorithmic technologies, practical governance (or governance *of* algorithms) is a key issue facing society today. The existence of autonomous weapons, self-driving cars, and, of course, The DAO, all throw into relief the challenge of socially integrating these technologies, through forms of risk management, internal design and development, market solutions, industry self-regulation, and state and government regulation (Saurwein et al., 2015).

Once the exploit of The DAO took place, the previously existing ideals of algorithmic authority held by The DAO developers and supporters were thrown into disarray, and the project entered crisis mode. Slock.it and others attempted to assure a nervous public that the exploit did not threaten any funds and that it was "business as usual" (in the end, no funds were actually stolen) (carloscarlson, 2016). Some of these community members saw the exploit as an expensive lesson in "real life" ("Let the DAO burn" wrote "GeorgesTurdBlossom," 2016), or perhaps one that would motivate further development in security for decentralized autonomous organizations. Others, however, thought that a solution lay in the realization that, despite ideals and heaps of rhetoric about decentralization and immutability, good governance was flexible and pragmatic. For instance, some argued that this was a "maturing of the ecosystem" (Floersch, 2016) or a "rite of passage" (Sirer, 2016). For these individuals, which included Buterin, a hard fork was an obvious choice when faced with an existential crisis of this nature (vbuterin, 2017).

In these discussions, the issue of "centralized" governance emerged in parallel to factions in the community. Hardliners saw Buterin's and the Ethereum Foundation's support of a hard fork as tantamount to the bank bailouts following the 2008 global credit crisis. "DonaldCruz" wrote, jokingly, "good thing we have a central authority to come to the rescue when shit hits the fan" (DonaldCruz, 2016). And "Eldakara" wrote, "Ah..[*sic*] So decentralized protocols come with centralized bailouts now" (Eldakara, 2016). By accepting "centralized" governance in the form of a hard fork, instead of sticking with flawed but pure algorithmic authority, "itworks123" believed it was "like saying we should delay democracy until things are 'perfect'' (itworks123, 2016). On the other hand, many community members pushed back against this logic, perhaps motivated by saving their personal investment stake in The DAO, or perhaps by a thicker sense of the social embeddedness of technological systems. Summarizing this position, "DavidMc0" wrote, "decentralized doesn't need to mean static, stupid, or powerless against attackers" (DavidMc0, 2016).

An important part of the model of practical governance for The DAO rests on the view that it made a break with past forms of governance and that the exploit merely highlighted the ways that reality had not yet caught up to these new models. Looking toward technical developments that would create forms of algorithmic authority enabling a more robust and nuanced mode of governance, "redditbsbsbs" writes: "we can argue about full decentralization and autonomy post Serenity" (redditbsbsbs, 2016). Here, "Serenity" is the name of a point in the Ethereum development roadmap, but tellingly, also a rhetorical emblem of an imagined state of affairs, when algorithmic governance reaches peace and serenity.

Experiments in distributed action

From the earliest days of The DAO, many community members acknowledged that the enormous complexity of decentralized and algorithmic governance required a new kind of experimental "science" (dm1n1c, 2016) to map the "uncharted territory" The DAO was entering (laughing__cow, 2016). This new science was understood as, and promised to be, governance *by* algorithms. Bringing to light this science of society, however, required both a pioneering spirit and a new model of distributed action.

This logic and rhetoric of "experiment," "confusion," and "newness" pervaded discussions about how action could be coordinated using a decentralized technology platform. Summarizing the tension between a sound "investment" and a "recipe for chaos," one Reddit member noted that this kind of collective action is "dependent on an experimental, first-of-its-kind DAO platform" (xxeyes, 2016). The DAO was also surprisingly complex in terms of coordinating actors, with vigorous debates about the role of Slock.it, curators, developers, miners, the Ethereum Foundation, and the community of token-holders. When the collective "community is in charge," people worried, where do rights and duties fall (cubefriendly, 2016)?

Coordinating interests and actions across a range of actors with often very different incentives is a central challenge to designing many decentralized information communication technologies, including the Internet. The development of The DAO, as a model for future decentralized autonomous organizations, was an ideal site of exploration for experimenting with these incentive structures. One of the key actors in this regard is Vitalik Buterin, who has demonstrated a sophisticated, if at times blinkered, view of incentive and distributed action. In his online writing, he has come up with numerous game theoretical models to assure honesty, compliance, and other means for distributed action, which, in turn, can be instantiated in algorithms to produce authority and governance. Buterin's emerging and much-lauded "Proof of Stake" algorithm (replacing the now, much maligned, "Proof of Work" algorithm originally used in Bitcoin) is one such direct result of this kind of musing. Perhaps because it is so amenable to implementation in technical systems (a form of "computationalism;" Golumbia, 2009), rational actor and game theory have become key ways of modelling complex social properties in blockchain and cryptocurrency systems.

The exploit of The DAO, however, inevitably belied much of this sophisticated theory. The exploit shone a light on the shortcomings of these assumptions, or at least, reminded the actors of the enormous complexity of socially-embedded systems. It was believed that action could be coordinated through technology, or at least enhanced by it, with the application or operationalization of games or bets. Beneath the methods of coordinating action, however, The DAO relied on a model of human behavior and social constitution notionally based on liberal ideologies, where humans act as rational, self-interested, and untrusting agents (see Reijers et al., 2016; Scott, 2014). Inevitably, however, when governance of The DAO deviated from the expected course of events (those modelled in game theory by the designers), the social actors fell back to traditional strong network ties. In doing so, governance of The DAO discredited its ideological underpinnings, and even exposed a worrisome lack of managerial prowess that would typically use forms of rationalizing behavior drawn from risk management or crisis mediation.

The resolution of the exploit, through the eventual and final hard fork, was ultimately a hurried private discussion among known individuals, and bore little resemblance to theoretical modes of incentivizing and distributing action (see Hallam et al., 2016). Despite The DAO's experimentation, operationalizing algorithmic governance in society still requires awareness of implied and undeclared social goods (Levy, 2017), and any future design will need to contend with these challenges.

Discussion

I have not written with the goal of any strong conclusions to the many contentious issues present in The DAO or the broader themes revealed in this chapter. Rather, I have identified some of the ways that governance was *believed to* function in decentralized autonomous organizations, and the ways that it *did* function.

The DAO is an important artifact for attempting to understand emerging forms of algorithmic authority, working through practical modes of governance for autonomous and decentralized systems, and for understanding the ways that designing incentives and modeling action can fail. Its emergence and technical structure formally relates to ongoing discussions about the ethics of autonomous warfare, automated and high-frequency finance, and big data. Despite the utopian rhetoric on the one hand, and the largely critical academic literature on the other, what remains unclear with these technologies is whether they constitute an extension of existing socio-technical apparatuses, or are a decisive break with the past. What is clear, The DAO proved, is that these technologies have significant potential for real impact and harm, and therefore ring early warning alarms for the critical investigation of modes of governance beyond those already designed.

After the exploit, The DAO was formally shuttered, but in the conflictual community response that ensued there lies an interesting coda to its broader narrative. When the hard fork was proposed as a "fix" to the exploit, a vocal minority opposed it. While it is not entirely clear who opposed the hard fork, in their opposition, many "miners" declined to accept the hard fork software and therefore continued to mine the old blockchain. In doing so, the incentives (and capabilities) of the miners became critically misaligned with the incentives of the majority of The DAO community. By mining the old blockchain, the miners forged a new cryptocurrency, later called "Ethereum Classic," or ETC. Ethereum Classic would itself become a strange investment vehicle that created economic "value" out of thin air (not unlike all cryptocurrencies), underpinned by nothing more than vague idealism and a dogged interest in financial returns.

In the end, I think Ethereum Classic represents the story of The DAO fairly well. For all the dreams and visions contained in the rhetoric about The DAO, tracing the history of The DAO left me wondering if more than a tiny handful of individuals ever actually believed in the possibility and true benefit of a decentralized autonomous organization. It struck me that, like so many cryptocurrency and blockchain technologies, The DAO might have been just a high-risk investment vehicle masquerading as a new way of doing things.

Despite my cynicism, The DAO also introduced an interesting, relatively small-scale technology for experimenting with governance issues and new models of society. Indeed, perhaps this characterization can also be extended beyond matters of governance and beyond The DAO itself – should we see cryptocurrencies and blockchain technologies more broadly as apparatuses for socio-technical experimentation in society? That is, in the end, perhaps The DAO simply did not survive long enough to work out the kinks in a promising new kind of governance. Or, perhaps hype and exuberance got in the way of a good idea, whose time will come someday, which was first charted by these intrepid explorers.

In this chapter I detailed the brief history of The DAO, and offered an analysis of its modes of governance. To do so, I performed retrospective, ethnographic research of The DAO community by focusing on online discourse. I found three key themes of governance emerge from this discourse: (1) the shift of legal authority from existing, juridical authority to algorithmic authority; (2) the difficulty of designing and governing algorithmic systems, and especially immutable and decentralized ones; and (3) the challenging ethical terrain of experimentation with forms of distributed action through autonomous, decentralized systems.

Acknowledgments

Funding for this research was provided by the University College Dublin Centre for Innovation, Technology, and Organization. I hold a small amount of crypto-currency for research purposes, including Ethereum and (previously) The DAO tokens.

Thanks to Gianluca Miscione, Paul Ennis, Donncha Kavanagh, and Bill Maurer for commentary and guidance. Thanks for Stephan Tual and Christoph Jentzsch for commentary on an early draft. Initial qualitative research on The DAO was also conducted by Melissa K. Wrapp and shared with me, providing an invaluable aid in the early stages of this research. Malcolm Campbell-Verduyn provided welcome editorial assistance.

Notes

1 Values and dates for The DAO were initially collected through online sources, but later confirmed and adjusted to correspond with internal data provided by Stephan Tual of Slock.it. The largest discrepancy between publicly reported values and internal values is the maximum US$-converted monetary value of The DAO, which online sources claimed reached a maximum of US$150 million. Using historical market data, Slock.it's internal data showed a maximum of US$250 million, from 11,944,260.98 ETH. Due to wild ETH price swings during this period, the US$-converted monetary value changed rapidly.

2 At the time of writing, examples include MakerDAO, Wings DAO, Digix Global, Augur, and TokenFunder.

3 It is even possible to have low-trust/high-honesty human input through an "oracle" arrangement. In the context of blockchain human–machine organizations, these oracles can use economically incentivized prediction markets (e.g., TrustCoin, Augur), a game-theory setup (e.g., SchellingCoin), or even just simple multiple-signature ledgers to reduce the possibility of human cheating when reporting answers to oracle questions.

4 There is also a group of individuals misleadingly called "curators," who are responsible for the overall maintenance of "The DAO" platform, but despite their title they do not control or curate which projects are funded.

5 One known risk about this arrangement, however, is the possibility of the majority robbing the minority. If a majority shareholder decided to create a rule that stipulated, say, all funds were to be disbursed to majority stakeholders only, then this (majority) stakeholder could also approve such a rule, and therefore rob the minority. Slock.it was aware of this issue, and designed an odd "split" mechanism for funders to leave a DAO before decisions could be implemented (which utilized built-in delays). The split mechanism was later used during the exploit, but the built-in delays prevented the attacker from successfully exiting The DAO with any funds.

6 The idea of a deodand is now part of legal lore, but with recent rulings such as *Citizens' United v. Federal Election Commission*, which effectively made it possible for corporations to act like people (at least for campaign spending), I argue that the idea of a deodand is no longer far-fetched.

7 A version of the attack was originally identified by Christian Reitwiessner, and reported to key developers four days prior (Vessenes, 2016).

8 It must be stressed that it is very unlikely this letter is authentic. Nonetheless, the letter beautifully crystalizes the views of many people in the community, and is therefore an important source for understanding the dynamics of governance in The DAO.

9 One must, however, use caution when extrapolating between cryptocurrency and blockchain communities, since each has its own history and values. For example, the Bitcoin community is famously anti-authoritarian in comparison with Ethereum or, even more so, any number of the financial technology organizations using blockchain and "distributed ledger technology." The latter tend to be incentivized to work within existing capital institutions, whereas the former tend to want to replace the existing economic system.

10 Performative discourse is an especially acute issue for cryptocurrency communities, which suffer from a well-known "pump and dump" problem. Individuals attempt to convince others of the value or future value of a currency that he or she already owns a stake in (using traditional rhetorical strategies or pseudo-scientific analytical "projections"), in order to drive up the currency price and then sell at profit.

11 Although it is rarely appreciated in cryptocurrency and blockchain discourses, Lessig's original (1999) version of the "code is law" slogan argued that algorithmic permissions obviate the very category of law – not that the code constitutes a new form of law. In Lessig's version, if code prevents the activity in the first place (such as sharing an MP3 file under a fair use/fair dealings exemption), the appropriate laws do not even have a chance to be invoked, since there is no (potentially illegal) action to be considered.

Bibliography

A2be. (2016). An historical note on the creation of The DAO. *DAOhub.org*. Retrieved April 7, 2017, from https://forum.daohub.org/t/an-historical-note-on-the-creation-of-the-dao/6377

Bichler, S., and Nitzan, J. (2004). Dominant capital and the new wars. *Journal of World-Systems Research, 10*(2): 254–327.

Campbell-Verduyn, M., Goguen, M., and Porter, T. (2017). Big data and algorithmic governance: The case of financial practices. *New Political Economy, 22*(2): 219–36.

carloscarlson. (2016). "No hard fork" does NOT mean "DAO holders lose all their ETH." This debate is being rushed – let's examine ALL options. *reddit*. Retrieved April 10, 2017, from www.reddit.com/r/ethereum/comments/4op69x/no_hard_fork_does_not_mean_dao_holders_lose_all/

Christoph. (2016). How to split the DAO: Step-by-step. *The DAO*. Retrieved April 7, 2017, from https://daowiki.atlassian.net/wiki/display/DAO/How+to+split+the+DAO%3A+Step-by-Step

cubefriendly. (2016). 'The DAO' does not invest in Slock.it, it will hire the slock.it team to build the USN (Universal Share Network) for "the DAO." *reddit*. Retrieved April 10, 2017, from www.reddit.com/r/ethereum/comments/4ij7d7/the_dao_does_not_invest_in_slockit_it_will_hire/

DavidMc0. (2016). Ether Safe – But DAO cancelled. We're getting a refund. *reddit*. Retrieved April 10, 2017, from www.reddit.com/r/TheDao/comments/4oisep/ether_safe_but_dao_cancelled_were_getting_a_refund/

dm1n1c. (2016). The DAO debate and the Ethereum Autonomous Finance DAO. *reddit*. Retrieved April 10, 2017, from www.reddit.com/r/ethereum/comments/4gz43z/the_dao_debate_the_ethereum_autonomous_finance_dao/

DonaldCruz. (2016). DAO IS SAFE. *reddit*. Retrieved April 10, 2017, from www.reddit.com/r/ethereum/comments/4oiib4/dao_is_safe/

Dunning_Krugerrands. (2016). Don't wait for Slock.it DAO announcement – there won't be any. *reddit*. Retrieved April 9, 2017, from www.reddit.com/r/ethtrader/comments/4dtlvc/dont_wait_for_slockit_dao_announcement_there_wont/

Eldakara. (2016). F*ck this DAO. *reddit*. Retrieved April 10, 2017, from www.reddit. com/r/ethtrader/comments/4oif5c/fck_this_dao/

Epstein, C. (2005). *The power of words in international relations: Birth of an anti-whaling discourse*. Boston: MIT Press.

Floersch, K. (2016). The Ether Review #31 – Aftermath, discussing the DAO hack. *ConsenSys Media*. Retrieved April 10, 2017, from https://media.consensys.net/the-ether-review-31-aftermath-discussing-the-dao-hack-8afcb52575f9

GeorgesTurdBlossom. (2016). We want unstoppable contracts. Let the DAO burn. *reddit*. Retrieved April 10, 2017, from www.reddit.com/r/ethereum/comments/4ozzdv/we_ want_unstoppable_contracts_let_the_dao_burn/

Glaser, B.G., and Strauss, A.L. (1967). *The discovery of grounded theory: Strategies for qualitative research*. Chicago: Aldine Publishing Company.

Golumbia, D. (2009). *The cultural logic of computation*. Cambridge, MA: Harvard University Press.

Hallam, G., Shihara, B., Buterin, V., et al. (2016). Untitled. *Pastebin.com*, Paste Site. Retrieved April 10, 2017, from https://pastebin.com/aMKwQcHR

IAMnotA_Cylon. (2016). Critical update RE: DAO vulnerability. *reddit*. Retrieved April 9, 2017, from www.reddit.com/r/ethereum/comments/4oiqj7/critical_update_re_dao_ vulnerability/

Introna, L.D. (2016). Algorithms, governance, and governmentality: On governing academic writing. *Science, Technology and Human Values, 41*(1): 17–49.

itworks123. (2016). Ether Safe – But DAO cancelled. We're getting a refund. *reddit*. Retrieved April 10, 2017, from www.reddit.com/r/TheDao/comments/4oisep/ether_ safe_but_dao_cancelled_were_getting_a_refund/

Jentzsch, C. (2016). *Decentralized autonomous organization to automate governance*. Retrieved August 25, 2017, from https://github.com/slockit/DAO/tree/develop/paper

laughing__cow. (2016). To the community. *reddit*. Retrieved April 10, 2017, from www. reddit.com/r/ethereum/comments/4p521a/to_the_community/

ledgerwatch. (2016a). Don't wait for Slock.it DAO announcement – there won't be any. *reddit*. Retrieved April 9, 2017, from www.reddit.com/r/ethtrader/comments/4dtlvc/ dont_wait_for_slockit_dao_announcement_there_wont/

ledgerwatch. (2016b). I think TheDAO is getting drained right now. *reddit*. Retrieved April 7, 2017, from www.reddit.com/r/ethereum/comments/4oi2ta/i_think_thedao_is_ getting_drained_right_now/

Lessig, L. (1999). *Code and other laws of cyberspace*. New York: Basic Books.

Levy, K.E.C. (2017). Book-smart, not street-smart: Blockchain-based smart contracts and the social workings of law. *Engaging Science, Technology, and Society, 3*(0): 1–15.

Lustig, C., and Nardi, B. (2015). Algorithmic authority: The case of Bitcoin. In IEEE, pp. 743–52. Retrieved April 28, 2016, from http://ieeexplore.ieee.org/lpdocs/epic03/ wrapper.htm?arnumber=7069744

Mark, D., Zamfir, V., and Sirer, E.G. (2016). A call for a temporary moratorium on "The DAO." Retrieved April 7, 2017, from https://docs.google.com/document/ d/10kTyCmGPhvZy94F7VWyS-dQ4lsBacR2dUgGTtV98C40/edit?usp=embed_ facebook

Merriam, S.B., and Tisdell, E.J. (2016). *Qualitative research? A guide to design and implementation*. 4th ed. San Francisco: Jossey-Bass.

Pasquale, F. (2011). Restoring transparency to automated authority. *Journal on Telecommunications and High Technology Law, 9*(235): 235–56.

Polycephal_Lee. (2016). Critical update RE: DAO vulnerability. *reddit*. Retrieved April 9, 2017, from www.reddit.com/r/ethereum/comments/4oiqj7/critical_update_re_dao_vulnerability/

redditbsbsbs. (2016). Ether Safe – But DAO cancelled. We're getting a refund. *reddit*. Retrieved April 10, 2017, from www.reddit.com/r/TheDao/comments/4oisep/ether_safe_but_dao_cancelled_were_getting_a_refund/

Reijers, W., O'Brolcháin, F., and Haynes, P. (2016). Governance in blockchain technologies and social contract theories. *Ledger, 1*(0): 134–51.

Ryan, D.M. (2016). *The DAO: An experiment in responsibility*. Retrieved April 7, 2017, from http://enterstageright.com/archive/articles/0516/dao.htm

Samman, A. (2015). Crisis theory and the historical imagination. *Review of International Political Economy, 22*(5): 966–95.

Saurwein, F., Just, N., and Latzer, M. (2015). Governance of algorithms: Options and limitations. *Info: the Journal of Policy, Regulation and Strategy for Telecommunications, Information and Media, 17*(6): 35–49.

Schroeder, K. (2014). Deodands: DACs for natural systems. *Ethereum Forum*. Retrieved May 12, 2016, from https://forum.ethereum.org/discussion/392/deodands-dacs-for-natural-systems

Scott, B. (2014). Visions of a techno-leviathan: The politics of the Bitcoin blockchain. *E-International Relations*. Retrieved April 30, 2016, from www.e-ir.info/2014/06/01/visions-of-a-techno-leviathan-the-politics-of-the-bitcoin-blockchain/

Shirky, C. (2009). A speculative post on the idea of algorithmic authority. *Clay Shirky*, blog. Retrieved April 7, 2017, from www.shirky.com/weblog/2009/11/ a-speculative-post-on-the-idea-of-algorithmic-authority/

Sirer, E.G. (2016). The Ether Review #36 – Emin Gün Sirer, Wrapping it all up. *ConsenSys Media*. Retrieved April 10, 2017, from https://media.consensys.net/the-ether-review-36-emin-g%C3%BCn-sirer-wrapping-it-all-up-4d6c4280faa4

"The Attacker." (2016). An open letter. *Pastebin.com*. Retrieved April 7, 2017, from https://pastebin.com/CcGUBgDG

Tual, S. (2016a). Announcing DAO Framework 1.1. *Slock.it Blog*. Retrieved April 7, 2017, from https://blog.slock.it/announcing-dao-framework-1-1-35249e2e001#.uav8dw16j

Tual, S. (2016b). DAOs, or how to replace obsolete governance models. *Slock.it Blog*. Retrieved April 9, 2017, from https://blog.slock.it/daos-or-how-to-replace-both-the-kickstarter-and-token-presale-models-1b2b8898d6e7

Tual, S. (2016c). No DAO funds at risk following the Ethereum smart contract "recursive call" bug discovery. *Slock.it Blog*. Retrieved April 7, 2017, from https://blog.slock.it/no-dao-funds-at-risk-following-the-ethereum-smart-contract-recursive-call-bug-discovery-29f482d348b#.dt2ssoywp

UntamedOne. (2016). Critical update RE: DAO vulnerability. *reddit*. Retrieved April 9, 2017, from www.reddit.com/r/ethereum/comments/4oiqj7/critical_update_re_dao_vulnerability/

vbuterin. (2017). Personal statement regarding the fork. *reddit*. Retrieved April 10, 2017, from www.reddit.com/r/ethereum/comments/4oj7ql/personal_statement_regarding_the_fork/

Vessenes, P. (2016). More Ethereum attacks: Race-to-empty is the real deal. *Peter Vessenes*. Retrieved April 7, 2017, from http://vessenes.com/more-ethereum-attacks-race-to-empty-is-the-real-deal/

xxeyes. (2016). The DAO: Risk-free short term investment; high-risk long term investment. Is this a recipe for chaos? *reddit*. Retrieved April 10, 2017, from www.reddit.com/r/ethtrader/comments/4h80xm/the_dao_riskfree_short_term_investment_highrisk/

9 Conclusion

Towards a block age or blockages of global governance?

Malcolm Campbell-Verduyn

What can be understood about governance in the contemporary global political economy by taking emergent technologies like blockchains seriously? This volume illustrated various manners in which new as well as traditional actors and processes underpinning global governance are (dis)empowered by applications of blockchain to Bitcoin and beyond. Examining Bitcoin and other applications of blockchains revealed how emergent technologies can be *used* to enhance the relative power of some actors over others, as well as how emergent technologies can *re-constitute* the interests and perceptions of their users. Parsing through the techno-dystopian and techno-utopian hype surrounding discussions of blockchains and Bitcoin, this volume provided more nuanced understandings of the governance implications of technological change in a digital age. Taking emergent technologies such as blockchain seriously offered insights into global governance in an era of increasingly complex and intense digital interconnections within and across nation-states.

In returning to the central framing questions and themes outlined in the introduction to this volume, this chapter summarises the specific insights generated by its interdisciplinary set of contributors, as well as maps out some further questions and topics that might be explored in further research. Most centrally, is governance in the global political economy truly at the cusp of the 'block age' in which applications of blockchain technologies are 'unblocking' longstanding problems? Or are applications of these emergent technologies enhancing existing 'blockages' and contributing to *new* problems in contemporary global governance? In short, a key question contemplated in this chapter is whether blockchain applications are improving on or further entrenching pathologies of contemporary governance. Rather than seeking to predict a fundamentally elusive future, insights into this question are gleaned by examining the actual roles and impacts of blockchains that were detailed in this volume and are stemming from increasingly nuanced interdisciplinary scholarship on these emergent technologies. Directions are then proposed for ongoing scholarly scrutiny of blockchains to Bitcoin and beyond that continue to stress the implications posed for global governance in an increasingly digital age. First, however, this chapter considers the fundamental question of what blockchains are and how they can be considered emergent technologies.

Blockchains as emergent technologies

The common conceptual point of departure for contributors to this volume was *what* emergent technologies are and *whether* blockchains can be conceived as such. Science and technology policy scholars consider emergent technologies to be novel types of knowledge whose practical application and integration into the global political economy remain largely, if not wholly, unsettled (Einsiedel, 2009; Rotolo *et al.*, 2015). The novelty of emergent technologies often lies in their assemblage of existing applications of knowledge, as innovations 'built on top of innovation' (Holley, 2015). It is in this sense of the term that contributors to this volume largely understood blockchains as emergent technologies. In unique manners blockchains bring together existing sets of knowledge, namely cryptographic and time-stamping technologies. Their applications – such as to Bitcoin and competing cryptocurrencies (CCs) – benefit from cheap and prevalent information and communication technologies (ICTs) such as computer processors, as Hütten and Thiemann emphasized in their contribution to this volume.

The undefined and uncertain paths from 'emergent' to 'established' technologies also characterise the short evolution of blockchains since the technical design of this technology was published in a white paper by one Satoshi Nakamoto in 2008. Technologies are considered to no longer be emergent when their previously rapid growth in funding and potential applications declines and they are abandoned by their key supportive communities (Einsiedel, 2009; Rotolo *et al.*, 2015). This scenario certainly does not yet appear to characterise blockchains, whose applications continue to benefit from the funding of several large and growing sets of supportive communities (e.g. KPMG, 2017). Even failed blockchain applications, such as The DAO, have not (yet) been completely abandoned by their supportive communities, as the chapter by Quinn DuPont in this volume explored. Nevertheless, it is not completely beyond the realm of possibility to contemplate Bitcoin disintegrating from its numerous internal contradictions, which have been exemplified most prominently in the ongoing 'civil war' over the 'scalability' of the leading blockchain (e.g. Walters, 2016). Neither is it unthinkable that blockchain technology more generally might one day be regarded as one of the many technological fads of the 2010s. Even the continuous support of powerful actors does not guarantee the eventual widespread establishment of emergent technologies in everyday practices and processes, as the 1980s battle between VHS and Betamax as well as the more recent example of Google Glass exemplified (Narayanan *et al.*, 2016).

Emergent technologies do become more established in the global political economy and its governance as their practical applications become *less* ambiguous and *more* widespread in activities beyond their initial niches (Rotolo *et al.*, 2015). It is the examination of this expansion process that broadens the analytical emphasis from the more descriptive stress on *what* technologies and *who* their supportive communities *are* towards what precisely technologies *do*. The growing interest in and application of blockchains by a wide variety of regulatory, professional, civil society, and business actors around the world is indicative of the increasingly established character of this technology. Yet, with very few exceptions, practical applications of blockchains beyond Bitcoin remain shrouded in highly ambiguous and uncertain 'proof of concept' phases.[1] Despite the considerable hype surrounding blockchain-based insurance, national currencies, registries, remittances, 'smart' contracts, and payment settlement systems of all kinds (Gartner, 2016; e.g. Schwab, 2016), so-called blockchain 2.0 and 3.0 applications largely remain theoretical. Indeed, these *potential* rather than *actual* applications of blockchains across the global political economy are illustrative of the fundamentally emergent character of this set of technologies.

Emphasising the emergent character of blockchains in turn enables a more nuanced appreciation of the implications technological change poses for governance beyond techno-utopian and techno-dystopian claims that assume predetermined paths and impacts of technologies. The stress on emergence induces analysis to, as DuPont succinctly puts it in his contribution to this volume, distinguish between 'the ways that governance was *believed to* function [...] and the ways that it *did* function'. Rather than the technological cycles and waves promoted by some governments and scholars in understanding technological change,[2] contributors to this volume stressed specific *contexts* and *phases* through which emergent technologies such as blockchains evolve. In their chapter, Rodima-Taylor and Grimes linked the general uncertainty and ambiguity of blockchain-based digital payment systems to particular local meanings of savings, debt, and innovation. Their analysis emphasised the importance of understanding individual choices and delving into specific legal systems, forms of organisation, and patterns of ownership. Meanwhile, by highlighting similarities and differences with precise parallels to the evolution of earlier technologies such as local currencies and 'e-moneys', sociologists Hütten and Thiemann as well as Mallard, Méadel, and Musiani stressed the unique development and impacts of blockchain applications. In their respective chapters, Campbell-Verduyn and Goguen as well as DuPont also argued against conceiving the reactions to, and the failures of, blockchain applications as predetermined, but rather in a continual state of flux that is fundamentally difficult to predict and anticipate.

A key insight gleamed from the stress on emergence by contributors to this volume is that particular actions enacted, or not enacted, by certain actors at specific moments in the evolution of technologies such as blockchains are influenced by the structures of existing processes and practices. Rodima-Taylor and Grimes situated the advent of blockchain-based remittances within wider structures of digital payment networks. Campbell-Verduyn and Goguen positioned the regulatory perceptions of CCs within broader and longstanding international efforts to combat money laundering in specific manners. Jia and Zhang stressed the longstanding roles of nation-states in the development of ICTs generally and the emergence and expansion of the Internet particularly. The evolution of blockchains and the implications of their applications for global governance were regarded as largely idiosyncratic matters, supporting the Skolnikoff principle emphasising the unpredictable evolution and impacts of technologies (Skolnikoff, 1993: 35). Yet that these implications are difficult to aniticipate does not mean that their consequences cannot be analysed and understood. As this volume has shown, varying insights for contemporary governance *by*, *with*, and *of* emergent technologies can be usefully gleamed by scrutinising the actual impacts and evolution of blockchains.

Implications for and insights into contemporary global governance

That even the leading and most prominent application of blockchain technology has neither replaced national moneys nor the plumbing of the global financial system in the manners that Satoshi Nakamoto and many original Bitcoin developers intended does not entail that these and other applications of blockchain technologies have had little impact on the global political economy and its governance. In navigating between the dystopian pessimism and utopian optimism, contributors to this volume illustrated more nuanced implications for and insights into intertwined forms of governance *by*, *with*, and *of* blockchain technologies.

Governance by blockchain technologies and its normative implications

This volume contributed to ongoing interdisciplinary efforts to open technological 'black boxes' (MacKenzie, 2005) and highlight how particular ideas underlying technical features of blockchains (re)constitute the interests and perceptions of their users specifically and contemporary global governance more generally. Existing claims that the computer codes underpinning blockchain applications are both implicitly as well as explicitly informed by libertarian ideas that constitute blockchain users in market-based relations (e.g. Atzori, 2017b; Karlstrøm, 2014; Scott, 2016) were supported by contributors to this volume. In their chapter, Hütten and Thiemann, for instance, chronicled how the anti-statist 'political vision' advanced by Bitcoin pitted its early promoters of 'free' markets, free banking, and 'frictionless e-commerce' in adversarial relations with longstanding state-regulated institutions and processes. In a surprising set of subsequent developments, incumbent multinational companies and governments sought to 'tone down' the libertarian ideas underlying blockchains by 'co-opting' and 'normalising' the emergent technology. Yet the ability to perform a 'cognitive split' and 'pacify' the politics underlying blockchains was regarded as fundamentally questionable by Hütten and Thiemann. Despite being rendered largely implicit, profoundly political ideas were shown to continually inform the perceptions of new users of the technology, such as central banks in their understandings of what money is and what it can be in increasingly cashless societies.

Other contributors to this volume also detailed the roles and implications of blockchains in governance *by* emergent technologies. Hsieh, Vergne, and Wang noted how the 'formative ideology' underpinning the computer-coded 'organisational rulebook' of most CCs advances decentralised forms of 'community governance'. With power and decision-making spread across user communities and traditional manager–employer relationships bypassed, individual CC users become incentivised to make decisions based on forces of market demand and supply. Similarly, DuPont detailed how The DAO was pre-programmed to encourage investor management of blockchain-based projects without the 'need for messy and inefficient human negotiation'. This chapter noted how investors in The DAO were also incentivised to 'act as rational, self-interested, and untrusting agents' by the liberal ideologies underpinning the 'technical makeup' of this application of blockchain technologies. The particular 'political vision' underpinning The DAO also rewarded risk-taking and inspired a 'vocal minority' of users to persistently stress the 'algorithmic authority' of its terms of service agreement in resisting centrally administered solutions to fix the computer code glitch revealed in the 2016 exploit.

Contributors to this volume also assessed the normative implications arising from forms of governance *by* blockchains. Their evaluations navigated beyond prominent framings of applications such as Bitcoin as either 'evil' (Krugman, 2013) or potentially 'the most efficient and equitable models for administering all transnational public goods' (Swan, 2015a: 31; e.g. Knieff, 2015). Campbell-Verduyn and Goguen, for example, stressed how the particular features and activities arising from blockchain applications such as CCs can be harnessed in manners that provide challenges as well as opportunities for combatting international money laundering. Rodima-Taylor and Grimes detailed the positive potential of blockchains for facilitating remittances in manners that support financial inclusion and development in the Global South. This first set of chapters pointed to how a 'block age' may help improve longstanding 'blockages' in global governance.

Contributors to this volume also contrasted the normative *promises* of liberal and libertarian modes of governance with their *actual* contributions to transparency, efficiency, fairness, and democracy. The chapter by Musiani, Mallard, and Méadel emphasised how, in facilitating a range of illicit activities, the efficiencies gained by applications of the emergent technology became more widely viewed outside crypto-communities as controversial. Meanwhile, Hsieh, Vergne, and Wang lamented how 'information asymmetries' between insiders and outsiders in CC communities, as well as the complexity of these blockchain applications, contribute to fundamentally unclear community-based democratic decision-making. Similar criticisms of the differences between theoretical and actual accountability processes were stressed in the shift of The DAO from decentralised towards centralised forms of democratic decision-making that DuPont detailed in his chapter, as well as the roles of 'benevolent dictators' in the 2013 Bitcoin 'fork' controversy that Musiani, Mallard, and Méadel traced in their chapter. This second set of chapters thereby indicated how a 'block age' fails to provide novel solutions to overcome longstanding problems of transparency, efficiency, fairness, and democracy in global governance.

Together, however, both sets of normative assessments by contributors to this volume provided much more nuanced understanding of governance *by* blockchains than the dichotomised and at times sensationalistic claims of many prominent observers. In distinguishing between potential and actual outcomes of the governance *processes* underlying blockchains, implications for the power and agency of specific *actors* underlying contemporary governance were also illustrated by contributors to this volume.

Governance with blockchain technologies and (dis)empowerment

Nuanced insights into who specifically becomes (dis)empowered in governance *with* emergent technologies such as blockchains were also provided in this volume. Contributors reinforced findings from initial studies of blockchain applications that certain groups of individuals as well as centralised companies and governments may be empowered to varying extents by blockchain technologies (e.g. DuPont and Maurer, 2015). Blockchains were shown to enhance the abilities of some actors to exercise relative power *over* others. For instance, technologists and coders have gained knowledge and skills enabling them to navigate through technical complexity and exercise decision-making power in becoming key 'insiders', as the chapters by DuPont as well as Hsieh, Vergne, and Wang revealed in the cases of CCs and The DAO, respectively. Musiani, Mallard, and Méadel also detailed how specialised journalists and CC users were empowered in gaining knowledge of the technical features and processes underlying applications of the emergent technology. Their chapter revealed further 'micro-hierarchies' and power asymmetries amongst small and large developers, between developers and intermediaries, as well as between users and 'a small oligarchy of mining pools'.

Contributors to this volume detailed how governance *with* blockchains empowers some historically underprivileged non-state actors, giving rise to new sets of actors in the increasingly digital global political economy. Invoking the idea of a 'networked world order' (Slaughter, 2004), the chapter by Rodima-Taylor and Grimes stressed the 'multiplicity of global and national standard-setting bodies, development agencies and experts, funders and philanthropists, financial institutions, fintech companies, retail agents, and consumers' involved in drawing blockchains into global remittance governance. In his chapter, DuPont noted how governance *with* emergent technologies can empower civil society actors such as charities, who can use blockchains to receive and transparently manage donations. Meanwhile, new actors can be empowered by drawing on blockchain to link crypto and mainstream economies, as the chapters by Hütten and Thiemann as well as Musiani, Mallard, and Méadel detailed with regards to CC-to-national money exchanges. Campbell-Verduyn and Goguen emphasised the growing importance of these new 'nodes' in global anti-money-laundering (AML) governance, as well as other new actors such as the Bitcoin Foundation and the Digital Asset Transfer Authority in providing education and elaborating governance principles, respectively. Finally, Hsieh, Vergne, and

Wang discussed how start-up businesses become empowered in employing blockchain technologies for their internal organisation in manners that replace longstanding forms of corporate governance.

Contributors to this volume, however, also stressed how governance *with* blockchains can further empower incumbent and historically powerful actors in the global political economy. Hütten and Thiemann pointed to how blockchains add to the pre-existing power of a 'priviledged tech-savvy male elite'. Rodima-Taylor and Grimes noted how, despite bypassing certain remittance operators and traditional financial intermediaries, crypto-remittances also empower banks, payment aggregators, and other incumbents in the 'last mile' of international money delivery. Other established firms are empowered by employing centrally governed CCs such as Ripple to perpetuate their dominance, as the chapter by Hsieh, Vergne, and Wang described. Campbell-Verduyn and Goguen discussed how individual nation-states and international organisations are further empowered in their collaborations with blockchain firms to monitor transactions, as well as in both 'races to the top and bottom' to gain competitive advantages over competing national jurisdictions and global governance institutions. The greater empowerment of these traditional actors in the global political economy is further illustrated in the increasingly formal and informal governance *of* blockchains.

Governance of blockchain technologies: centralised coercion and decentralised flexibility

This volume provided further insights into both the merits and limits of centralised and decentralised approaches to the governance *of* emergent technology. On the one hand, contributors emphasised the utility of and boundaries to 'top–down' forms of centralised coercion involving explicitly 'hands-on' government actions in stamping out the least desirable features of blockchain applications, such as the volatility of CCs and their facilitation of illicit activity. Formal bans in Russia and other countries reduced risks related to the former features of blockchain technologies, as the chapter by Jia and Zhang noted. The latter risk of illicit activities being facilitated by the use of Bitcoin in 'dark web' markets such as Silk Road was reduced, albeit only temporarily, by coercion of the American Federal Bureau of Investigation (FBI), as the chapter by Musiani, Mallard, and Méadel detailed. Contributors to this volume also stressed the limits to formal coercion in the governance *of* blockchains. Several chapters emphasised how overly coercive and prohibitive approaches undermined opportunities presented by emergent technologies such as blockchains for attending to and improving upon longstanding governance problems. Rodima-Taylor and Grimes discussed how the finding by the Central Bank of Kenya that Bitcoin is an unregulated currency ultimately harmed efforts to integrate CC transfers into existing remittance payment platforms in that East African country. Coercive governance responses were also regarded less as *resolving* than merely *shifting* illicit activities elsewhere. The re-establishment of 2.0 and 3.0 versions of the

Silk Road noted in the chapter by Campbell-Verduyn and Goguen illustrated limits to even internationally coordinated coercive governance *of* emergent technology. Short of shutting down the entire Internet, more coercive governance can be escaped through distributed blockchain-enabled activities with relative ease.

On the other hand, contributors to this volume provided nuanced assessments of seemingly more flexible approaches to the governance *of* emergent technologies. Jia and Zhang stressed how 'laissez-faire' responses do not necessarily entail a *lack* of formal governance. Rather, less restrictive approaches to the governance *of* emergent technology often still involve formal regulations at multiple levels of governance. Flexible and more 'experimentalist' (Sabel and Zeitlin, 2008) approaches to the governance *of* blockchains have permitted individual states and non-state actors to trial various governance approaches, some of which appear more coercive than others. In the United States, for instance, New York State developed a 'Bitlicense' that the chapter by Campbell-Verduyn and Goguen noted was perceived as highly restrictive by members of the blockchain industry, some of whom subsequently relocated to other jurisdictions, such as Panama. Key actors in the international AML regime, such as the Financial Action Task Force (FATF), developed a flexible approach that allowed some actors and jurisdictions to 'race to the top' in distinguishing themselves as AML-compliant. The intentions of more flexible approaches appear less to be experimentation merely for the sake of experimentation than *learning* and *disseminating* successful strategies for achieving common governance goals (see also Overdevest and Zeitlin, 2014). Yet like all formal forms of governance, risks remain with such flexible and decentralised approaches. As Jia and Zhang stressed, states pursuing flexible approaches remain vulnerable to capital flight and the volatility associated with leading applications of blockchains, such as CCs.

A further contribution of this book then was to illustrate various overlaps between seeming dichotomous centralised coercive and more decentralised flexible governance strategies. Jia and Zhang, for example, identified a middle ground approach to the governance *of* emergent technology that bridges flexible and coercive strategies. Although focused on the 'prudent enthusiasm' of key Chinese state actors, Jia and Zhang argued that other countries confronting emergent technologies might similarly seek to balance risks and opportunities presented by technological change. The next sub-section highlights several intersections between the forms of governance *by*, *with*, and *of* blockchains illustrated in this book.

Limits, shifts, and interrelationships between contemporary forms of governance

Analysing blockchains provides nuanced insights into the overlaps and interrelationships between contemporary forms of governance *by*, *with*, and *of* emergent technologies. Significant limits pertain to each of these forms of governance, as this volume illustrated in analysing blockchains. Governance *by* blockchains is grounded in inflexible pre-programmed computer codes; governance *with* blockchains can perpetuate status quo power relations in empowering dominant actors and processes; and governance *of* blockchains is restricted by the digital and distributed nature of activities enabled by block-chain technologies. These limits in turn can induce shifts between forms of governance. The chapter by DuPont revealed how key actors, such as the founder of Ethereum, exercised governance *with* blockchains in overcoming the flaws of governance *by* blockchains following the exploit of The DAO in 2016. This attack induced what appeared to both community members and to outside observers as an explicit shift from governance *by* blockchains towards governance *with* blockchains.

Yet more mundane and everyday relationships between the forms of con-temporary global governance illustrated in Figure 9.1 also occur in more mundane manners beyond periods of attention-grabbing crisis and contestation. In a first instance are interactions between forms of governance *by* and *with* emergent technologies. The influence of the former upon the latter was illus-trated with how several technical features of blockchains enable certain actors to be empowered over others, as the chapter by Musiani, Mallard, and Méadel illustrated in discussing 'benevolent dictators'. Hsieh, Vergne, and Wang sim-ilarly noted how the seemingly technical specifications of pre-mined CCs induce the empowerment of concentrated sets of actors. Specific ideas and ideologies underpinning traits of emergent technologies such as blockchains were regarded by contributors to this volume as shaping, but not wholly determining, *who* becomes (dis)empowered by technological change.

Yet, the relationships between governance *by* and *with* emergent technologies are not simply one-way. The specific forms of ideas and ideologies underlying emergent technologies are also influenced, but not wholly determined, by *who* pro-grammes and designs blockchains. As several chapters in this volume stressed, privileged individual programmers, frequently operating in the Global North, insert their particular biases and perceptions of the world into supposedly 'neutral' technical designs. Investors are also further empowered by blockchain applications and are able to shape, though not wholly determine, the reach of governance *by* the emergent technologies. In hunting for returns, investors are able to promote the market values of more centralised CCs with 'clear strategic directions and organ-isational mandates' over decentralised CCs characterised by forms of 'community governance' and slower, potentially more acrimonious decision-making, as the chapter by Hsieh, Vergne, and Wang illustrated. Through forms of governance *with* blockchains, these powerful sets of actors can thereby influence the shape and scope of governance *by* blockchains.

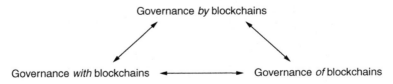

Figure 9.1 Interrelationships between governance *by*, *with*, and *of* blockchains.

Forms of governance *of* and *by* blockchains also interact in subtle manners. Hütten and Thiemann pointed to how applications of blockchains have become slowly integrated within formal regulatory institutions, despite the positioning of early Bitcoin developers explicitly against such formal governance arrangements. This chapter stressed the continual importance of formal 'political authority that creates moral and legal space for financial markets to operate and consolidates and legalizes a professional domain for particular financial practices'. The chapter by DuPont similarly emphasised how applications of emergent technologies occur in the space between algorithmic and juridical forms of authority, in between governance *by* and *of* blockchains. Campbell-Verduyn and Goguen furthermore pointed to how particular features of formal governance *of* blockchains in the international AML regime influenced, but did not wholly determine, a bifurcation of blockchain applications. Policies and regulations underlying the governance *of* blockchains have implications, for instance, the development of CCs promising total anonymity that then in turn structure the activities of their user in particular manners.

Once again, however, interrelationships between forms of governance *by* and *of* blockchains are not unidirectional. The former also influence, but do not wholly determine, the specific form and shape of the latter. For instance, pre-programmed traits and ideologies underlying applications of blockchains structure not only their users but also regulatory perceptions of the emergent technology. The chapter by Campbell-Verduyn and Goguen detailed how the perception of the quasi-anonymous and decentralised features of CCs as threats to key actors in the international AML regime influenced the subsequent formal approaches taken to the governance *of* the emergent technologies. Decentralised forms of governance were regarded as having been shaped, yet not entirely determined, by the features of blockchains and underlying forms of governance *by* blockchains.

Finally, mundane interrelationships between forms of governance *of* and *with* blockchains were identified in this volume. The chapter by Musiani, Mallard, and Méadel detailed a range of individuals influencing, but not wholly determining, how formal governance *of* blockchain applications unfolds at some times and fails to unfold at other times. Their chapter stressed the structuring and performative effects of certain narratives that give rise to specific conceptions of the types of formal governance that do and do not make sense, and which delimit the range of legitimate policies and regulatory responses. The chapter by Hsieh, Vergne, and Wang also specified how certain traditional and social media actors promote or discourage formal governance *of* the emergent technology in their normative judgements of the failings, successes, and implications of blockchain applications. Formal governance *of* blockchains influences the actors empowered over others in forms of governance *with* blockchains. As the chapter by Campbell-Verduyn and Goguen detailed, flexible approaches pursued in the international AML regime empowered actors such as CC-to-national currencies exchanges, as well as industry governance bodies, to implement market-based money laundering policies.

Examining blockchains and their applications in the contemporary global political economy illuminates not only varying governance *by*, *with*, and *of* emergent technologies, but also the intricate relationships between these forms of contemporary governance. The following section makes the case for further investigations of these and other relationships underpinning governance in an increasingly digital global political economy, as well as identifies further paths that future interdisciplinary research might productively take.

Future avenues of inquiry

Needless to say, there exist numerous avenues to further elaborate the implications of and insight into contemporary governance that applications of blockchain technologies provide. In scrutinising the novelty of the 'block age' and whether applications of emergent technologies such as blockchains are enhancing existing 'blockages' or contributing to new problems of governance in the contemporary global political economy, many different paths can productively be taken. In contemplating avenues for ongoing research, however, it remains essential to recognise that the impacts and insights emergent technologies provide for contemporary global governance are uncertain and difficult, if not impossible, to accurately predict. Perhaps the only 'known unknown' is that the evolution of blockchains, like all technologies, remains characterised by a general 'messiness' (Mayer *et al.*, 2014: 15) pertaining to the 'untidy, uneven processes' through which applications of novel knowledge sets emerge (Jasanoff, 2004: 4). As innovation policy scholars Rotolo, Hicks, and Martin (2015: 1831) observe, understanding even the range of 'probabilities associated with each possible outcome (e.g. potential applications of the technology, financial support for its development, standards, production costs) may be particularly problematic' (see also Hesse-Biber, 2011).

Rather than reviewing the numerous predictions pervading emerging literature on blockchains (for overviews see Swan, 2015a; Vigna and Casey, 2015), this section instead emphasises several areas identified by contributors to this volume that continual scholarly investigations might scrutinise in providing futher nuanced understanding of the global governance implications of blockchains and other emergent technologies. Three interrelated themes for further research are mapped out in this section: hybrid forms of contemporary governance; the materiality of Bitcoin, other blockchain applications, and emerging ICTs more generally; as well as the ethics and legitimacy of blockchains and governance *of*, *with*, and *by* emergent technologies. Each avenue proposed for future research stresses how interdisciplinary studies engaging a range of analytical perspectives could enable further nuanced understandings of the implications posed by blockchains and emergent technologies pose for governance in an increasingly digital global political economy.

Hybridity in global governance

A first avenue for further investigating the nexus of blockchains, emergent technologies, and global governance is engagement with research on 'hybrid' forms of governance that are being increasingly explored in global political economy and the social sciences more generally (Hurt and Lipschutz, 2015; Aoyama and Parthasarathy, 2016). Hybridity in a broad sense refers to a range of social processes and temporalities between continuity and upheaval (Adam, 2004; Campbell-Verduyn, 2013). In the more specific sense identified by Rodima-Taylor and Grimes in their contribution to this volume, hybridity refers to 'organisational forms' combining traditional and modern features of global governance. Rodima-Taylor and Grimes located hybridity in both organisations and practices linking formal and informal forms of contemporary governance. Extending this governance-specific conception to other recent efforts in GPE and beyond to elaborate notions of hybridity may help overcome artificial analytical separations that tend to hamper more nuanced understanding of the complexities underpinning contemporary governance, such as between centralisation and decentralisation, as well as between public and private spheres (Best, 2014; Porter, 2014; Sheller and Urry, 2003). Further research might specifically investigate whether forms of hybrid governance, such as the 'prudent enthusiasm' identified by Jia and Zhang in this volume, are becoming more widely replicated in the governance *of* blockchains. Parallels might be identified between the mix of formal and informal forms of blockchain governance in China and the so-called 'regulatory sandboxes' set up in, as well as between, Switzerland, the United Kingdom, and a number of Commonwealth jurisdictions, including Australia, Hong Kong, Malaysia, Singapore, Thailand, and the Canadian province of Ontario (Australian Securities and Investments Commission, n.d.; Bank of Thailand, 2016; Bank Negara Malaysia, 2016; Financial Conduct Authority, 2015; Hong Kong Monetary Authority, 2016; Sharp, 2017). The latter novel forms of contemporary governance relax existing formal laws in providing informal spaces for 'controlled experimentation'. Formal laws are not *eliminated* as in a typical regulatory 'race to the bottom'. Yet certain products, services, and processes located awkwardly within existing laws are allowed to be trialled and tested under continual regulatory scrutiny. The ostensible purpose here is to accrue the benefits of innovation whilst minimising risks of harm to citizens and to society more generally. State scrutiny involves not only monitoring, but similar types of formal and informal dialogue between regulators and industry actors that Jia and Zhang highlighted with the 'prudent enthusiasm' approach to Bitcoin governance in China. Once again, a continual 'shadow of state regulation' is implicitly and at times explicitly underpinning such dialogue and the understanding that experiments will be shut down should they jeopardise socioeconomic stability.

As with all approaches to the formal governance *of* technology, however, risks pertain to even the most conventional 'hybrid' forms of governance. Regulatory capture in both its 'material' as well as 'cognitive' or 'cultural' forms tends to be overlooked by advocates and analysts of 'sandbox' approaches (Maupin, 2017). Frequent contacts between regulators and the regulated industry, as well as shared outlooks and professional backgrounds of personnel, can induce various forms of 'regulatory capture'. The blurring of broader social welfare and the interests of particular groups identified in numerous areas of global governance (e.g. Baker, 2010; Novak, 2013; Campbell-Verduyn, 2017) remains relevant to novel hybrid forms of blockchain governance for at least two reasons: first, because of the high degree of individual movement between personnel of regulatory and industry institutions. A prominent case of this 'revolving door' in the United States was the departure of the first New York State Superintendent of Financial Services to a consultancy specialising in compliance with the very Bitlicense he shaped and developed (Freifeld, 2015). Another reason for which risks of capture appear particularly pertinent to hybrid governance *of* blockchains is the shared technical and professional backgrounds of industry and regulatory personnel. The high degree of technical literacy required for comprehending most blockchain-based activities can induce an uncritical reliance by regulators on industry knowledge and insights.

Understanding the risks of regulatory capture in the governance *of* emergent technologies such as blockchains requires further integration with existing efforts to identify how such problems might be both prevented and conceptualised (Carpenter and Moss, 2013; Pagliari, 2012). Whether or not regulatory capture is an inevitable process, for example, could be examined in studies enhancing scrutiny of the specific actors programming the seemingly neutral technical codes of blockchains and other ICTs. Whether and how wider benefits are actually accrued to society more generally, rather than just to certain actors in forms of hybrid governance, needs to be continually scrutinised as 'regulatory sandboxes' gain in popularity (Aitken, 2016; Sharp, 2017). Finally, whether concepts like 'regulatory capture' are themselves sufficient for conceiving the intricacies of symbiotic relationships between regulatory and industry actors can be elaborated in taking the governance *of* emergent technologies such as blockchains seriously.

The materiality of blockchains and digital technologies

Hütten and Thiemann concluded their contribution in this volume with the provocative claim that the most lasting contribution of CCs may be returning a focus to longstanding debates on the materiality of money, as well as advancing new perspectives on the roles of monetary governance in increasingly cashless societies. Further interrogations of the wider governance implications of the 'practical materiality' (Maurer *et al.*, 2013) and 'material embeddedness' (Karlstrøm, 2014) of CCs can provide fruitful insights into contemporary forms of global governance, as Campbell-Verduyn and Goguen as well as Musiani, Mallard, and Méadel revealed in this volume with their respective focus on the 'socio-technical environments' in which international regimes operate and the technical 'Internet infrastructure and infrastructure as Internet politics'. Specifically, exploring questions of materiality might help understand whether CCs can be understood as ' "hybrids" of conventional money' (Leander, 2015: 951–2), as Hütten and Thiemann discussed in their contribution to this volume. Elaborating such insights on CCs may in turn more widely inform scholars, policy-makers, businesses, and the general public on the evolving nature of conventional currencies, and specifically whether or not CCs and other electronic monetary tokens are transforming conventional money 'from within' (ibid.).

The material contexts in which CCs have arisen and blockchain applications are being developed might be further investigated in several manners. For example, future studies could interrogate whether the actors and processes associated with modes of 'platformisation' identified by Rodima-Taylor and Grimes are replacing, adding onto, or combining existing governance infrastructures. How might new and old material infrastructures be interacting with the forms of governance underpinning what GPE scholars had identified as 'platform capitalism' (Langley and Leyshon, 2016)? Recent efforts in GPE and the wider social sciences to return to the longstanding scrutiny of the material infrastructures enabling market activities and their governance could productively be extended to the governance *of*, *with*, and *by* blockchains (e.g. Cerny, 1994; Edwards, 2003; Jeffs, 2008; Maurer and Swartz, 2017; Musiani *et al.*, 2016; Star, 1999).

Another avenue for further investigating the materiality of CCs and other applications of blockchain technologies is their interrelationship with the natural environment. As with most commentary on blockchain applications, the environmental implications of CCs have attracted sensationalist headlines in media outlets. For instance, Bitcoin mining has been likened to an 'unsustainable' (Malmo, 2015) 'real-world environmental disaster' (Gimein, 2013; see also *The Economist*, 2015). Some nuanced and more detailed analysis has compared the considerable computing power required to verify and maintain Bitcoin transactions in particular (Hayes, 2015)[3] with nearly the annual energy consumption of countries such as Ireland and Paraguay. Such environmental impacts might stem from the physical location of CC mining 'farms' in regions where electricity is cheap yet environmentally unfriendly, such as coal power in western China and eastern Ukraine. These material impacts might, however, also be due to the specific design of the leading CC. Do Bitcoin competitors such as Solarcoin truly reduce the environmental impacts of CCs, and if so, how exactly? How does the energy consumption of CCs compare with that of more traditional payment systems (e.g. Malmo, 2017)? While some scholars have begun to address the environmental 'dark side' of CCs (Carney, 2013; e.g. McCook, 2014; O'Dwyer and Malone, 2014), much remains to be done before any conclusive claims can be made regarding the impacts of these and other applications of blockchain technologies. In addressing the materiality of blockchains, further research might more widely contribute to debates on the desirability of technological 'silver bullets' as governance solutions to complex environmental problems, such as solutions to climate change (Kuehr and Williams, 2003; Galaz, 2014).

Ethics and legitimacy of blockchains and global governance

Changes in the earth's climate, in technology, and in global governance all tend to be considered by scholars and policy-makers alike in technical manners that background the important ethical underpinnings and implications of such dynamic processes (Brassett and Holmes, 2010). Against this, and as summarised in this chapter, several contributors to this volume stressed the normative implications of forms of blockchain-based governance. For example, DuPont concluded how the case of The DAO highlights 'the challenging ethical terrain of experimentation with forms of distributed action through autonomous, decentralised systems'. In foregrounding the normative implications of pre-programmed and automated activities, this chapter provided an important avenue for wider scrutiny of the *desirability* that applications of emergent technologies provide for contemporary global governance. Yielding potentially significant efficiencies in organisation and management of activities across and within national borders, such as in minimising human corruption and error, automated technologies can also involve significant risks and inspire fears of out-of-control decision-making (e.g. Harris, 2012). Yet, as contributors to this volume stressed, neither technologies nor specifc actors are alone in 'complete control' or entirely 'out of control' of contemporary governance. Rather, technology and social actors tend to co-constitute one another and evolve in dialectical manners that are hard to predict, as Campbell-Verduyn and Goguen stressed in their analysis of the specific case of global AML governance.

Further research might seek less to provide the most accurate predictions of how technologies and global governance are likely to co-evolve than to try to identify normative implications arising from technological change that are pertinent to the everyday decisions made by a variety of actors underpinning contemporary global governance. Further dystopian warnings of out-of-control technologies and utopian visions of magnificent technology-enabled futures are less required than explicitly normative analysis that, for example, renders visible the implications of competing visions of how the world *should* be governed. In doing so, future research on blockchains and other emergent technologies might productively integrate and build on existing interrogations of the implicit ideas programmed in various automated systems that increasingly underly processes of governance in the global political economy (e.g. Coeckelbergh and Reijers, 2016: 177). Studies might specifically ask whether alternative applications of emergent technologies advance less individualistic visions and more collective social goals (e.g. Scott, 2016; Zeilinger, 2016). Whether existing blockchain applications can harness individual autonomy to herald more communal activities and processes should be investigated further, as Rodima-Taylor and Grimes call for in this volume. Do applications of blockchains such as 'e-residency' identity documents (re)constitute actors as citizens or merely consumers (e.g. Sullivan and Burger, 2017)? Might governance *by* bockchains give rise to less market-based outcomes when actors beyond a privileged male technocratic elite are involved in the coding and technical designs?

These questions and calls for further research also point to the need to further consider the legitimacy of emergent technologies and contemporary global governance. Both the effectiveness of outputs and representativeness of inputs in blockchain-based organisations and decision-making processes might be further scrutinised in ongoing studies of this emergent technology (Scharpf, 1999). Who precisely is involved in programming blockchains, as well as in using blockchains and in implementing formal and informal governance *of* blockchains might be explicitly linked to the *input* legitimacy of emergent technologies. Meanwhile, whether or not applications of blockchains help in addressing long-standing 'blockages' in global governance, or simply reinforce existing problems and give rise to new pathologies, might be related to their *output* legitimacy. The novel forms of remittance detailed by Rodima-Taylor and Grimes, as well as the more controversial blockchain-based derivatives that legal scholars have investigated (Shadab, 2014), may pose profoundly different implications for the legitimacy of blockchains. Explicit attention to issues of ethics and legitimacy may provide further insights into the governance dynamics underlying *other* novel technologies with autonomous features, from the Internet-of-Things (IoT) to self-driving cars and forms of artificial intelligence, whose emerging presence in the global political economy and overlaps with blockchains tend to be considered in largely technical and apolitical manners (Atzori, 2017a; Christidis and Devetsikiotis, 2016; Omohundro, 2014; Swan, 2015b).

Conclusion

This book sought to shift beyond largely sensationalistic, economistic, legalistic, and technical existing debates on blockchain applications to Bitcoin and beyond towards more nuanced appreciations of the wider implications posed by these and other emergent technologies for the specific actors and processes underpinning contemporary global governance. Even a dedicated volume, however, cannot tease out *all* of these implications. This book was intended as an *initial* rather than the *sole* bridge linking broader social scientific analysis of blockchains with the analytical insights of GPE scholarship into issues of authority, power, and governance. This merely provisional final chapter has tied the insights of contributors to this volume together in clarifying interlinked forms of governance *by*, *with*, and *of* emergent technologies, as well as in proposing directions that future research might productively take for generating further insights into the contemporary governance of global political economy. GPE scholars and scholars from the wider social sciences and humanities alike are invited to take up these suggested research avenues in further exploring governance in a period that may or may not be labelled by future historians as the 'block age', but surely will be identified as one characterised by novel experimentations with emergent technologies.

Acknowledgements

The support of the Social Sciences and Humanities Research Council of Canada (fellowship no. 756-2015-0474) as well as the editors at Routledge and the RIPE Global Political Economy Series, especially Eleni Tsingou, is gratefully acknowledged.

Notes

1 Entailing efforts to demonstrate the feasibility and practical application of what remains a concept or prototype.
2 Such as www.acq.osd.mil/chieftechnologist/publications/docs/TRA2011.pdf. See also the Schumpeterian waves or Konkratieff cycles that have been criticised for over-emphasising the self-driving momentum of technologies (Fritsch, 2014).
3 For real-time statistics see http://digiconomist.net/beci

Bibliography

Adam, B. (2004). *Time*. Cambridge: Polity.
Aitken, R. (2016, 2 November). Switzerland eyes Europe's fintech crown with lower regulation. *Financial Times*.
Aoyama, Y., and Parthasarathy, B. (2016). *The rise of the hybrid domain: Collaborative governance for social innovation*. Cheltenham: Edward Elgar.
Atzori, M. (2017a). Blockchain-based architectures for the internet of things: A survey. Available at SSRN: https://papers.ssrn.com/sol3/papers.cfm?abstract_id=2846810
Atzori, M. (2017b). Blockchain technology and decentralized governance: Is the state still necessary? *Journal of Governance and Regulation*, 6(1): 45–62.
Australian Securities and Investments Commission. (n.d.). *Regulatory sandbox*. Retrieved 26 August 2017 from http://asic.gov.au/for-business/your-business/innovation-hub/regulatory-sandbox/
Baker, A. (2010). Restraining regulatory capture? Anglo-America, crisis politics and trajectories of change in global financial governance. *International Affairs*, 86(3): 647–63.
Bank of Thailand. (2016). *Regulatory sandbox*. Retrieved 26 August 2017 from www.bot.or.th/Thai/FIPCS/Documents/FPG/2559/ThaiPDF/25590251.pdfthai
Bank Negara Malaysia. (2016, 18 October). *Financial technology regulatory sandbox framework*. Retrieved 26 August 2017 from www.bnm.gov.my/index.php?ch=en_announcement&pg=en_announcement&ac=467&lang=en.
Best, J. (2014). *The return of the public in global governance*. Cambridge: Cambridge University Press.
Brassett, J., and Holmes, C. (2010). International political economy and the question of ethics. *Review of International Political Economy*, 17(3): 425–53.
Campbell-Verduyn, M. (2017). Capturing the moment? Crisis, market accountability, and the limits of legitimation. *New Political Science*, 39(3).
Campbell-Verduyn, M. (2013). Between continuity and upheaval: Hybridised global financial policy in the post-crisis period. *Paterson Review of International Affairs*, 13: 33–68.
Carney, M. (2013, 16 December). Bitcoin has a dark side: Its carbon footprint. *Pando*.
Carpenter, D., and Moss, D.A. (eds) (2013). *Preventing regulatory capture: Special interest influence and how to limit it*. Cambridge: Cambridge University Press.

Cerny, P. (1994). The infrastructure of the infrastructure? Toward "embedded financial orthodoxy" in the international political economy. In R.P. Palan, and B. Gills (eds) *Transcending the state-global divide: A neostructuralist agenda in international relations* (pp. 223–49). Boulder, CO: Lynne Reinner.

Christidis, K., and Devetsikiotis, M. (2016). Blockchains and smart contracts for the internet of things. *IEEE Access, 4*: 2292–2303.

Coeckelbergh, M., and Reijers, W. (2016). Cryptocurrencies as narrative technologies. *ACM SIGCAS Computers and Society, 45*(3): 172–8.

Der Derian, J. (2003). The question of information technology in international relations. *Millennium, 32*(3): 441–56.

DuPont, Q., and Maurer, B. (2015, 23 June). Ledgers and law in the blockchain. *King's Review*.

Edwards, P. (2003). Infrastructure and modernity: Force, time, and social organization. In T.J. Misa, P. Brey, and A. Feenberg (eds) *The history of sociotechnical systems: Modernity and technology* (pp. 185–226). Cambridge, MA: MIT Press.

Einsiedel, E. (2009). Making sense of emerging technologies. In E. Einsiedel (ed.) *Emerging technologies: From hindsight to foresight*. Vancouver: UBC Press.

Financial Conduct Authority. (2015, November). *Regulatory sandbox*. London: Author.

Freifeld, K. (2015, 28 July). Former NY financial watchdog counters criticism on bitcoin work. *Reuters*.

Fritsch, S. (2014). Conceptualizing the ambivalent role of technology in international relations: Between systemic change and continuity. In M. Mayer, M. Carpes, and R. Knoblich (eds) *The global politics of science and technology, Vol. 1* (pp. 115–39). Berlin: Springer Berlin Heidelberg.

Galaz, V. (2014). *Global environmental governance, technology and politics: The Anthropocene gap*. Cheltenham: Edward Elgar Publishing.

Gartner. (2016, 16 August). Gartner's 2016 hype cycle for emerging technologies identifies three key trends that organizations must track to gain competitive advantage. Retrieved 26 August 2017 from www.gartner.com/newsroom/id/3412017

Gimein, M. (2013, 12 April). Virtual bitcoin mining is a real-world environmental disaster. *Bloomberg*.

Harris, R. (2012). *The fear index*. New York: Random House.

Hayes, A. (2015). *A cost of production model for Bitcoin*. New School for Social Research, working paper 05/2015.

Hesse-Biber, S. (ed.) (2011). *The handbook of emergent technologies in social research*. Oxford: Oxford University Press

Holley, E. (2015, 28 October). Linq launches blockchain platform Linq at Money 2020 in Las Vegas. *Banking Technology*.

Hong Kong Monetary Authority. (2016, 6 September). *Fintech supervisory sandbox*. Retrieved 26 August 2017 from www.hkma.gov.hk/media/eng/doc/key-information/guidelines-and-circular/2016/20160906e1.pdf

Hurt, S., and Lipschutz, R. (eds) (2015). *Hybrid rule and state formation: Public-private power in the 21st century*. New York: Routledge.

Jasanoff, S. (2004). The idiom of co-production. In S. Jasanoff (ed.) *States of knowledge: The co-production of science and the social order*. London: Routledge.

Jeffs, J. (2008). The politics of financial plumbing: Harmonization and interests in the construction of the international payment system. *Review of International Political Economy, 15*(2): 259–88.

Kaminska, I. (2016, 17 March). More decentralized autonomous organisation (DAO) mysticism. *Financial Times.*

Karlstrøm, H. (2014). Do libertarians dream of electric coins? The material embeddedness of Bitcoin. *Distinktion: Scandinavian Journal of Social Theory, 15*(1): 23–36.

Knieff, B. (2015). Blockchain: What is it good for? Absolutely something. *Aite Group.*

KPMG. (2017). *The pulse of fintech Q4 2016.* Retrieved 26 August 2017 from https://assets.kpmg.com/content/dam/kpmg/xx/pdf/2017/02/pulse-of-fintech-q4-2016.pdf

Krugman, P. (2013, 28 December). Bitcoin is evil. *New York Times.*

Kuehr, R., and Williams, E. (2003). *Computers and the environment: Understanding and managing their impacts.* Vol. 14. Berlin: Springer Science and Business Media.

Langley, P., and Leyshon, A. (2016). Platform capitalism: The intermediation and capitalisation of digital economic circulation. *Finance and Society*, early view.

Leander, A. (2015). Theorising international monetary relations: Three questions about the significance of materiality. *Contexto Internacional, 37*(3): 945–73.

MacKenzie, D. (2005). Opening the black boxes of global finance. *Review of International Political Economy, 12*(4): 555–76.

Malmo, C. (2017, 7 March). A single Bitcoin transaction takes thousands of times more energy than a credit card swipe. *Vice Motherboard.*

Malmo, C. (2015, 29 June). Bitcoin is unsustainable. *Vice Motherboard.*

Maupin, J. (2017). *Blockchains and the G20: Building an inclusive, transparent and accountable digital economy.* Centre for International Governance Innovation, Policy Brief 101.

Maurer, B., and Swartz, L. (2017). *Paid: Tales of dongles, checks, and other money stuff.* Cambridge, MA: MIT Press.

Maurer, B., Nelms, T.C., and Swartz, L. (2013) 'When perhaps the real problem is money itself!': The practical materiality of Bitcoin. *Social Semiotics, 23*(2), 261–77.

Mayer, M., Carpes, M., and Knoblich, R. (2014). The global politics of science and technology: An introduction. In M. Mayer, M. Carpes, and R. Knoblich (eds) *The global politics of science and technology Vol. 1* (pp. 1–38). Berlin: Springer Berlin Heidelberg.

McCook, H. (2014). *An order-of-magnitude estimate of the relative sustainability of the Bitcoin network.* Retrieved 26 August 2017 from www.scribd.com/doc/228253109/The-Relative-Sustainability-of-the-Bitcoin-Network-by-Hass-McCook

Musiani, F., Cogburn, D.L., DeNardis, L., and Levinson, N.S. (eds) (2016). *The turn to infrastructure in Internet governance.* New York: Springer.

Narayanan, A., Bonneau, J., Felten, E., Miller, A., and Goldfeder, S. (2016). *Bitcoin and cryptocurrency technologies: A comprehensive introduction.* Princeton, NJ: Princeton University Press.

Novak, W.J. (2013). A revisionist history of regulatory capture. *Preventing Regulatory Capture: Special Interest Influence and How to Limit It*, pp. 25–49.

O'Dwyer, K., and Malone, D. (2014). *Bitcoin mining and its energy footprint.* 25th IET Irish Signals and Systems Conference, pp. 280–5.

Omohundro, S. (2014). Cryptocurrencies, smart contracts, and artificial intelligence. *AI Matters, 1*(2): 19–21.

Overdevest, C., and Zeitlin, J. (2014). Assembling an experimentalist regime: Transnational governance interactions in the forest sector. *Regulation and Governance, 8*(1), 22–48.

Pagliari, S. (2012). *Making good financial regulation: Towards a policy response to regulatory capture.* London: Grosvenor House Publishing.

Porter, T. (2014). Constitutive public practices in a world of changing boundaries. In J. Best, and A. Gheciu (eds) *The return of the public in global governance*, pp. 223–42. Cambridge: Cambridge University Press.

Rotolo, D., Hicks, D., and Martin, B. (2015). What is an emerging technology? *Research Policy, 44*(10): 1827–43

Sabel, C., and Zeitlin, J. (2008). Learning from difference: The new architecture of experimentalist governance in the EU. *European Law Journal, 14*(3): 271–327.

Scharpf, F.W. (1999). *Governing in Europe: Effective and democratic?* Oxford: Oxford University Press.

Schwab, K. (2016). *The fourth industrial revolution*. Geneva: World Economic Forum.

Scott, B. (2016). Blockchain technology for reputation scoring of financial actors. *Ethics in Finance, Robin Cosgrove Prize Global edition 2014–2015*: 128–39.

Shadab, H. (2014, 9 October). *Regulating Bitcoin and block chain derivatives*. Written statement to the Commodity Futures Trading Commission Global Markets Advisory Committee Digital Currency Introduction – Bitcoin.

Sharp, A. (2017, 23 February). Canada's securities regulators launch fintech 'sandbox' program. *Globe and Mail.*

Sheller, M., and Urry, J. (2003). Mobile transformations of public and private life. *Theory, Culture and Society, 20*(3): 107–25.

Skolnikoff, E. (1993). *The elusive transformation: Science, technology, and the evolution of international politics*. Princeton, NJ: Princeton University Press.

Slaughter, A.M. (2004). Sovereignty and power in a networked world order. *Stanford Journal of International Law, 40*: 283.

Star, S.L. (1999). The ethnography of infrastructure. *American Behavioural Scientist, 43*(3): 377–91.

Sullivan, C., and Burger, E. (2017). E-residency and blockchain. *Computer Law and Security Review*, early view. https://doi.org/10.1016/j.clsr.2017.03.016

Swan, M. (2015a). *Blockchain: Blueprint for a new economy*. Farnham: O'Reilly Media.

Swan, M. (2015b). Connected car: Quantified self becomes quantified car. *Journal of Sensor and Actuator Networks, 4*(1): 2–29.

The Economist. (2015, 31 October). Blockchains: The great chain of being sure about things.

Vigna, P., and Casey, M.J. (2015). *The age of cryptocurrency: How bitcoin and digital money are challenging the global economic order*. London: St. Martin's Press.

Walters, R. (2016, 11 February). Bitcoin's future threatened by software schism. *Financial Times.*

Zeilinger, M. (2016). Digital art as 'monetized graphics': Enforcing intellectual property on the blockchain. *Philosophy and Technology*: 1–27.

Index